FASHION DESIGNER'S
RESOURCE
BOOK

FASHION DESIGNER'S
RESOURCE BOOK

SAMATA ANGEL

B L O O M S B U R Y
LONDON · NEW DELHI · NEW YORK · SYDNEY

About Author

Samata Angel is a womenswear designer, public speaker and author who has her own fashion label, Samata. In 2007 Samata became the first British female to showcase during the New York Nolcha Fashion Week and has received a host of industry awards and nominations including *Cosmopolitan* magazine's 'Future Fashion Star of 2008'. She has been named in the 'Black Women in Europe: Power List 2010', and in March 2011 was listed as one of *Red* magazine's 'One to Watch: Top 20 women under the age of 30'. At the same time she was also announced as the winner of Suzy Amis Cameron's international dress design contest *Red Carpet Green Dress*, creating an Oscar worthy gown from sustainable materials. Samata is currently the Global Campaign Director of the contest working between Los Angeles, New York and London. Samata is a guest lecturer at the London College of Fashion and has written for *Fashion Capital*, *Cision*, *The Guardian* and *Vogue* UK. Samata has been invited to Number 10 Downing Street to meet former Prime Minister Gordon Brown and has addressed Prime Minister David Cameron and an audience of MPs, entrepreneurs and media at the launch of StartUp Britain.

First published in Great Britain 2013
Bloomsbury Publishing Plc
50 Bedford Square
London WC1B 3DP
www.bloomsbury.com

ISBN: 978-1-4081-7089-2

A CIP catalogue record for this book is available from the British Library

Publisher: Susan James
Cover design: Eleanor Rose
Page design: Evelin Kasikov
Page layouts: Susan McIntyre
Index and assistance: Kate Jervis

This book is produced using paper that is made from wood grown in managed, sustainable forests. It is natural, renewable and recyclable. The logging and manufacturing processes conform to the environmental regulations of the country of origin.

Printed and bound in China

CONTENTS

PREFACE

The global fashion industry is one of the most exciting and dynamic industries to work in. Full of taste-makers and trend setters, it is an industry which thrives (and depends) on innovation, hard work, multi-culturalism and relationships. I started out in the fashion industry in London as a young teen, studying at the London College of Fashion. I quickly learnt how all consuming the industry can be, and the importance of maintaining a balanced and healthy lifestyle whilst navigating it, a topic this book touches on. My personal experiences of the fashion industry, particularly the British fashion scene, whilst character forming and enlightening, also showed me how tough this industry is to navigate and mark your mark on. As Chairman of the British Fashion Council I am constantly in conversation with designers, seeking events and initiatives to support and strengthen their work. Fashion is big business. The British industry has a net worth of £21 billion and is globally respected, with platforms like London Fashion Week launching careers every season. But fashion is a 24-hour non-stop clock and each second something new is being created, discussed and having its fate decided. For a young designer starting out and trying to choose a career path it can be intimidating, with modern tools that, whilst holding the potential to launch careers, also pose challenges if information on how to most effectively use them is not readily available. Social media has transformed the way designers talk about themselves to the industry and to their customers, for example.

Designers also struggle with financing their ambitions, and at the start of their career often need to wear many hats: PR agent, sales representative, social media manager and more.

The wealth of available information and pertinent guidance needs to be made digestible. This is why books like this, written from the relatable perspective of a young fashion entrepreneur, are an important addition to the available resources for designers. Not just designers whose goal is to work within fashion houses, but also those who aim to set up their own business – fashion entrepreneurs.

This book provides a useful overview of the fashion industry globally, and actionable advice and guidance that will help anyone with the passion and ambition to succeed.

Harold Tillman CBE, former Chairman of the British Fashion Council

A long-time supporter of British fashion, Tillman's name is synonymous with iconic British brands Aquascutum and Jaeger. In 2006 he launched a £1 million scholarship fund at his alma mater, the London College of Fashion. In his role as chairman of the British Fashion Council he has nurtured many emerging British designers.

INTRODUCTION: A BRAND NEW PERSPECTIVE

The idea to write this book came as a result of my experiences, conversations and debates with aspiring creatives, emerging and established fashion designers, students, graduates and alumni, mentors, fashion industry influencers and many other colourful characters within the industry from around the globe over a period of 10 years. As any creative person knows, experiences can be the real driving force behind some of your best ideas and some of my most enjoyable adventures have taken place in the fashion industry. Likewise some of the most inspirational and talented people I have met (and been lucky enough to share time, thoughts and ideas with) work in that same industry.

I have been working in the fashion industry since 2001 in a number of roles, ranging from creative (design) to business (PR). Interestingly, I did not study Fashion Design. I have a BSc in Economics, Finance and Management from Queen Mary and Westfield University, London and hence have always looked at the fashion industry from a business perspective as well as creatively. I have worked hard to understand the business side of fashion and secure relevant work experience, and as a result I am often asked to mentor emerging designers who need guidance or to be pointed towards useful resources. As a guest lecturer at the London College of Fashion I am in constant contact with students and know some of the issues they face. This book is my 'light bulb moment': instead of waiting for 15 years to write down everything I have learnt, I have decided to write about what I know now in the hope I can help fellow designers tackle issues that are arising.

The fashion industry is dynamic, demanding, exciting and mysterious. It's fully understood by few but ventured into by many. I have written this book to connect some of the dots for aspiring designers, entrepreneurs, creatives, students and for those who are simply curious about taking the leap to work in fashion, and want to know more. My main aim is for this book is to provide insight and a learning opportunity presented through the eyes of a creative with business experiences that she wants to share.

I believe that to stand a chance of successfully working within this high-value and tough industry, you need encouragement, guidance and creative inspiration but also, crucially, business inspiration. It is vital that fashion designers are informed about both the business side of the industry – particularly in the current economic climate and in the face of constant global change – and the creative lifestyle needed to stay inspired, to be able to stand any chance of making a living and enjoying themselves.

First things first: getting your mind around the industry

As Bernard Arnault, Chairman and CEO of LVMH (Louis Vuitton Moët Hennessy) said: 'It's not enough to have a talented designer, the management must be inspired too.' Although speaking from the perspective of a global fashion brand this quote touches on a hugely important point. It is crucial that designers are able to understand the relationship between creative talent and business management because business acumen and support are equally important requirements for success in the fashion industry. At the very least, I have always felt that understanding as much of the business side of things as possible can only help and not hinder. Designers need to be able to access industry intelligence, interpret that intelligence and know how to use it.

Lifestyle

Understanding how to manage a fashion designer/ entrepreneur's lifestyle is important simply because a career can be all consuming. It is rarely possible to leave your work in the office; it follows you everywhere you go because fashion is all around us. In this book I have sought to address what I believe is a very important topic – the need for designers to be given creative sanctuary and room to breathe. In other words, I have set out to discuss the well-being of a fashion designer and how they can best stay inspired and happy within a stressful and pressurised environment (see chapter 10, Emotional wellbeing). For example, on p.179 you can find the playlist I design to and the sense stimulators I use when I want an energy boost. I have recommended these to a few designer friends and they now swear by these

Fashion is not something that exists in dresses only. Fashion is in the sky, in the street, fashion has to do with ideas, the way we live, what is happening.

Coco Chanel

Who is this book for?

The Fashion Designer's Resource Book is for those thinking of:
- Taking a step into the fashion industry; to study or work
- Pursuing a career path within fashion
- Setting up a fashion venture such as a clothing label

methods to help balance and reduce levels of stress during fashion week.

Becoming a fashion entrepreneur

One thing I have tried to do in this book is to give the term 'fashion entrepreneur' the cache it really deserves. This term has been in circulation since around 2007/2008; when it first emerged it required much more explanation than it does today. Increasingly fashion designers are now waking up to the realisation that to be successful in this industry they need to fully embrace the skills of the 'entrepreneur'.

As will now be clear it is my hope that this book will serve as a comprehensive resource and will provide both creative inspiration and business acumen. It covers a range of topics such as different types of designers, top global fashion colleges, how to create your fashion portfolio, networking in the industry and building your contact base, volunteer work, ethical fashion, managing your own PR and much more. It can be used as a guidebook, a lifestyle book or a thought piece, offering a fresh perspective and a clear approach that will hopefully encourage upcoming fashion entrepreneurs.

You may finish reading this book and be inspired to set up a fashion house or to work as a stylist. But more than anything else, I hope this book offers you a brand new perspective.

CHAPTER 1

AN OVERVIEW OF THE INDUSTRY:

Understanding the fashion industry

There are several definitions of the word 'fashion' and these vary depending on your perspective, whether you are a fashion designer, fashion buyer, stylist or photographer for example. Looking from a designer's point of view, I see fashion as a form of creative expression through clothing. Most of the definitions you will come across feature words like 'style', 'design' and 'art', implying fashion is inherently creative. However, whenever I take part in talks or workshops with emerging designers one of the first things I tell them is that when considering the fashion industry is not simply about creativity – in reality it is as corporate as the banking industry so don't let its appearance fool you. According to the US Bureau of Labor Statistics, the global fashion industry reached a value of US$1,781.7 billion by the end of 2010.[1] In the UK alone a comprehensive overview carried out by the New Landmark Report revealed an industry worth £21 billion to UK Economy as of September 2010.[2] The fashion industry has rules and regulations and trades through demand and supply. It is full of watchdogs,

Fashion can be understood in many ways. It is both an industrial and cultural phenomenon, one that goes to the heart of what we understand as design.[3]

Fifty Dresses that Changed the World, Deyan Sudjic

Definitions

Fashion (*n*):
A popular trend, esp. in styles of dress, ornament, or behaviour;[4] consumer goods (especially clothing) in the current mode.[5]

organisations providing market intelligence, news and reports, designers, manufacturers, buyers, PR specialists, stylists, editors, journalists and other key groups who all work together in an interconnected way. They directly and indirectly influence one another, so if you are interested in getting into fashion it will benefit you greatly to understand its characteristics and the relationships that help it to function.

Doing your own research

Learning how these relationships work and impact each other is a gradual but very necessary pursuit for any aspiring fashion designer. By doing research anyone can obtain a basic introduction and practical overview of the industry to further their

Why not try...

I suggest that you write down your initial observations and conclusions about the industry in your early days and then review them after spending a few years working within it. You will be surprised to see how your opinions change in both a positive and negative way.

understanding. Industry critique and commentary can be found in magazines, journals, newspapers, television programmes, fashion websites, blogs and other sources. Interested designers can join online forums (online resources are very easy to find) and read industry publications such as *Drapers* or WWD.com for industry news and intelligence. A website such as Fashionista.com offers a collection of fashion news, criticism and career advice and produces daily business stories on the big brand names, interviews with industry personalities and guidance on getting into and succeeding in all facets of the fashion world. Self-started research is the best first step for any aspiring fashion designer.

The *global* fashion industry

Having been based in London, showcased in New York, gone on buying trips to Paris, sourced fabrics from New Delhi, marketed for a Japanese clothing brand in Tokyo, represented designers from Columbia, in addition to falling for the World Wide Web's magical way of communicating with fashion followers around the globe, I fully embrace

Above: Images like this are seen on billboards and in magazines across the world. A global network of people, from textile manufacturers to seamstresses, makeup artists and photographers, has been required to make this one image possible. Below: traditional batik dyeing in Bali, Indonesia.

the fact that this industry is best viewed *globally*. The fashion industry, commonly thought to have first developed in America and Europe[6], now represents a thriving global market of revenue, investment, trade and source of employment. In the 19th century advancements in technology such as the introduction of sewing machines led to an improvement in manufacturing capabilities, while increased trade between countries such as the USA, UK, India, Italy and China resulted in higher demand and for products to be delivered with a faster turnaround. It became common that clothing had been 'designed in one country, manufactured in another and sold in a third.'[7] Many items in your closet are likely to have made a global journey. For example, a dress bought in Saks department store, New York, could have been designed in the USA, made from fabric sourced in Italy and manufactured in Indonesia before being shipped to New York for sale.

A textile factory in Africa.

The underlying backbone of the fashion industry is the textile industry. Touching every corner of the globe from China to Italy to Thailand, the textile industry connects to the fashion industry at each stage of production, with the end products residing in our wardrobes. For example:

Suppliers of natural and man made raw materials such as Lycra™, cotton, wool and polyester work with and sell to manufacturers of textiles.

Textile manufacturers work with and sell to fashion designers and clothing manufacturers.

Designers and clothing manufacturers work with and sell to customers, retailers and wholesalers.

How did the manufacturing industry for fashion develop into a global business and what are the implications?

1

THE ROLLING BALL: A RISE IN CHEAP IMPORTED CLOTHING

Between 1980 and 1996 the production of clothing in industrialised countries decreased. However, during the same period it increased in developing countries such as Indonesia and Bangladesh.[8] In 2005 the Multi-Fibre Arrangement (MFA), which put quotas (limits) on the garments and textiles that developing countries could export, ended, and as a result countries such as the UK saw an influx of clothing from developing countries. These countries could hire a low-wage work force and source inexpensive textiles to produce garments at a comparatively minimal cost. [9]

2

THE KNOCK-ON EFFECT: UK MANUFACTURING SPLIT

In response to this change, the UK manufacturing industry has split, concentrating either on specialist fashion clothing or luxury products for wealthy consumers in developed countries.

HOW HAS THIS IMPACTED ON FASHION DESIGNERS?

As a result of these changes, designers who could not afford manufacturing in the UK or did not have the capability to do their production in-house felt the need to look overseas to have their garments made. Others simply moved away from fashion design into other areas.

3

HOW WILL THIS CONTINUE TO AFFECT THE INDUSTRY?

Trend forecasters predict that in the future the UK fashion market will continue to be driven by retailers rather than manufacturers, with a division of the market into discounters (as seen in fast, cheap fashion) and full-price retailers.

4

For a clothing designer, where manufacturing takes place, how effective it is and its quality can make or break a brand, and manufacturers are constantly competing with each other to secure a designer's business. I am always getting involved in conversations with other designers about who the big players are and where the new go-to destination is for manufacturing. Today the largest apparel manufacturers and exporters are countries such as China, Hong Kong, India, Italy, Pakistan, the Philippines, Thailand, the UK and the USA. The increased number of global interaction 'points' has also inspired a more 'trans-cultural' approach to design, increasingly facilitated by the rapid share of images and information through the Internet. In 1984 an exhibition of Yves St. Laurent's work was staged in Beijing, China. A year later the streets of Beijing were full of YSL knock-offs. The Chinese who saw the exhibition were inspired by his work, in spite of the fact that they had never been exposed to European fashion.[10] Gianni Versace's 'Evening Ensemble', from his 1994 Spring/Summer collection, took the sari as a source of inspiration and over a decade later, for the Spring/Summer 2007 collection, Christian Dior collection featured a bright beaded collar inspired by the Masai people and kimono sleeves inspired by Japanese tradition style. Japanese artistic elements were also John Galliano's inspiration for his Dior Handbags collection, the Dior Samourai 1947 Woven bag which was released in celebration of Dior's 60th anniversary. In Paul Smith's Spring/Summer 2010 collection the Sapeurs of the Congo (a subculture of dandy men that love to dress up in fine clothing despite living in near poverty conditions) were transformed into a runway statement during London Fashion Week. In the face of an increasingly global fashion industry, the trend towards a 'trans-cultural' approach to design is still just as relevant as it was twenty years ago.[11]

It is also easy to see the speed with which these influences are shared through tools such as the Internet. This means that a design can be picked up and translated to the other side of the globe, with accurate detail, in no time at all. For instance, the cut, material and detailing of Kate Middleton's chosen wedding frock was replicated within days of her stepping out of her wedding carriage. Before the royal wedding a bridal designer named Jim Hjelm told the *New York Times* that his company would send sketches digitally to factories in China, who would create mock ups of the dress within 24 hours, making for a short turnaround for brides hoping to emulate princess style on their big day.[12]

Designer Nova Chui was inspired by the ethnic groups in Shangri-La, China (her homeland) for her Shangri-La collection with co-designer Jeff Archer. The collection was shown at the London College of Fashion BA Show, June 2011.

Key countries in the fashion industry

The Global Language Monitor (GLM) is an innovative company that documents, analyses and tracks trends. It has used its data to rank the top fashion centres of the world.[13] According to Bekka Payack, the Manhattan-based Fashion Director at GLM:

At the Global Language Monitor, we began to rank the Global Fashion Capitals (GFC) as a way to focus on fashion as a means of empowerment for the industry, for the emerging cities and regions, and especially for women themselves, providing means of self-expression and personal fulfilment. We decided early on to highlight emerging fashion capitals on all five continents, to emphasize native, indigenous, and environmentally conscious fashion trends.

Listed below are the top 50 fashion capitals according to the GLM. As of August 2011, London has overtaken New York, knocking the US city off the top spot for the first time in several years. London also beat Paris, Milan and Los Angeles.

2011 Ranking	City	Previous ranking	Comment
1	London	(3)	Kate Middleton and Alexander McQueen help raise the City to No.1 status.
2	New York	(1)	New York is strong but London has Kate. 'Nuff said.
3	Paris	(4)	No. 1 in our hearts but No. 3 in the media.
4	Milan	(6)	The Earth has returned to its proper orbit: The Big Four once again occupy the top four spots.
5	Los Angeles	(5)	LA solidifying her hold on No. 5.
6	Hong Kong	(2)	Down from No. 2 but tops again in Asia.
7	Barcelona	(10)	The Queen of the Iberian Peninsula. Once again.
8	Singapore	(15)	Up seven spots and into the Top Ten.
9	Tokyo	(14)	Third Asian city in the Top Ten.
10	Berlin	(18)	Completes a long climb into elite status.
11	Sydney	(7)	Drops a bit but leaves Melbourne in the dust.
12	Madrid	(11)	Iberia now has two cities firmly ensconced in the top echelon.
13	Rome	(22)	The Eternal City set the tone for fashion throughout the Empire for a millennium. Today the tradition continues, though on a smaller scale.
14	Shanghai	(12)	Shanghai shines along with Hong Kong in the Middle Kingdom.
15	Monaco	(Debut)	The principality debuts at No. 15 more than doubling the ranking of the next newbie.
16	Las Vegas	(16)	Las Vegas and Monaco virtually tied on the Top Fashion Capitals ranking.
17	Melbourne	(9)	Though a Top 20 fashion capital, slips a bit in its on-going battle with Sydney (No. 11).
18	Moscow	(20)	More billionaires (79) call it home than New York City and its continual move up the fashion rankings reflects it.

2011 Ranking	City	Previous ranking	Comment
19	Amsterdam	(17)	Moves up two spots; now No. 10 in Europe.
20	Buenos Aires	(24)	Dramatic rise as she moves into the Top 20.
21	Bali	(32)	The world is discovering the allure that has been a secret for centuries.
22	Mexico City	(29)	The vast metropolis now claims the No. 2 spot in Latin America.
23	Rio de Janeiro	(19)	Ever readying for the Summer Olympics, also strengthening its fashion knowhow beyond swimwear.
24	Mumbai	(28)	Mumbai is beginning to display the swagger of old Bombay.
25	Sao Paulo	(13)	A burgeoning fashion scene and a bustling fashion industry.
26	Miami	(8)	More than just swim- and leisurewear town.
27	Dubai	(21)	Top in its region but feeling the pressure from intense global competition.
28	Stockholm	(33)	Stockholm and Copenhagen both moving up in tandem.
29	Copenhagen	(34)	Up five on the rankings, as was Stockholm.
30	Santiago	(31)	A strong No. 5 in the Latin America region.
31	Florence	(Debut)	Firenza undergoing a Renaissance in 21st century fashion.
32	Bangkok	(35)	Quietly moving up the rankings.
33	Warsaw	(36)	No. 2 in the Middle and Eastern European region.
34	Toronto	(38)	Now known for more than its fine Film Festival.
35	Vienna	(27)	This once Imperial City is staking a 21st century claim in its own right.
36	Chicago	(38)	City of the Big Shoulders stretching out toward world-class fashion.
37	Dallas	(40)	For Western Wear, please see Fort Worth.
38	San Francisco	(Debut)	Makes the list, like Austin, for its quirky, eclectic style.
39	New Delhi	(30)	A strong, emerging presence on the Global Fashion scene.
40	Austin	(Debut)	Eclectic? Outlandish? Even Green Fashion? Austin has it all.
41	Johannesburg	(25)	Maturing fashion industry a boon to a city in transition.
42	Abu Dhabi	(Debut)	Attempting to break into the world of fashion at the highest ranks.
43	Frankfurt	(38)	Holding its own amidst a thriving European fashion scene.
44	Antwerp	(Debut)	The legend of old becomes the reality of today. A fine debut.
45	Atlanta	(40)	Learning the ropes of competing globally, with a definite Southern flair.
46	Cape Town	(23)	In the process of gaining evermore attention for a worthy effort.
47	Krakow	(38)	One of the world's cultural treasures with a penchant for the eclectic.
48	Prague	(26)	Bohemian fashion influence is moving into its 2nd millennium.
49	Montreal	(Debut)	A strong debut into the Top 50.
50	Caracas	(40)	Despite internal turmoil, fashion savvy can be hard to ignore.

Reproduced courtesy of the Global Language Monitor. Report first published on 21 August 2011.

The GLM ranks the cities based on the frequency, contextual usage and appearance of fashion words and phrases like 'Haute Couture' and 'Mode' in the media, blogosphere and on the Internet, analysing what we say about fashion and how often.

The global dynamics of fashion centres is interesting to watch and important to be aware of, for instance the 'Big Four', originally New York, Paris, London and Milan, are no longer the only key fashion centres receiving all of the media attention. New and innovative fashion centres are getting a look in: Tokyo, Sao Paulo, Sydney, Moscow and Madrid particularly have been noted for their impressive progress.[14] In addition, Berlin and Singapore also made it into the GLM's influential list for the first time in 2011. It is important to widen the international arena to enable centres yet to build a global reputation to break in (such as Lima in Peru, which

launched its first fashion week in 2011), as new fashion centres may hold the key for dynamic fashion innovation and development.

All of the fashion centres, big or small, are important because of the unique qualities they offer and the role they play defining and maintaining trends and styles across fashion globally. The industry could not solely rely on one centre, and nor would it want to. Where New York and London are the top 'economic and media fashion capitals',[15] Paris is better known for couture fashion design.

Another tool for measuring the perception of leading fashion centres is the Anholt-Gfk Roper Nation Brands Index (NBI), which measures the global image of 50 countries by surveying 20,000 adults.[16] It measures global perception of countries across several dimensions (governance, culture, people,

exports, tourism, investment and immigration). According to the NBI for example, the UK is seen as an important fashion centre by other important global fashion centres, namely France, Italy and the United States. In 2007 their respondents ranked the UK 4th, 3rd and 4th respectively.[17] The fact that there is now a system to measure the success of the global fashion centres is an indicator of how increasingly important they are, and how competitive things are getting. In the words of Simon Anholt, policy advisor and co-founder of Anholt-Gfk Roper Nation Brands Index, 'The rapid advance of globalisation means that every country, every city and every region must compete with [each] other for its share of the world's consumers, tourists, investors, students, entrepreneurs, international sporting and cultural events, and for the attention and respect of the international media, of other governments, and the people of other countries.'[18]

When we talk about the global fashion industry a key group of countries are often referred to including the United Kingdom, the United States, France, Italy, China, South Korea, Spain, Germany, Brazil, India and Japan. Each country is known for its unique contribution and plays its own, defined role. For example, China is known for its manufacturing capabilities and India as a great source of fabric. These dynamics are gradually changing with time, but as an example of the strong and separate fashion identities of different countries here are case studies of six locations that are arguably the best known places for design style and industry talent: US (New York), United Kingdom (London), France (Paris), Italy (Milan), China (Hong Kong) and Japan (Tokyo).

*Case
Study*

British fashion design, leading fashion capital: London

London as a fashion capital balances commercial appeal with innovative and fashion-forward (i.e. early mass adoption) trends and this is what makes it unique. London is not defined by the sophistication and opulence of Milan, or the romantic couture-influence of Paris. Instead, one of the capital's unique selling points is its design creativity and diversity. British national fashion treasures such as Kate Moss, the late Alexander McQueen, the Duchess of Cambridge, Paul Smith, alongside elegant areas such as King's Road, Sloane Street and Savile Row and thriving shopping areas such as Oxford Street, Regent Street and Portobello all ensure London is at the top of the league in the style stakes. For me, the magic of London is its traditional heritage, a multicultural dynamism and prestige. Iconic brands like

Burberry and Aquascutum have set global trends, with both brands credited with the invention of the trench coat (Aquascutum claims that theirs dates back to the 1850s and Thomas Burberry, founder of Burberry, submitted a design in 1901.[19])

London has design credibility built from the Swinging Sixties, to the 70s Punk style, to the Cool Britannia image of the 1990s, but it also has versatility. Whilst at one end of the spectrum British style can be described as being classic, traditional and smart, at the other it can be seen as cutting edge, modern and casual. Some well-known and notable UK fashion brands include Burberry, Christopher Kane, Paul Smith, Reiss, Vivienne Westwood, Stella McCartney, Jasper Conran and Alexander McQueen. The influence that London (and the

UK overall) has had on the global fashion industry is undeniable, from the aforementioned clothing brands to world-renowned art colleges where many of the designers shaping the industry today have studied. Likewise, London Fashion Week (which attracts global visitors every season) and the many institutions that educate the public about the history of fashion, such as the Victoria and Albert Museum and the National Portrait Gallery, have all put London firmly on the global fashion map.

Case Study

My experience of London

I grew up in Cambridge, a beautiful university town, known for its attractive scenery, the River Cam and the world-renowned University of Cambridge. I loved growing up there but as I grew older I felt the pull of the 'Big City' of London, the fashion capital of the UK – after all it was only 50 miles away! I eventually moved to London to study Economics, Finance and Management at Queen Mary and Westfield University in Mile End, East London. Once there, it was impossible to ignore the fashion scene and I was keen to be part of it. There was definitely something about living in London that flicked a switch on in my creative mind. I loved exploring, travelling around Portobello Road and Notting Hill on a Sunday, seeing one-offs and vintage clothing being sold at Portobello Market. I enjoyed venturing into the East End to watch the street style on Brick Lane, Hoxton Square and in other popular areas, comparing the boho chic of the west with the hipster cool of the east. I felt inspired by the hustle and bustle of the capital city and people watching was heaven for the voyeur in me. In my opinion, if you are in the UK and it's fashion that you're into, London is at the centre of the buzz.

Flea markets in London are good places to find vintage clothing and inspiration.

Case Study

American fashion design: leading fashion capital New York

> 'New York – If I can make it here, I can make it anywhere…'
>
> Theme from *New York, New York*, composed by John Kander, with lyrics by Fred Ebb (1977).

New York is one of the four leading fashion capitals in the world, ranked by economic and media success. Many designers I have spoken to think of New York as the most important market in which to achieve success, because if you can become a big fashion brand in New York, then the doors to other global fashion capitals will (supposedly) open for you.

The world's first ever formally organised Fashion Week was held in New York in 1943. Nowadays New York Fashion Week officially kicks off the global fashion calendar in February, immediately followed by London, Milan, and Paris. Home to brands such as Ralph Lauren, Michael Kors, Marc Jacobs, Betsey Johnson, Tom Ford, Donna Karan, Anna Sui,

Calvin Klein and Diane Von Furstenberg, it holds a bright allure. Everything in New York seems to be done on a larger scale: longer runways, brighter lights, more celebrities lining the front row. Whatever happens in the rest of the fashion world, New York seems to do it bigger, and in fashion the biggest and most glamorous is often considered to be the most successful.

New York is home to around 5,000 showrooms and is the base for leading global marketing firms, media companies and consumer publications such as *Vogue* and *Women's Wear Daily*. As a trendsetting base, New York sees diverse 'block-to-block' fashion, from the Gossip Girl Manhattanites on the Upper East Side, right across to the urban chic worn in Harlem. Inspiration for fashion designers can be found everywhere, from the iconic Metropolitan Museum of Art with its well-stocked fashion division displaying over 30,000 garments from across five continents, to the

museum at the Fashion Institute of Technology (a design school with alumni including Michael Kors and Nina Garcia). And of course for any fashion lover, an invite to Anna Wintour's Benefit Gala, hosted at the Costume Institute, is the most coveted ticket in town.

New York is undeniably the fashion capital of America, although Miami and Los Angeles all have a strong presence. I showcased in New York 2007 and was blown away by the scale of its grandeur from the length of the runway to the sea of photographers: it felt simply huge. From numerous visits to New York I would say, when describing the street style, that it is a seemingly effortless layered look, which creates balance. Pieces are cleverly paired to contrast fit or textures, one simple example being denim skinny jeans worn with an oversized knitted jumper and silk scarf.

Case Study

French fashion design: leading fashion capital Paris

couture' not only originated from France but is also protected by law there. (See p.70.)

Paris has always had a strong influence over the direction of the global fashion industry. Since the early 19th century and the birth of haute couture, when the rich and powerful dictated the fashions of the day, France has always borne trendsetters. A typical example of this was the creation of Christian Dior's famous 'New Look' collection, which showcased in Paris in 1946 and heralded a significantly more curvaceous shape to the female silhouette, sparking a trend which ricocheted across the fashion world. The lure of Paris as a fashion centre draws aspiring designers for apprenticeships, learning experiences and dreams of showcasing their design work. Paris is a fashion capital known for its chic, refined, sophisticated style but it is also a go-to destination when shopping for quality accessories and shoes (it is the home of Louis Vuitton and luxury shoe design Christian Louboutin after all). Through the strong fashion capital of Paris, France has long been seen as the arbiter of what is *au courant* with the GLM describing it as 'No. 1 in our hearts but No. 3 in the eyes of the media.'

Paris is the couture fashion capital of the world and one of Europe's best loved. It is easy to fall for the charm and elegance of Paris, birthplace to global mega brands such as Chanel, Yves Saint Laurent and Dior. Most designers dream of showcasing their collections in Paris at a least once. This romanticism could be attributable to several aspects of the city: the fashion super brands which showcase their collections there, such as Lanvin and Givenchy; the beautiful architecture and art like the Notre Dame; or the infamous 'golden triangle' between the Champs-Elysées, the Avenue Marceau and the Avenue Montaigne, where Louis Vuitton, Givenchy, Rochas, Dior, Chloe, Celine, Chanel, Donna Karan and Hermes can all be found. The term 'haute

Case Study

Italian fashion design: leading fashion capital Milan

Milan, a beautiful city in northern Italy, is firmly placed on the global fashion map. Consistently in the 'Big Four' it is known for sophisticated and sleek fashion. Its architecture seamlessly blends traditional and modern styles. Its breathtaking landmarks such as the Centro Storico (historical centre), Duomo (cathedral) and La Scala (opera house) make it the perfect place from which to draw inspiration, while its natural glamour makes it an exciting and vibrant fashion centre. Versace, Gucci, Valentino, Prada, D&G, Armani and Bottega Veneta can be found in and around the influential 'Quadrangle of Fashion', the district between Via Montenapoleone, Via Gesu, Via Andrea, Corso Venezia and Via della Spiga. Italian style is known for being sophisticated and glamorous with a focus on stylish, ready-to-wear pieces despite a high-end haute couture presence. Milan's fashion week was established in 1958 and has successfully managed to keep the global spotlight with fierce determination and attitude. In February 2010 when the editor of American *Vogue*, Anna Wintour, had to cram Milan Fashion Week into four days, organisers had to scramble to make it happen. Two of Italy's strongest brands, Prada and Fendi decided to go on with their scheduled shows, with or without Wintour's presence. 'You have to believe in what you are worth,' Silvia Venturini Fendi, the second generation Fendi designer, said after the show. When the lights went up, Wintour was seen gracing the front row at both shows. Milan's designers certainly have attitude but the basis of this attitude lies clearly in the knowledge that they are worthy. The impact of the 'economic crisis' on the fashion industry, noticeably in 2008[21] and again from 2011 caused Milan to tighten its spending belt. Designer Frida Giannini may have successfully coined the phrase for Milan's adapted approached to global recession, by referring to it, when interviewed in February 2010, as 'controlled opulence'.[22] As it stands, as a fashion centre Milan is all about a sense of glamour, distinctiveness and bold sophistication. Milan, Florence and Rome are the main bases for Italian fashion houses Valentino Garavani, Dolce & Gabbana, Bottega Veneta, Etro, Emilio Pucci, Roberto Cavalli, Versace, Giorgio Armani, Fendi, Prada, Alberta Ferretti, Moschino, La Perla and Missoni.

Case Study

Japanese fashion design: leading fashion capital Tokyo

Tokyo's influence on global fashion is rising in the monitors. Whereas in the early 1990s the 'Big Four' – New York, London, Milan and Paris – heavily dominated, now the work of designers from other fashion capitals is drawing the spotlight and Tokyo is a strong example of this. By the start of the 21st century Japan was becoming known for its popular 'street fashion', where individuals were creatively mixing and personalising mainstream trends. Tokyo is an exciting example of Japanese style, which can be visibly observed as fashion-forward, adventurous and uniquely eclectic, where contrasting pieces are mixed and matched in unique colour combinations, cuts and textures. Well-known Japanese designers include Issey Miyake, Yohji Yamamoto, A Bathing Ape, Kenzo and Comme des Garçons's cutting innovator Rei Kawakubo, who developed a new way of cutting and whose design style focuses on innovation and challenging convention. Kawakubo's cutting has been compared to Madeleine Vionnet's innovation in the 1930s which saw fabric being uniquely cut on the bias allowing for more freedom of movement and a more 'natural elasticity'. The youth streetwear of Harajuku (a popular area in Japan where fashionable young people hang out every Sunday and seen as a popular fashion centre) and Shibuya (also a popular fashion centre) is well-known globally alongside the gothic-lolita and punk styles. Designers who have been inspired by Japanese fashion include Elie Saab, Karl Lagerfeld and John Galliano. Givenchy's Haute Couture Spring/Summer 2011 collection, all worn by East Asian models, was an obvious heavy nod in the Japanese direction with its inspiration being taken from Japanese dancer Kazuo Ohno and the futuristic world of Gundam fighters. Popular shopping areas include the Omotesando (in the Harajuku district) and 'The Ginza' which is to Tokyo what Fifth Avenue is to New York and what Bond Street is to London. Respected fashion schools Bunka Fashion College and Mode Gakuen are also found in Tokyo.

Case Study

Chinese fashion design: leading fashion capital Shanghai

Market analysts predict that China will become the largest luxury market by 2020, with Chinese consumers buying more than 44 percent of the world's luxury goods.[23] In addition, China is one of the most important manufacturing countries on the global fashion scene with international fashion houses opening up more stores and increasing their presence there (Net-a-Porter launched there in 2012). This global influence can be clearly seen – in April 2012 Gucci presented its first Chinese fashion show (men and women's Fall/Winter 2012 collections) on the Shanghai Bund – and abroad. Well-known Chinese-American designers, or designers of Chinese origin include Vera Wang, Jimmy Choo, Derek Lam, Phillip Lim, Anna Sui and Jason Wu. Are the streets of Shanghai, Hong Kong or Beijing any indication of what is to come for the global fashion industry?

At the Autumn/Winter 2012 Christian Dior show at Paris Fashion Week, Jessica Michault (Online Style Editor of the *International Herald*) tweeted a photograph of five gorgeous Chinese women sitting together in the front row, with the caption 'The future of the fashion world's front row.' Indeed a number of leading global fashion brands have a head office in Hong Kong. The relevance of Shanghai (described as the 'Paris of the East') as a leading fashion capital should be self-explanatory despite being less well established than the leading fashion centres (20-30 years younger than Hong Kong for example). It first gained exposure to western fashion when it was opened as a commercial port in 1843, and a western influence is still visible today, with the Chinese showing support for western brands such as Louis Vuitton, Chanel, Dior, Burberry, Comme des Garçons and others. Despite this, the reputation of China's creative domestic talent is building a name for itself locally and internationally. Designers to look out for include Lan Yu (a bridal wear designer who has earned the title of 'China's Vera Wang') Guo Pei, Li Xiaofeng (who collaborated with Lacoste in 2010).

Bustling Shanghai is an exciting example of Chinese style, which can be described as bold and creative, featuring a unique blend of colours, styles, fabrics and shapes. The fusion of western influence combined with the elegance of eastern tradition can result in a daring, in-your-face, colourful look or one which is well put-together yet simple. As it is such a young fashion capital Shanghai style is still emerging and evolving. Let's see what it holds over the next few years.

Key fashion events

The events in everyone's calendars are, of course, the global fashion weeks. Fashion weeks are when the industry is at its most visible in the global mainstream media; when all of the key figures and influencers come out to socialise, network, showcase their work and most importantly to do business. Phones are buzzing, designers are sourcing models, working non-stop on collections to be ready in time for showing, organising exhibitions and presenting their collections; photographers are selling work, getting accreditation to cover the various runway and backstage events; press (such as journalists, bloggers and editors) are finding out what each respective capital has to offer and who the rising and falling stars are; buyers are watching fashion shows, visiting showrooms and placing orders. The exact dates for the various fashion weeks vary, but as a rule, the main fashion week months are February and September when New York, London, Milan and Paris (in that order) each host a fashion week. Fashion weeks run for 5–7 days and showcase collections by designers and brands through a series of runway fashion shows or exhibitions/showcases. Press and media attention is crucial as designers vie for attention and business. For some emerging designers fashion week is a time to watch fashion show after fashion show with a wistful, 'one day it might be me' feeling. There's always something to excite, whether it's the front row celebrities, the designer's publicity stunts (such as when Yasmin Le Bon walked the runway for Issa during London Fashion Week for the brands Autumn/Winter 2011 collection; how the crowd roared to see the seasoned model make a rare runway appearance!), or simply seeing fashion hit the runway knowing you have witnessed the key trends to come months ahead of time. Fashion week symbolises a period of excitement but also stress for the fashion industry.

In addition to the official fashion weeks there are also smaller, independent fashion weeks, which can be less expensive to enter and showcase for new and emerging designers. Vauxhall Fashion Scout (www.

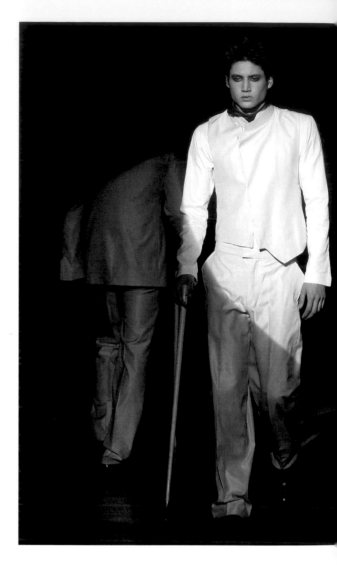

vauxhallfashionscout.com), for example, is a London-based independent showcase which promotes new and seasoned designers to an international audience via catwalk shows, presentations, fashion films and exhibitions. Another is On|Off (www.onoff.tv), the UK's independent fashion showcase during London Fashion Week which connects the gap between 'on and off' schedule designers. It seeks to help boost designers' profiles and sales via exposure to top UK and international press and buyers. Fashion East (www.fashioneast.co.uk), also in London, gives womenswear and menswear designers the opportunity to showcase catwalk collections during London Fashion Week. In New York, Nolcha Fashion Week (www.nolchafashionweek.com) is an event for

independent fashion designers to showcase their collections and in Toronto, |FAT| Arts & Fashion Week (http://fashionarttoronto.ca) is a multi-arts event which features 200 national and international fashion designers. Independent fashion weeks like these can be found in other cities also.

Fashion seasons

The industry is divided into two key seasons: Spring/ Summer and Autumn/Winter, also known as Fall/ Winter. The transition from one season to another is marked by the introduction of new styles, colours and silhouettes and can be characterised by fabrics and styles for warm and cold weather. Designers create collections for these seasons and work all year around from January to December, showcasing collections six months ahead of their in-store delivery. This means that Autumn/Winter or Fall/Winter collections which designers show in February will hit the stores around August/September. Inter-seasonal collections clothing will arrive in November/December. Likewise, designers showcase Spring/Summer collections in September, which will be in stores around February/ March. Inter-seasonal clothing will arrive in June/July. On an individual and country to country basis, stores and designers may deviate from these timings. Inter-seasonal collections are usually referred to as Resort/ Cruise or Pre-Fall (before Autumn/Winter).

Official global fashion weeks

EUROPE

Albania Fashion Week Albania
MQ Vienna Fashion Week Austria
Belorussian Fashion Week Belarus
Sarajevo Fashion Week Bosnia Herzegovina
Bridal Fashion Week Bulgaria
Men's Fashion Week Bulgaria
Plovdiv Fashion Week Bulgaria
Sofia Fashion Week Bulgaria
Dubrovnik Fashion Week International Croatia
Dreft Fashion Week Zagreb Croatia
Cyprus Fashion Week by Harper's Bazaar Cyprus
Prague Fashion Week Czech Republic
Copenhagen Fashion Week Denmark
Paris Fashion Week France
Mercedes-Benz Fashion Week Berlin Germany
Fashion Week Athens Greece
Hellenic Fashion Week Greece
Budapest Fashion Week Hungary
Iceland Fashion Week Iceland
Africa Fashion Weekend Ireland
Belfast Fashion Week Northern Ireland
Motorola Dublin Fashion Week Ireland
Alta Roma Alta Moda Italy
Milan Fashion Week Italy
Milano Moda Pre-Collezioni Italy
Riga Fashion Week Latvia
Mercedes-Benz Malta Fashion Week Malta
Amsterdam International Fashion Week
Netherlands
Oslo Fashion Week Norway
Fashion Philosophy Fashion Week Poland
ModaLisboa/Lisbon Fashion Week Portugal
Cluj Fashion Week Romania
Eurasian Fashion Week Russia
Mercedes-Benz Fashion Week Russia
Volvo Fashion Week Russia
Glasgow Fashion Week Scotland
Belgrade Fashion Week Serbia Montenegro
Andalusian Fashion Week Spain
Barcelona Bridal Week – Noviaespaña Spain
Cibeles Madrid Fashion Week Spain
Valencia Fashion Week Spain
Mercedes-Benz Fashion Week Stockholm Sweden
Stockholm Fashion Week Sweden
Lviv Fashion Week Ukraine
Ukrainian Fashion Week Ukraine
Liverpool Fashion Week United Kingdom
London Fashion Week United Kingdom
Middlesbrough Fashion Week United Kingdom
Oxford Fashion Week United Kingdom
Urban Fashion Week Europe United Kingdom
Wimbledon Fashion Week United Kingdom

NORTH AMERICA

Aspen Fashion Week USA
Atlanta International Fashion Week USA
Austin Fashion Week USA
Baltimore Fashion Week USA
Boston Fashion Week USA
BOXeight Fashion Week Los Angeles USA
Charleston Fashion Week USA
Cincinnati Fashion Week USA
Columbus Fashion Week USA
Connecticut Fashion Week USA
DC Fashion Week USA
Detroit Fashion Week USA
Emerald City Fashion Week USA
Fashion Week Cleveland USA
Fashion Week El Paseo USA
Fashion Week San Antonio USA
Fashion Week San Diego USA
Fashion Week Tampa Bay USA
Funkshion: Fashion Week Miami Beach USA
Haute.Lanta Fashion Week USA
Houston Fashion Week USA
Kansas City Fashion Week USA
Los Angeles Fashion Week USA
Los Angeles Fashion Weekend USA
Maryland Fashion Week USA
Mercedes-Benz Fashion Week Swim Miami USA
Mercedes-Benz Fashion Week New York USA
Miami Fashion Week USA
New Jersey Fashion Week USA
North Carolina Fashion Week USA
Northern Virginia (NOVA) Fashion Week USA
OKC Fashion Week USA
Omaha Fashion Week USA
PBH Philadelphia Fashion Week USA
Philadelphia Fashion Week USA
Phoenix Fashion Week USA
Portland Fashion Week USA
Sacramento Fashion Week USA
Saint Louis Fashion Week USA
San Francisco Fashion Week – Re-Invent USA
Scottsdale Fashion Week USA
Seattle Fashion Week USA
Virginia Fashion Week USA
Wisconsin Fashion Week USA

CANADA

Alberta Fashion Week Canada
Atlantic Fashion Week Canada
British Columbia Fashion Week Canada
Eco Fashion Week Vancouver Canada
Edmonton Fashion Week Canada
Frugal Fashion Week Canada
LG Fashion Week Beauty by L'Oreal Paris Canada
Montreal Fashion Week Canada
Vancouver Fashion Week Canada
Western Canada Fashion Week Canada

CENTRAL/SOUTH AMERICA

Argentina Fashion Week Argentina
Pinamar Fashion Week Argentina
Islands of the World Fashion Week The Bahamas
Fashion Rio/Rio De Janeiro Fashion Week Brazil
São Paulo Fashion Week Brazil
Pereira Fashion Week Colombia
República Dominicana Fashion Week Dominican
Republic
Fashion Week Honduras
Caribbean Fashion Week Jamaica
Fashion Week Mexico
Mercedes-Benz Fashion Mexico
Asunción Fashion Week Paraguay
Puerto Rico High Fashion Week Puerto Rico
Fashion Week Trinidad & Tobago

AFRICA AND MIDDLE EAST

Cairo Fashion Week Egypt
Liberia Fashion Week Liberia
Lagos International Fashion Week Nigeria
Nigeria Fashion Week Nigeria
Ethnica Fashion Week Agadir Morocco
Africa Fashion Week South Africa
Audi Joburg Fashion Week (A/W) South Africa
Cape Town Fashion Week South Africa
Durban Fashion Week South Africa
Joburg Fashion Week (S/S) South Africa
Mpumalanga Fashion Week South Africa
SA Fashion Week South Africa
Swahili Fashion Week Tanzania
Fashion Week Tunis Tunisia
Coca-Cola Light Zambia Fashion Week Zambia
Zimbabwe Fashion Week Zimbabwe
Accra Fashion Week Ghana

ASIA

Bangladesh Fashion Week Bangladesh
Dhaka Fashion Week Bangladesh
China Fashion Week China
Hong Kong Fashion Week S/S China
Hong Kong Fashion Week F/W China
International Fashion Week China
Shanghai Fashion Week China
Bangalore Fashion Week India
Chennai International Fashion Week India
Kolkata Fashion Week India
Lakmé Fashion Week India
Van Heusen India Men's Week India
Wills Lifestyle India Fashion Week India
Bali Fashion Week Indonesia
Jakarta Fashion Week Indonesia
Japan Fashion Week Japan
Malaysia-International Fashion Week Malaysia
Fashion Pakistan Week Pakistan
Islamabad Fashion Week Pakistan
Karachi Fashion Week Pakistan
PFDC Sunsilk Fashion Week Pakistan
Philippine Fashion Week Philippines
Singapore Fashion Week Singapore
Seoul Fashion Week South Korea
Colombo Fashion Week Sri Lanka
Ho Chi Minh City Fashion Week Vietnam

OCEANIA

Rosemount Australian Fashion Week Australia
MHCC Fiji Fashion Week Fiji
Air New Zealand Fashion Week New Zealand
iD Dunedin Fashion Week New Zealand

Global fashion organisations

It is important to be aware of the various organisations that exist within the fashion industry that offer information and support. Not least because emerging designers need assistance in key areas such as business planning, marketing, finance, retail and product development but also because these organisations facilitate a sense of belonging. Being part of a group of like-minded individuals is crucial, not only for inspiration and sounding board sessions but also to help develop a network. Life as a fashion designer can sometimes be a solitary existence so industry organisations and groups provide the opportunity to share opinions, concerns and boost energy levels. The number of industry organisations, networking groups and support organisations has risen meteorically in recent years and help is now much more readily available.

BRITISH FASHION COUNCIL (BFC), UK

The BFC is an organisation that aims to support and showcase British designers and promote London as a leading fashion capital. They achieve this via high profile events, such as London Fashion Week, where international press and buyers view established and establishing UK designers. The BFC is also behind the 'BFC Colleges Council Initiative', which helps forge links between fashion graduates and key industry bodies. Other initiatives include 'New Gen' and 'Fashion Forward' which are schemes offering a range of support to designers and creatives from mentoring and sponsorship to competitions and seminars. Also see p.103.

www.britishfashioncouncil.com

COUNCIL OF FASHION DESIGNERS OF AMERICA (CFDA), USA

The Council of Fashion Designers of America (CFDA) is a non-profit trade association that leads industry-wide initiatives and whose membership consist of over 400 of America's foremost womenswear, menswear, jewellery and accessory designers. The organisation hosts the annual CFDA Fashion Awards, which recognise and reward the top creative talents in the industry. The Council also offers programs that support professional development, and offer scholarships including the CFDA/*Vogue* Fashion Fund, the Geoffrey Beene Design Scholar Award, the Liz Claiborne Scholarship Award, and the CFDA/*Teen Vogue* Scholarship.

www.cfda.com

IMG FASHION (INTERNATIONAL MANAGEMENT GROUP), GLOBAL

IMG Fashion is part of the global sports, entertainment and media company IMG Worldwide and plays a crucial part in global fashion events including the New York Fashion Week by supporting their promotion and operations. IMG Fashion owns and operates worldwide fashion weeks and events, represents designers, models, photographers, art directors and stylists.

www.imgworld.com

THE CHARTERED SOCIETY OF DESIGNERS, GLOBAL

The Chartered Society of Designers is a professional body for designers and the main authority on professional design practice. It is the world's largest chartered body of professional designers with members in 33 countries and represents designers in all disciplines.

www.csd.org.uk

THE FASHION GROUP INTERNATIONAL, GLOBAL

The Fashion Group International, whose founding members include Elizabeth Arden, Eleanor Roosevelt and Helena Rubinstein, is a global, non-profit, professional organisation with over 5000 fashion industry members. The organisation seeks to assist its members to develop their individual careers.

www.fgi.org

WORLD GLOBAL STYLE NETWORK (WGSN), GLOBAL

WGSN is an online trend analysis and research service providing creative and business intelligence for the apparel, style, design and retail industries.

www.wgsn.com

NOTES

1. Bureau of Labor Statistics website, 'Apparel Manufacturing: NAICS 315', http://stats.bls.gov/iag/tgs/iag315.htm; accessed 17 October 2012

2. British Fashion Council website, 'New Landmark Report: Value of Fashion' (September 2010), http://www.britishfashioncouncil.com/news_detail.aspx?ID=228; accessed 17 October 2012

3. Deyan Sudjic, *Fifty Dresses that Changed the World* (London: Conran Octopus, 2009)

4. Definition from Google Dictionary

5. Definition from wordnetweb.princeton.edu/perl/webwn

6. Bureau of Labor Statistics website, 'Apparel Manufacturing: NAICS 315', http://stats.bls.gov/iag/tgs/iag315.htm; accessed 17 October 2012

7. http://proxy.mbc.edu:2312/EBchecked/topic/1706624/fashion-industry

8. Fashion Products website, 'Fashion Apparel Industry Overview', http://www.fashionproducts.com/fashion-apparel-overview.html; accessed 17 October 2012

9. British Fashion Council website, 'Value of Fashion Report' (September 2010), http://www.britishfashioncouncil.com/news_detail.aspx?ID=228; accessed 17 October 2012

10. G J Sumathi, *Elements of Fashion and Apparel Design* (New Delhi: New Age International, 2007)

11. Valerie Mendes and Amy de la Haye, *20th Century Fashion*, (London: Thames and Hudson, 1999)

12. Ruth La Ferla, 'Waiting for the Dress', *The New York Times* website (22 April 2011), http://www.nytimes.com/2011/04/24/fashion/24knockoff.html?pagewanted=all&_r=0; accessed 17 October 2012

13. Global Language Monitor website, 'London Overtakes New York as Top Global Fashion Capital' (August 2011), http://www.languagemonitor.com/olympics/london-overtakes-new-york-as-top-global-fashion-capital/; accessed 17 October 2012

14. Global Language Monitor website, '2009 Fashion Capital Research', www.slideshare.net/TrendsSpotting/2009-fashion-capital-survey; accessed 17 October 2012

15. Global Language Monitor website, 'London Overtakes New York as Top Global Fashion Capital' (August 2011), http://www.languagemonitor.com/olympics/london-overtakes-new-york-as-top-global-fashion-capital/; accessed 17 October 2012

16. GfK America website, 'Anholt-GfK Roper Nation Brands Index', http://www.gfkamerica.com/practice_areas/roper_pam/nbi_index/index.en.html; accessed 17 October 2012

17. Simon Anholt, '2007 Anholt-GfK Roper Nation Brands Index'; available at http://www.simonanholt.com/Publications/publications-other-articles.aspx, accessed 17 October 2012

18. Simon Anholt, 'Competitive Identity: A New Model for the Brand Management of Nations, Cities and Regions', *Policy and Practice*, Issue 4, Spring 2007 (Belfast: Centre for Global Education); available at http://www.developmenteducationreview.com/issue4-focus1, accessed 17 October 2012.

19. Wikipedia, 'Trench Coat', http://en.wikipedia.org/wiki/Trench_coat; accessed 17 October 2012

20. Global Language Monitor website, 'New York Regains Fashion Capital Crown from Milan' (August 2010), http://www.languagemonitor.com/fashion-capitals/new-york-regains-fashion-capital-crown-from-milan; accessed 17 October 2012

21. Global Times website, 'Fashion Tightens Belt' (September 2011), http//www.globaltimes.cn/NEWS/tabid/99/ID/677537/Fashion-tightens-belt.aspx; accessed 17 October 2012

22. Jess Cartner-Morley, 'Dolce & Gabbana and Gucci lead Milan Fashion Week's Fightback', *The Guardian* website (1 March 2010), http://www.guardian.co.uk/lifeandstyle/2010/mar/01/dolce-gabbana-gucci-milan-fashion-week; accessed 17 October 2012

23. CLSA website, 'China to Become the World's Largest Market for Luxury goods over the Next decade' (February 2, 2011), http://www.clsa.com/about-csla/media-centre/2011-media-releases/china-to-become-the-worlds-largest-market-for-luxury-goods.php; accessed 25 October 2012

VENTURING IN

Vision and goals

After you have taken a good, close look at the industry and decided that you want to build a career within it, you might start to feel rather overwhelmed about exactly where to begin your journey. The comforting truth is that there is more than one way to get where you want to be. It is not uncommon for a designer who does not hold a fashion design degree to work for a fashion house as a design intern and gain experience this way, or for a stylist to get work without an official qualification because he/she simply has a natural talent. I have no intention of trying to downplay how difficult it is to forge forward without a certain level of education in such a competitive industry, but opportunities do exist for those who are willing to work hard and create them.

Never lose sight of the fact that hurdles, although challenging, are also character building (and character is something you will need a lot of in fashion). The nature of the industry can be quite unpredictable, meaning that you may find yourself getting swept in any direction the fashion wind is blowing at the time. For this reason, I think it is extremely important to know what 'making it' really means to you. Attaining and maintaining a clear image of what your personal success looks like will make it easier to achieve and to stay focused on your path.

What does 'making it' mean to you?

What exactly do you want to achieve within the fashion industry? When you picture 'success' do you imagine achieving any of the following?

- getting paid to dress people;
- international recognition;
- freedom to do what you love, all day every day;
- freedom to work with talented people;
- the feeling being able to create gives you;
- getting the trends the world wears;
- money and fame.

All of the above? None of the above? Thinking about what success means to you will influence the decisions you make and how you approach your career. For example, if success means recognition for quality design work within the fashion industry then you will need to start to pay more attention to detail and invest in high-quality materials, even when this means going a little further out of your way to source them.

Also remember that if you understand your goal you will be able to stay motivated. Motivation can be defined as being either intrinsic (motivated by your personal feelings) or extrinsic (motivated by specific needs/objectives and goals). You will probably be motivated by a combination of intrinsic and extrinsic factors. Personally, I am motivated by the good feelings I derive from creating unique designs and also by the feeling of excitement I get from working in an industry where creative talent is all around me (intrinsic factors). I am also motivated by the lifestyle I would like to lead, to live comfortably, to travel and visit different parts of the world (extrinsic factors). Setting goals and defining what motivates you can help you to channel your focus and work in the right direction.

Success is not all about a high IQ

Whatever your opinion is about what determines success, I hope that you will agree with this one statement, that success is achieved due to a combination of factors and not just one single factor. Being skilled is not enough, nor is just being hard working. For my own personal journey into the fashion industry, the three factors I believe have played a role in my progress are determination, ambition and consistency. Looking beyond my own personal efforts I acknowledge that my upbringing has also contributed since hard work was always highly valued when I was growing up. When I consider my most successful friends within this industry, I see they are not always the ones who attended leading fashion colleges and took home all of the design prizes year after year, but they all have drive, ambition, talent, focus, determination, the ability to self-motivate and have built a support network of some kind. I think Malcolm Gladwell offers an interesting perspective on success in his book *Outliers*.[1] He writes, '[*Outliers*] grew out [of] a frustration I found myself having with the way we explain the careers of really successful people. You know how you hear someone say of Bill Gates or some rock star or some other outlier – "they're really smart", or "they're really ambitious"? Well, I know lots of people who are really smart and really ambitious, and they aren't worth 60 billion dollars.' Gladwell then goes on to try to find a better set of explanations for success. He addresses the importance of the individual's characteristics, personality traits and habits but also looks at the surrounding factors such as their community, culture and family. As he says, 'We've been looking at tall

trees, and I think we should have been looking at the forest.' The importance of networks and relevance of certain character traits are discussed later in this book; see pp.86–91 and p.66.

Can you identify your strengths?

It's important to be honest with yourself about where your strengths lie to increase your chances of making progress. Working towards mastering your strengths will bring you one step closer to your goals and will help you to understand and maybe even improve on your areas of weakness. You may be a great illustrator and communicator but not have a great ability to sew, in which case presenting and sharing your ideas will be one of your strongest tools but you'll need to find an experienced seamstress to act as a mentor or someone more capable to sew for you. Be realistic and open to finding help. Even if you are capable of everything, if you plan to start your own clothing label a time will come when you need to employ someone to help you develop your business. I used to think that asking for help or relinquishing control meant I was not coping or wasn't good enough, but in many ways it means the opposite, that you are not only managing but you are allowing yourself (and your clothing label) to grow.

What do you want to do in the fashion industry?

Now you've considered what success means to you and you're familiar with your strengths, it is time to start asking yourself some questions. Do you want to be the boss or the employee? To design for a brand or to be the creative director? Do you truly enjoy being a solo or team player? Some designers dream of setting up and running a company specialising in making products they love. Others hope to work for a prestigious and well-respected brand. Whatever your dream job, you are going to have to work hard to get it and keep it, as it's a certainty that the same dream

Identifying where your strengths lie is important. Are you someone who can predict future trends? Is your passion for textile design? Do you have an eye for visual merchandising? What part of the global fashion industry most appeals to you?

will be shared by many others. There are a number of exciting and challenging jobs in the fashion industry, which you may work in or interact with at some stage in your career. Descriptions of some of these follow.

Fashion/retail buyer

A fashion buyer plans, selects and buys the clothing and accessory ranges sold in retail outlets. They need to be able to analyse and understand fashion trends in addition to customer preferences and buying patterns. Buyers know how to manage budgets for their shop/department, in addition to understanding the style of their store and its customers. A fashion buyer can look at global fashion trends and translate them to the shop-floor level, buying clothing from

Jobs in the fashion industry

- fashion buyer;
- fashion and textile designer;
- fashion forecaster;
- fashion journalist;
- fashion merchandiser;
- fashion promotions/ public relations (PR);
- fashion retailer;
- fashion stylist.

designers and manufacturers that is on trend but also introducing edgy and unique fashion to the shop if required. Buyers need to have a thorough knowledge and understanding of their competitors. A good head for figures is important when it comes to collating financial information such as profit and loss reports. Buyers may spend a great deal of time travelling to source clothing – this involves visiting fashion weeks, exhibitions or trade shows - and negotiating with designers and clothing manufacturers. The job comes with its own unique pressures as a miscalculated forecast or investing in the wrong type of clothing for the store could risk job loss. Buyers need to have a lot of nerve and the ability to cope with stress.

Fashion or trend forecaster

A fashion forecaster predicts future market trends ranging from a few months to a few years. This role relies on three main elements: a sharp instinct for fashion, an understanding of trends and style, and an ability to read and interpret 'industry intelligence' such as trend analysis, reports, industry news headlines and market research data. Forecasters assist designers and retailers by giving them the first idea of what they should be making and buying. Forecasting involves a great deal of travelling to known 'trend hot spots'. A successful fashion forecaster pays close attention to what people are wearing on the streets, in magazines, on television and all around, in addition to asking the question 'why?'. Forecasters need to be well read in cultural and social topics too as these have an impact upon fashion. Constantly on the lookout from the high street to the Internet, a forecaster is forever researching and then translating research into fashion facts and figures for different markets in order to let people know what is to come and what to buy. Forecasting jobs can be in-house or freelance.

Fashion merchandiser

Merchandisers ensure products appear at the point of sale at the time they are wanted by customers in the right quantities to meet demand. They understand the importance of display and presentation and those known as 'visual merchandisers' also work with accessories and props such as mannequins and busts to ensure clothing is displayed in the best way possible. Merchandisers work with the buying teams to select the clothing and product lines and ensure they are bought in the right quantities. In smaller companies and/or departments the merchandiser and buyer is the same person due to the crossover in responsibilities. It is the main role of the fashion merchandiser to set price and work on product promotions and discounts to generate the most profit. The fundamental aim of their role is to ensure products sell well so a good head for figures is necessary to monitor performance, sales figures and oversee stock. Merchandisers will analyse why a product is doing well and why particular colours, price points and styles are flying off the shelves.

Fashion promotions/ public relations (PR)

Fashion PR agents aim to capture a target audience in line with a company's selling strategy using carefully planned and implemented campaigns for products and brands. Regular tasks involve writing press releases and releasing content to media, dealing with press – such as journalists and bloggers – and organising events such as fashion shows and launches. A Fashion PR agent is constantly communicating with industry contacts to get their job done, which is why a strong book of contacts, and excellent communications skills are an absolute must. A PR agent needs to have an understanding of the product and brand they represent in order to target the most relevant media and audience; they must also work hard to keep both the client and the media happy. PR may be employed by a range of organisations from a fashion house to individual

Visual merchandisers are responsible for the selection of clothing on sale in a store and how it is presented.

designers to industry organisations such as the British Fashion Council or the Council of Fashion Designers of America. There are three types of PR: in-house/corporate PR working within a large organisation to promote them; agency/consultancy PR working for a number of clients as part of an agency; freelance/consultancy PR, working as an individual/independent selling PR services. For a good, general overview of PR visit http://www.kent.ac.uk/careers/workin/PR.htm.

Fashion stylist

Fashion stylists work with designers, photographers, hair and makeup artists and art directors to create visual images and looks for models, celebrities, musicians and high profile clients in addition to others. These are used across platforms such as in magazines, on TV, online and at events. Individuals, fashion houses, magazines, advertising agencies and design companies can employ stylists, but they can also work individually on a freelance basis. Stylists understand fashion and have a natural eye for selecting the clothes and accessories to best compliment a look and convey the desired final image. Stylists often borrow, hire or buy garments for photo shoots so it is in their interest to build and maintain relationships with as many fashion designers and clothing manufacturers as possible, in addition to fashion PR. Powers of persuasion are high up the list of desired attributes! Being trend aware is crucial as well as understanding how to work with different body shapes and skin tones, alongside colours, style and cut. (Also see pp.72–3.) Stylists need excellent communication skills as they need to be able to discuss the overall concept for a look with everyone involved including the designer, model and photographer.

Fashion retailer

The role of a fashion retailer can vary greatly depending on the size of the shop – whether it is a huge high street department store or a small independent shop and boutique. Depending

Case Study

Above, Anne Look, and right, the cover of *FIASCO* magazine featuring Gillian Anderson by Dave Wise, styled by Anne Lock.

Interview with stylist Anne Look

Anne Look is a fashion stylist from Sydney who has worked with the likes of Gillian Anderson, Daniel Bedingfield and Sophie Delila. Anne has previously contributed to and worked with *International Life* magazine, The British Hairdressing Awards, The Fashion Business Club, *Every Model Magazine*, Matthew Curtis Hair Design, Glam Media, and has styled collections for countless emerging, graduate and established designers. Now, Anne divides her time between London and Sydney and writes fashion trend articles for picture giant Big Pictures as well as running her styling, writing and consulting business through her popular site Stylist And The City. Her website www.stylistandthecity.com showcases fashion features, how to style the latest, street style, interview and global trend news.

WHAT MADE YOU WANT TO BE A STYLIST?

It actually happened by accident! Growing up in Sydney in the 80s and 90s I found that there were only a few bookshops I could visit to find out more about the international fashion scene and what clothing designs were being created across the globe. Fashion styling was always just an interest that developed for me as my background was in sport so I did not know anybody in the fashion world.

I had friends who loved gossip magazines and would look at fashion with an eye to buy. I always knew I had a different take on it, instead wanting to create looks with the clothes as my tools. I wasn't really interested wearing it myself or buying – I just wanted to create that fantasy look! I loved considering the way an outfit was put together in a creative way and it wasn't until some time after that I researched the role of the stylist and exactly what it meant to be one and how.

HOW DO YOU DEVELOP RELATIONSHIPS WITH DESIGNERS?

I didn't know any designers when I started out but the relationships come with time. If a designer works alone that is one thing but if not then the public relations and press teams behind the designer become the major factor for a stylist. They are the communicators between the stylist and the designer.

HOW IMPORTANT ARE THESE RELATIONSHIPS?

Crucial. It is in fact, everything. The designer and their team need to understand your aesthetic and angle and it needs to fit with what they want to achieve. It's a constant and evolving communication.

HOW CAN A STYLIST WORK WITH A FASHION DESIGNER TO DEVELOP THE BEST POSSIBLE IMAGES?

I work on projects where as a stylist I work closely with the fashion designer to create a certain look. For example, I have a client (a musician) who wants to work directly with a fashion designer to produce something individual as an artist. I think there is a huge difference between working with designers on a catwalk show or for an editorial shoot or for an individual. Like most things in life, it's all about communicating. In the world of image, it's talking in pictures – which is a developed skill.

HOW IMPORTANT IS IT FOR A DESIGNER TO UNDERSTAND THE ROLE OF A STYLIST?

Again, crucial. It's funny really, when I talk to people who work outside of the industry – they always wonder what a stylist is and what they do, they can't understand why a designer needs a stylist. When you speak to people in the industry, the designer will often refer to the stylist as part of them, like their other arm. A designer needs to focus on their collection and the individual pieces making up that collection. A stylist is a vault of information, research and outside influences. We look at the bigger picture and how the collection should come together and be consistent as well as cohesive.

HOW CAN A DESIGNER KNOW IF A STYLIST IS ANY GOOD OR NOT?

To be honest it is often trial and error. It is also about looking at what they have done in the past and knowing if its a good fit for you or not. A stylist who doesn't work with a particular designer doesn't mean they won't work for another. It's all very subjective. Stylists starting out should test, test, test! And network!

WHAT DO YOU DO WHEN LOOKING FOR PRESS COVERAGE?

You must consider who you are dressing and what they are like as a person. You don't get results if the person is uncomfortable with the way they have been dressed. In saying that, it's very rewarding to work with someone who has a certain image or a way they have always been portrayed and they are trying to change that idea. It's showing the world another dimension or side to that person. It can be very beneficial if they are up for it and trusting in their stylist.

on this size and structure, responsibilities could involve visual merchandising, buying and managing stock, processing deliveries clothing or handling payment. For example, retailers working in a role which involves sales will be liaising with customers in the shop on a regular basis, working on visual merchandising, in the changing room or at the point of sale. A fashion retailer with managerial responsibilities could be responsible for management and operation of the shop and staff. Working as a fashion retailer requires good communication skills and an ability to work as part of a team as well as a genuine and enthusiastic interest in customer relations and fashion retail.

Fashion journalist

Fashion journalists work for local and national newspapers, magazines and journals, trade press, TV channels, independent TV and radio and news agencies. They research and write pieces about the fashion industry, nationally and/or internationally. Fashion journalists write about an industry that is predominantly visual so they must have the language skills and vocabulary to be able to tell a good story. Topics can range from industry news and trends to interviews and fashion events. Part of the job is to interview people working in the industry and to attend fashion shows and trade shows. Relationships are key – for example, if working for a fashion magazine, journalists may need to develop relationships with PR companies, designers and organise photo shoots. They also need to be able to sniff out a good story and develop it. Nowadays social media skills are becoming increasingly important as journalists are required to work online through platforms such as Facebook and Twitter.

Career paths

The roles described on the previous pages are some of the key jobs within the fashion industry that I have interacted with as a fashion designer. There are many more that I haven't mentioned, such as photographers, hair and makeup artists, event and trade exhibition organisers, graphic designers and so on. For every job there is a level of experience you need to have or a particular skill set. If you study the lives of world-renowned fashion designers you may find that some skipped higher education and landed work experience in a studio as a design assistant or apprentice and from there worked their way up, gaining experience as they went along. Other designers went to leading fashion colleges, walked out with numerous awards and went straight into running their own brand. Some didn't even start out by working in the fashion department at all. I really enjoy reading designer's biographies on Wikipedia or Biography.com. You learn so much about a specific designer and so often you will discover that their paths were not cookie cutter copies of each other. Career paths are very individual depending on your goals and strengths. Everyone has to find his or her own way to dream big, but at the same time you need to be realistic. It is not possible to leap into a role as Creative Director for a leading fashion house without having done any work in the field of fashion design before!

Believe in yourself; it's never too late

From the outside, fashion appears to be an industry for the 'younger generation' but this is really not the case, especially when it comes to pursuing a career in fashion design. You often hear the term 'emerging designer', but this refers to the age of the company not the age of the designer, and being relevant and successful in the fashion industry is not based on how old you are, it is about the fashion you create. Some people have discovered their love for fashion design in their late twenties, thirties, forties and beyond. Dress designer Vera Wang is said to have begun designing when she became engaged at age 39, and simply

couldn't find a suitable wedding gown for the mature first-time bride. Whilst many designers start at a young age, maturity and life skills are invaluable, so value the lessons you have learnt from whatever you have done. If you studied business at university like I did, then view this as experience giving you an advantage when it comes to understanding the business side of the industry.

Another myth to dispel is that of overnight success. Marc Jacobs is nearly 50 years old, born on April 9th 1963 and has worked in the industry since he was 15 years old, yet only started to become well-known in his mid to late thirties. It takes time to build your legacy. To help you put individual career paths into perspective, I have investigated the two very different journeys of Bridal and Womenswear designer Vera Wang and fashion designer Marc Jacobs. When emerging designers start up a business they are often advised to allow five years before their brand becomes profitable. I believe that roughly the same time frame can be applied to your own career path. Be willing to invest three to five years to discover what you enjoy, what you are good at and the best direction for you to go in.

Work experience, internships and work

Definition

'Employability' refers to a person's 'capability of gaining initial employment, maintaining employment, and obtaining new employment if required.'[2]

Once you have an idea of the kind of work you want to do in the fashion industry, the next step is to secure it. You may be asking yourself, 'how do I make myself more employable?' Education (see pp.52–6) is a key part of developing your employability but it is not the only factor. To increase your chances of securing initial employment or work, in addition to gaining an education, it is important to secure valuable work experience and to develop key skills such as teamwork, communication, leadership, time management, creative thinking, organisational and problem solving. Personally, I have never known whether or not a job would really suit me until I tried it out, because as we all know, theory is one thing but practical reality is quite another. Even fashion designers who do not want to work for a fashion house and intend to set up their own clothing label need to have work experience and develop these skills for their own success and growth. Work experience and internships are opportunities worth their weight in gold, and can even lead to a job so however inconsequential the opportunity may seem – grab it. I can confidently say that every bit of work experience I have ever had has proven useful even if I did not enjoy doing it at the time.

Case Studies

Vera Wang

Vera Ellen Wang is a Chinese American fashion designer based in New York City. After graduating from The Chapin School in 1967, she attended the University of Paris and earned a degree in Art History from Sarah Lawrence College. While in high school, alongside a passion for ballet, Wang trained as a figure skater and competed at the 1968 US Figure Skating Championships. After failing to get into the US Olympics team, she entered the fashion industry at 22 years old for a change in career and due to an interest in fashion. Starting at *Vogue* as the fashion director's assistant she became a senior fashion editor within a year, a role she held for 15 years. She left the role after being turned down for the editor-in-chief position (currently filled by Anna Wintour).[3] Wang then took a job as a design director at Ralph Lauren before spotting a niche in bridal wear. Frustrated after failing to find her own wedding dress she stated, 'I wanted something more elegant and subdued, but there wasn't anything. I realized the desire to fill that niche.'[4] She went on to design modern dresses with traditional elegance, luxurious fabrics and exquisite detailing. With a combination of talent and financial support from her father, Wang opened her own store in 1990. She has since gained a loyal following for her bridal collections and her dresses have been selected by the likes of Chelsea Clinton, Jennifer Lopez and Uma Thurman. Alongside her bridal collections, Vera Wang is also now known for fragrance, jewellery and shoes.[5] She also revisited her love of figure skating, designing a hand-beaded ensemble for skater Nancy Kerringan for the 1994 Olympics.

Marc Jacobs

Marc Jacobs was born in New York on April 9 1963. Following the death of his father Jacobs went to live with his grandmother. During his childhood he was given a great deal of freedom to explore his surroundings and life in general. 'No one ever told me anything was wrong. Never. No one ever said, "You can't go out at night because you're 15 and 15-year-olds don't go to nightclubs."'[6] Jacobs focused on his creative talent attending the High School of Art and Design, whilst gaining retail experience working in an upscale boutique after school. He soon began designing hand knit sweaters for the boutique and over time his work experience and talent gained him admission to the prestigious Parsons School for Design. There he won the Perry Ellis Gold Thimble Award and Design Student of the Year at graduation.[7] He went on to create his first collection for Reuben Thomas, Inc., under the 'Sketchbook' label. After becoming the youngest designer to ever win the Council of Fashion Designers of America Perry Ellis Award for New Fashion Talent, he designed for womenswear brand Perry Ellis. Branching out with his own company in 1986 with a show supported by Naomi Campbell and Linda Evangelista, Jacobs became a leading global fashion brand. His name is also synonymous with Louis Vuitton (Jacobs has been the Creative Director of Louis Vuitton since 1997). In 2010 Jacobs was named on *Time Magazine*'s '2010 Time 100' list of the most influential people in the world.[8]

Internship or work experience?

An internship is a system of on-the-job training, similar to an apprenticeship. Interns are usually college or university students, but they can also be high school students or postgraduate adults seeking skills for a new career. Student internships provide opportunities for those in education to gain experience in their field, determine if they have an interest in a particular career, create a network of contacts, and in some cases it can count towards school coursework and grades.[9]

Work experience is the experience gained by a person who has been working, or works in a specific field or occupation. The phrase is sometimes used to mean a type of volunteer work that is commonly intended for young people – often students – to get a feel for professional working environments. This usage is common in the United Kingdom, while the American equivalent is intern.[10]

Often the phrases intern and work experience are used interchangeably, the definition and conditions for each depending on the company and country in which you are working. Finding work experience or an internship – and ultimately work – is hard, so be open to taking a step in a direction which may not be exactly what you are looking for, viewing it as a way to develop and build your CV. Getting your foot in the door is the main aim, so acknowledge that there are more doors (and windows) open to you than the obvious front one. Use work experience or interning as an opportunity to soak up atmosphere, meet people and learn processes first hand and, crucially, to find out whether or not the industry is the place for you. Even the most monotonous of tasks can teach you a great deal about the fashion industry, including the parts you aren't as interested in which you need to know about later in life. Watching, learning and then taking an informed step in the right direction reduces the chances that you will make a mistake early on in your career. Remember, in many cases work experience and internships can lead to paid employment, so before you start looking there are some questions worth asking yourself:

◆ What type of experience do I want to get?

◆ Do I want to understand the theory of fashion design more?

INTERNSHIP/ APPRENTICESHIP

• Normally secured when studies have been completed or are nearing completion;

• Greater responsibility than work experience and can lead to paid work;

• The longer it lasts, the greater the likelihood it will result in full time work;

• Can be paid or unpaid (where travel expenses may be covered for you);

• Typically lasts a few months.

WORK EXPERIENCE

• Usually lasts for a few weeks and is unpaid;

• Can lead to paid internship or work;

• Typically gained whilst in education for example, at school or university, or at the early stages of your career.

- Would I like to design and work for a fashion house?
- Would I like to start my own clothing label one day?
- Do I need more business experience or more practical experience?
- What part of running a clothing label most appeals to me?
- Would there be benefits for me to seek further education, for example at design college?
- Do I want to get a mentor?
- Would I like to get an apprenticeship?
- What are my career goals?
- What do I hope to get out of this?

Where to find opportunities

You can find work, internships or work experience opportunities through a range of places such as your school or college career office, through online fashion forums and job websites as well as your own independent research by putting pen to paper (or fingers to keyboard keys) and sending out your CV. Put out the word that you are looking for work to your nearest and dearest – email friends and family or consider sharing through online communities such as Facebook. An opportunity may come through your network from a first, second or third hand connection. Other ways could be through a mentor, an industry contact or by tapping into fashion business groups or networking communities such as LinkedIn. If you are currently studying, make good use of your careers advisor or tutor as helping you to increase your employability is a key part of their job. You can also go to a company directly, as nowadays most have a 'Careers' section on their website, failing that you can get in touch with the company of interest and ask for the contact details of Human Resources department.

Part of my work experience took the form of weekend work experience assisting a boutique owner in Covent Garden, London. I initially worked in a visual merchandising role but by the end I was helping the owner out with PR, giving designers (who were stocked in the boutique) customer feedback and assisting backstage at fashion shows. This opened my eyes to the type of production and planning that goes into fashion shows. I witnessed firsthand the sheer number of people involved in these shows and the importance of backstage organisation. It helped me to become aware of what I did and didn't enjoy, and gave me an insight into the bigger picture. This is why I strongly believe that whether you are after workshop experience or time in the buying department, grab whatever experience you can with both hands. For example, use your time in an atelier to learn everything you can about the design process: visit fabric manufacturers and watch the negotiation process between designer and fabric manufacturer. Use your time spent in a buying office to learn about the administrative office-based elements such as making calls, managing relationships with suppliers and customers and doing stock checks.

Volunteer for as many responsibilities as you can handle and build up relationships, as the people you meet during this time are potential contacts for your future career. Don't make the mistake of solely

My personal first-hand experience, having studied at the London College of Fashion, was then to become an apprentice to a menswear distribution company. I worked in every department in that business before I was given the opportunity to design my first collection. This initiated my entrepreneurial awareness.[11]

Harold Tillman, former Chairman of the British Fashion Council

setting your sights on the 'big' companies. There are just as many, if not more opportunities for work experience if you target smaller ones where you are more likely to be given a broader responsibility, spanning different functions. In my case, working for a small boutique gave me the chance to sit with the owner, pick her brains for advice and offer my opinion. The bottom line is: don't dismiss any opportunity, wherever it is. A fellow designer once told me his personal motivation for getting work experience: 'I know that I am going to make mistakes in my career. To be honest with you I would rather make those errors at the beginning of my career and on someone else's pound!' This sounds mercenary but it's a valid point. When you first start out, the chances are you may work for a fashion house even though your future goal is to venture out on your own. Many fashion houses can actually be supportive of your personal ambitions as long as you deliver good work in their time. Before venturing out on their own Marc Jacobs worked for Perry Ellis, Karl Lagerfeld for Balmain and the legendary Alexander McQueen worked on Savile Row clocking up the hard miles and learning invaluable skills.

Getting work experience in a fashion house or another fashion start-up business is a great way to see first-hand what's involved with running a business in your industry. Don't just focus on getting into the large fashion houses though. Whilst there is a certain cache of working in a recognisable 'brand' the benefit of working in a start-up/small company is that you're likely to get a broader range of exposure and experience and may even get to work alongside the founder of the business. The experience can help you gain confidence, skills, knowledge and contacts which will stand you in good stead for when you launch your own venture.[12]

Rajeeb Dey, CEO of Enternships.com

When to look for opportunities

The best answer to this question is when you feel ready for it. It doesn't matter if you are a student, already working in the industry in some capacity or at a more inquisitive stage. That said, fashion design students should definitely be looking for work experience or internship opportunities before they reach their final year of study, preferably in their penultimate year if not before. Several fashion houses such as Stella McCartney and Vivienne Westwood have quite visible graduate recruitment and internship programmes on their website.

Writing a great CV

During mentoring sessions with aspiring fashion designers I go over their CVs to help them identify experience and core skills. During these sessions we discuss the best terminology to use to elevate their CV and highlight core skills for employability. For example, replacing 'I worked in a retail shop at the weekend on the till and dressed the shop floor', with 'whilst studying at college I successfully managed my time, working at a womenswear boutique during the weekend. I was responsible for handling transactions at the point of sale, in addition to visual merchandising on the retail floor.' Any preparation you do, even simply visiting the website of the company you plan to send your CV to, will make you more informed and help you to put together a more effective CV and covering letter.

It is easy to be intimidated when applying for a position if you feel that you do not yet have a strong enough working history, but for work experience or internship positions, employers

This is a sample CV of an imaginary person called Mark Edwards who wants to get into fashion.

Mark Edwards

Flat 1, Designers Lane,
London, UK A1 2BC
T   +44(0)77777 77777
E   markedwards@email.com

PERSONAL PROFILE

A professional creative graduate with an excellent understanding of the high-end luxury goods market and a keen interest in fashion alongside runway fashion show experience. I am an enthusiastic, reliable and flexible hard working person with a mature attitude towards work. I believe I have the right frame of mind and skills required for me to be an asset to any company. I believe that my willingness to learn, my unwavering work ethic combined with my desire to learn everything about the fashion industry will make me a valuable asset to the fashion business.

EDUCATION

2003–2008
Seven GCSEs achieved in Maths, English, Art, Design Technology Graphics, Physical Education, Information and Communication Technology and Religious Education

2008–2010
Studied A-Levels in Business Studies, Marketing and Design Technology

2010–present
London College of Fashion studying a degree in Fashion Design & Marketing; areas of specialism: Fashion Design, Graphic Design, Marketing

SKILLS

Fashion Design
Pattern Cutting
Hand and Machine Sewing
Trend Analysis and Marketing Research
Knowledge of Mac and Windows applications, including Microsoft Excel and Database
Knowledge of Macromedia Dreamweaver, InDesign, Photoshop, Illustrator and Flash

AWARDS

I was awarded a fashion design project where I had to design a swimwear collection using the latest computer design software (Adobe Photoshop and Illustrator)

WORK EXPERIENCE

Miriam Em Womenswear,
February 2011–November 2011
Studio Assistant
- Working closely with the designers and improving my pattern cutting skills
- Producing patterns for toiles and final garments
- Draping on stand, machine and hand sewing
- Fabric research
- General organisation of the studio environment

Designer, Le Lu London,
October 2010–February 2011
Studio Assistant
- Worked on the AW Ready-to-Wear collection for London Fashion Week
- Worked with Studio Director on Trend Research for themes, shapes, colours and implementation
- Drawing and moulding prototypes
- Proposition of colour palettes and patterns.
- Specialised in cutting chiffon

Designer Collective Boutique,
January 2010–April 2010
Visual Merchandising Assistant
- Organised visual merchandising for Designer Collective Boutique London
- Market research and fashion trends analysis for Boutique owner
- Managed suppliers of clothing including domestic and direct import items

Referees available upon request.

My work experience

Author, Samata Angel

I secured work experience when I was at university (from 2001–2004) and working in London before launching my label in 2007. When I graduated, I wasn't one hundred percent sure what area I wanted to work in although I was drawn to marketing. I sought out jobs via referrals, looking on fashion job boards, networking and asking around. My first job after graduating was as Head of Marketing for a Japanese clothing label, although marketing was not my only responsibility. I tackled everything from relationship management with stockists, buyers and retailers, to ordering stock, filling in purchase order forms, chasing payments from suppliers and monitoring trade publications like *Drapers* for news about events and the industry as a whole. In a later job I worked as Fashion Editor of *The Talent Magazine* which included such responsibilities as writing articles, researching industry trends and styling photo shoots. I learnt a great deal about how magazines function, the importance of advertising, the strength of the cover shoot and page layout, right down to the details of sourcing images from image libraries. Magazines earn the majority of their revenue from advertising and so part of my job was to put together media kits for potential advertisers. This experience taught me how to present facts and figures in a targeted way and also the importance of understanding your market.

understand that experience can be quite limited and as a result they will also be looking for potential. For example, in the Careers section of the Vivienne Westwood website the introductory text encouragingly states, 'If you are passionate about fashion, have a bubbly and dynamic personality and would like to be part of an exciting environment then have a look at our openings and see if any opportunity suits your profile.'[13] A truckload of experience is not expected so do not let the application process wobble your already shaking knees. Your work experience will be reviewed alongside your potential fit with the company, personality, enthusiasm and interests. Still, the more you can put on your CV the better, as it will help you stand out when competing against other designers for an opportunity.

What to expect from internships or work experience

Once you have secured work experience, be prepared for all eventualities. Be prepared to make coffee, count buttons, photocopy and bind health and safety manuals, type data into an excel spreadsheet, and other tasks you may find boring and humdrum. And to be fair, in comparison to your expectations of excitement and glamour they really are! But absolutely everyone I know in the industry has had at least one monotonous job. Just view it as part of your journey, suck it up and do these tasks in an exemplary manner. Work hard, be reliable and consistent and most importantly be polite to everyone. This will not guarantee you a job at the end of it – although in some cases it can – but it will increase your chances of translating the experience into something more.

Going to fashion college

What is the first word that springs to mind when you hear the word 'education'? For me it is nearly always 'school.' But by a wider definition, and to highlight how many different ways there are to get it, 'education in the broadest sense is any act or experience that has a formative effect on the mind, character or physical ability of an individual.'[14] With this definition in mind, consider some of the many places you can learn from.

◆ Educational institutions – schools, colleges, universities, museums, libraries;

◆ Experts – an individual with special knowledge or ability i.e. professors, entrepreneurs, CEOs, mentors;

◆ Experiences – knowledge or skill from doing, seeing or feeling things;

◆ Online resources – library databases, blogs, websites such as Wikipedia;

◆ Offline resources – books, magazines, DVDs, conferences, industry groups;

◆ Work experience/placements – on-the-job experience, volunteer or apprentice work;

◆ Peers – people around you of equal standing within your group;

◆ Support groups – group membership, mentor, tutor, industry experts and groups;

◆ Networking communities – Facebook, LinkedIn.

All of these places are touched on at some point in this book but as I said, the first thought I had was 'school'. Most designers want to study fashion design at a revered institution where the quality of teaching is renowned and there are strong relationships with industry and support networks. 'We live in a brand name society, and having the name of a good school behind you really does help,' says Carol Mongo, Director of the Fashion Department at Parsons School of Design, Paris.[13] Famous design institutions such as Central St Martins in London and Parsons in New York are given added cache and desirability due to the fact they were home to the likes of Alexander McQueen and Marc Jacobs. Likewise, the London College of Fashion is fortunate to have Jimmy Choo (a former student) as a guest lecturer. One of the other advantages of studying at a reputable design colleges is that students tend to work side-by-side with high profile fashion industry events such as the global fashion weeks and in conjunction with fashion retailers, key industry organisations and publications. The college-to-industry connection also helps students when it comes to securing work placements at the desirable fashion houses, fabric manufacturers or retailers. For example, luxury department store Harrods has worked alongside Central St Martins in London to promote new talent by awarding the 'Harrods Design Award', a cash prize and two weeks working in their window display department to an exceptionally talented MA course graduate. Previous winners have included Christopher Kane.

Students at the London College of Fashion waiting for a show to start.

Don't be intimidated

If you have the opportunity to study fashion design at a renowned institution then professionals who know the industry inside out will guide you through the different areas of clothing design and help you understand the industry. At some colleges the tutors still actively work in the fashion industry. However, not following this route is far from the end of world! You can learn through other routes, developing your strengths and acquiring information in the areas where your knowledge is limited. It is so important to remember that your success is determined by much more than your academic achievements. It is about your own personal bid to get noticed and get yourself out there. I do not have the same credentials as every other designer and it is precisely these differences that make us unique. Do not allow yourself to be intimidated by the 'creds' if you do not have them.

Course content

Fashion Design, Fashion Design Development, Fashion Design Technology, Pattern Design and Technology are all recommended courses for any aspiring fashion designer. These courses teach both design and technical skills, giving you the practical knowledge needed to work in the industry. Course content varies according to the area of design that the student is interested in, such as womenswear, menswear, knitwear or accessories, each focusing on the principals of fashion design, both technical and theoretical. Typically there will be modules such as fashion history and theory, practical and technical fashion design, pattern making, sewing, cutting, fine arts classes, drawing, colour composition and form, buying and merchandising, sales and distribution, fashion marketing and fashion PR (and many more). The teaching structure will be a variety of tutorials, seminars, projects, research and independent study or team work. These days, many designers are keen to combine business elements with their fashion training, so courses such as Fashion Design and Marketing are becoming increasingly popular. There are other options such as apprenticeships which offer work-based training and knowledge-based learning and/or certificates which cover core units such as drawing development and materials, fashion design and garment manufacture, pattern-grading and IT. A typical fashion degree course runs for three to four years with a placement at some stage, or shorter courses are available. For example, you could pursue a foundation degree (typically lasting a year), which is an introduction to the basics of pattern-cutting, design and construction and industry roles such as designing, buying and styling.

Applying for courses

A college's website will guide you through the application process. Ensure that you read all the available information with regard to deadlines, entrance requirements and qualifications. Each course will have different minimum requirements but a typical application procedure involves:

◆ filling in a detailed application form;

◆ submitting a CV and covering letter;

◆ writing a personal statement;

◆ submitting references;

◆ submitting your portfolio (a collection of images and sketches of your work.

If your application is successful, you may be selected for interview. Following that, you may receive an offer or rejection. Offers are either 'unconditional' which means you're being offered a place based on the experience and qualifications you already possess, or conditionally which means dependent on attaining certain grades at various examinations relevant to the course. Some good advice to follow at the application stage is to really take your time. Before you submit, read your application through thoroughly to ensure you have not made any mistakes. Most application forms can be completed online these days but for all handwritten or typed forms, take your time to ensure that your application is legible and neat. Your personal statement is an opportunity to express your passion and interest in the fashion course you are applying for. You'll be required to write the reasons why you

want to be considered, so be sure to support your statement with your experiences, goals and vision. You should be able to demonstrate a good understanding and assessment of the industry. Show confidence because if you do not believe in yourself it will be hard to convince others you deserve a place. References add to your credibility so try to select someone who knows your ability – a teacher or mentor for example. It is also important to ensure you have up-to-date and pertinent information on your CV. Highlight the relevant skills, which will be most beneficial to the course you are applying for, and list all work experience, even if you cannot see how it directly relates to fashion. Experience gained in another industry can still boost a CV because many skills are transferable.

APPLYING: CREATING A GOOD PORTFOLIO

Many colleges will ask you to submit a portfolio (a display of your work i.e. sketches, photos or samples) as part of the application process. It is helpful to hold a copy of your portfolio in digital format (on a USB or CD) as well as hard copy, so that it can be quickly emailed if required. For both formats, good presentation of your work is crucial.

Portfolio of fashion stylist Matthew Fox. Stylists, designers, photographers, hair and makeup artists use portfolios to showcase their work.

Some portfolio tips

1

KNOW THE DIFFERENCE
Every artist has a draft version of their work but it is important to know the difference between an unfinished presentation and a relevant display of your current ability.

2

THE SILENT VOICE OF YOUR PORTFOLIO
Your portfolio is an expression of yourself and by sharing it you are allowing an audience to become privy to your thoughts, perceptions, inspirations and most importantly, ability. Your work will be critiqued so prepare yourself to receive feedback. Criticism can be difficult to hear, but try not to take it personally.

3

CREATE A THEME
Grouping work by style or theme makes it digestible and easier to appreciate so keep it simple and allow your different design techniques to be seen through your story.

4

DIVERSITY
Techniques are part of the show. Your portfolio should demonstrate an ability to try new styles and techniques and make them your own.

5

LESS IS MORE
Keep your portfolio as simple as possible but keep it strong. Sometimes three amazing pieces of work can have more impact than seven OK ones.

6

EDIT
'Editing is one of the most important things when it comes to making a portfolio. It is a sign that they can't distance themselves from their work and look objectively so you don't really see what is good or bad.' Roger Szmulewicz, Fifty One Fine Art Gallery.[16]

7

INVEST IN YOURSELF
Your portfolio communicates your ability and seriousness to the course so invest in decent cases and present your work well.

8

SELL YOURSELF
You sell your portfolio, not the other way around. Your work does not stand-alone; it is only half of the offering. Your passion, energy and vision are also part of the package.

9

KEEP IT UP-TO-DATE
From my own personal experience I know that chance meetings happen all the time so always have your most up-to-date work available, which best reflects your present abilities.

What to expect from the fashion design experience

Being at fashion college is a different experience for everyone. Some people love their course, the campus and their peers whereas others find that it is not what they expected. You will only know how you feel about student life when you start your course. You may find the workload easy to juggle and the course content easy to follow. To get an idea of what to expect you can visit your fashion college's website, most websites have some content from students there, along the lines of 'A day in the life', and the forums show an accurate depiction of what is really going on. Through pictures and interviews with current and past students you can get a rough idea of what you could expect. You can also arrange to visit the campus and have a wander around during term time to get a real feel for the space. Here are some general tips for how you can really enjoy and make the most out of student life, the main one being to enjoy it!

◆ Go to Open Days and talk to students who are on the course you would like to do or are planning to do.

◆ Make an effort to talk to people, everyone is in the same boat and hoping to make friends and connections.

Author awards final year student Nova Chiu with Collection of the Year Award 2011, alongside Dean Frances Corner of London College of Fashion

◆ Join groups and organisations, whether the social committee or an athletic group of some sort – these groups provide you with the opportunity to make friends and get involved in student life.

◆ Go to lectures! It is tempting to miss them but it is really pointless. You can have fun when lectures are finished and won't have to cram desperately at the end of the year wishing you had not missed a lecture to go shopping.

◆ Talk to your lecturers. As you reach the end of your final year when being in lectures matters and coursework carries a high value, they may become your best friend!

NOTES

1. Malcolm Gladwell, *Outliers: The Story of Success* (New York: Little, Brown and Company, 2008)
   Also see www.gladwell.com/outliers/index.html.

2. Hillage J, Pollard E, *Research Report RR85* (London: Department for Education and Employment, November 1998); http://www.employment-studies.co.uk/pubs/summary.php?id=emplblty; accessed 5 November 2012

3. Vera Wang, *Vera Wang on Weddings* (London: HarperCollins, 2001)

4. Biography.com, 'Vera Wang', http://www.biography.com/people/vera-wang-9542398; accessed 17 October 2012

5. Vera Wang website, www.verawang.com; accessed 17 October 2012

6. Biography.com, 'Marc Jacobs', http://www.biography.com/people/marc-jacobs-594096 ; accessed 17 October 2012

7. Bibby Sowray, 'Marc Jacobs', *British Vogue* website (7 March 2012), http://www.vogue.co.uk/spy/biographies/marc-jacobs-biography; accessed 17 October 2012

8. *Time Magazine* website, 'The 2010 Time 100', http://www.time.com/time/specials/packages/0,28757,1984685,00.html; accessed 17 October 2012

9. Wikipedia, 'Internship', http://en.wikipedia.org/wiki/Internships; accessed 17 October 2012

10. Wikipedia, 'Work Experience', http://en.wikipedia.org/wiki/Work_experience; accessed 17 October 2012

11. Harold Tillman in conversation with the author in June 2012

12. Rajeeb Dey in conversation with the author 31st May 2011

13. Vivienne Westwood website, http://www.viviennewestwood.co.uk/w/contact/career-opportunities; accessed 17 October 2012

14. Wikipedia, 'Education', http://en.wikipedia.org/wiki/Education; accessed 17 October 2012

15. Fashionnet, 'How to Become a Fashion Designer', http://www.fashion.net/howto/fashiondesigner/; accessed 5 November 2012

16. Roger Szmulewicz in conversation with the author

Directory of fashion schools and colleges across the world

Fashionista.com is a fashion news website showcasing a collection of fashion news, criticism and career advice in addition to business stories and interviews. It has compiled an excellent list of the top 50 colleges around the world including details of the programmes, number of students and tuition fees.

AUSTRALIA

ROYAL MELBOURNE INSTITUTE OF TECHNOLOGY (MELBOURNE)

Programmes: Fashion Design and Technology, Textiles, Footwear, Fashion and Textile Merchandising
Number of Students: Fashion Undergrads: 588
Tuition: $19,500–$20,000 depending on programme
Misc: There are 2 schools within RMIT to study fashion; lots of diploma courses, too.
Famous Grads: Toni Maticevski, Karen Webster
The Bottom Line: A strong design programme and innovative, high-tech textiles programme are the highlights here.

http://www.rmit.edu.au

TAFE INSTITUTE OF TECHNOLOGY (SYDNEY)

Programmes: Fashion, Costume, and Millinery Design
Number of Students: Total 70,000 students at 7 campuses
Tuition: $32,000
Misc: Two colleges within the system offer fashion programmes: Ultimo College & St.George
Famous Grads: Dion Lee, Nicky Zimmermann, Lisa Ho, Akira

Isogawa
The Bottom Line: A huge university system with lots of resources; it has been churning out high-profile Aussie designers at a frightening pace.

http://www.sit.nsw.edu.au

WHITEHOUSE INSTITUTE OF DESIGN (MELBOURNE/SYDNEY)

Programmes: Fashion Design; Styling and Creative Direction
Number of Students: 470 students total (Melbourne and Sydney); just over half of these are fashion students
Tuition: AUD $24,680 (Note that this is the International fee– domestic is a bit less.)
Misc: You can start studying here in Year 11 and 12 (HS equivalent)
Famous Grads: Camilla Freeman Topper (Camilla & Marc); Yeojin Bae
The Bottom Line: A relatively young school (founded 1988) that has nonetheless managed to carve a niche for itself in fashion design.

http://www.whitehouse-design.edu.au

MELBOURNE SCHOOL OF FASHION (MELBOURNE)

Programmes: Applied Fashion Design and Technology, Retail Management, Styling
Tuition: $17,000
The Bottom Line: A vocational training programme that offers solid instruction in the adjunct fashion professions.

http://www. melbourneschooloffashion.com

FBI FASHION COLLEGE (SYDNEY)

Programmes: Fashion Design; Fashion Business
Number of students: 500

Tuition: $4,200–$14,000
Misc: Could be tricky for international students. They offer flexible part time classes, but you have to be a full time student to get a visa.
The Bottom Line: A newer school that offers part-time classes, perfect for someone looking for a second career.

http://www.fbifashioncollege.com.au

AUSTRIA

UNIVERSITY OF APPLIED ARTS (VIENNA)

Programmes: Fashion Design
Number of Students: Total: 1,100
Total who graduate/year: 120
Tuition: €1,525 ($2,000)
Misc: You must speak German; subsidized tuition.
The Bottom Line: Karl Lagerfeld, Jil Sander, Victor & Rolf, and Helmut Lang have all cycled through as guest lecturers.

http://www.dieangewandte.at

BELGIUM

ANTWERP ROYAL ACADEMY OF FINE ARTS (ANTWERP)

Programmes: Fashion Design
Number of Students: 140
Tuition: €6,000 ($8,000) Tuition is highly subsidized by the government, even for foreign students)
Misc: Required Dutch language proficiency.
Famous Grads: Ann Demeulemeester, Dries Van Noten, Dirk Bikkembergs, Walter Van Beirendonck, Dirk Van Saene, Marina Yee (The Antwerp Six), Martin Margiela, Veronique Branquinho, Haider Ackermann, Peter Pilotto, Bruno Pieters.

The Bottom Line: The Royal Academy is an elite design school. It's known for its serious students – many drop out because they can't handle the workload. Since the Antwerp Six put the school on fashion's map in the early 1980s, it's continued to produce all-star designers. If you're exceptionally dedicated, with an experimental, innovative, and avant garde sensibility, this may be the place for you.

http://www.antwerp-fashion.be

LA CAMBRE (BRUSSELS)

Programmes: Fashion Design; Styling
Number of Students: 630
Tuition: €1,487–€1,984 ($1,900–$2,600)
Misc: Must be French-speaking; 5-year fashion design programme
The Bottom Line: A more traditional art school alternative to the Antwerp school, definitely with a French design point of view.

http://www.lacambre.be

CANADA

RYERSON UNIVERSITY SCHOOL OF FASHION (TORONTO)

Programmes: Fashion Design; Fashion Communication
Number of Students: Undergrads: 26,000; Fashion: 600
Tuition: CAD $17,498 to $18,665 ($17,400–$18,500)
Famous Grads: Erdem Moralioglu (Went to RCA after Ryerson)
The Bottom Line: An impressive list of industry associations, a solid design programme, and a reasonable price. Fantastic value.

http://www.ryerson.ca

GEORGE BROWN COLLEGE (TORONTO)

Programmes: Fashion Design, Fashion Management, Fashion Business Industry, Jewellery
Number of Students: 800 Fashion Students
Tuition: CAD $10,780– $13,750 ($10,700–$13,600)
The Bottom Line: All the design courses also have a practical focus on the business side of fashion (for example, students run a retail store).

http://www.georgebrown.ca

LASALLE COLLEGE INTERNATIONAL (MONTREAL; SATELLITE CAMPUSES WORLDWIDE)

Programmes: Fashion Design, Fashion Marketing
Number of Students: 900 Fashion Students (Montreal campus)
Tuition: $6,800 per session (1–6 sessions total, depending on the programme)
The Bottom Line: A huge educational system that offers consistent instruction no matter which country's school you attend; they have a vocational bent.

http://www.lasallecollege.com

DENMARK

COPENHAGEN ACADEMY OF FASHION DESIGN (COPENHAGEN)

Programmes: Fashion Design
Tuition: DKK 68,000 ($12,140)
The Bottom Line: A classic European design education.

http://www.modeogdesignskolen. dk/index.aspx?id=20

FRANCE

ECOLE DE LA CHAMBRE SYNDICALE (PARIS)

Programmes: Fashion Design & Technique
Number of Students: 240 students
Tuition: €10,450 ($13,230)
It is the school associated with the regulating commission that determines which houses are eligible to be true couture houses.
Famous Grads: André Courreges, Issey Miyake, Valentino, Yves Saint Laurent, Nicole Miller
The Bottom Line: Prestigious French school that offers world-renowned couture classes. They offer baccalaureate-level programmes, but often don't accept some students until after they finish a design course elsewhere first.

www.modeaparis.com

ESMOD (PARIS PLUS 21 SCHOOLS IN 14 COUNTRIES)

Programmes: Fashion Design/ Fashion Business
Number of Students: 700
Tuition: €12,000 ($15,990)
The mannequin and measuring tape were invented here.
Famous Grads: Christophe Decarnin
The Bottom Line: The world's first and oldest French fashion design school, it has a 75%–85% placement rate post-graduation.

http://www.esmod.com

STUDIO BERCOT (PARIS)

Programmes: Fashion Design
Number of Students: 200
Tuition: €9000 ($11,440) – the third year is FREE (apprenticeship)
Misc: You must be fluent in French.
Famous Grads: Martine Sitbon, Lolita Lempicka, Isabel Marant, Sophie Theallet, Nicole Farhi

The Bottom Line: A very tightly run and prestigious design school with tons of connections in the industry.

www.studio-bercot.com

FINLAND

UNIVERSITY OF ART AND DESIGN (HELSINKI)

Programmes: Textile Art, Fashion, and Clothing Design
Tuition: NO TUITION, even for non-EU international students
Misc: Finland provides free university education for everyone, even international students. The university is looking into charging non-EU students in the future, but right now they don't.
The Bottom Line: Yes, it's free, but you have to be VERY talented to get in.

http://arts.aalto.fi/en

INDIA

NIFT NATIONAL INSTITUTE OF FASHION TECHNOLOGY (NEW DELHI)

Programmes: Design (Fashion, Leather, Textile, Accessory, Knitwear), Management, and Technology (Apparel Production)
Tuition: Non-resident Indian: Rs 40,000 ($880) Other international students: Rs. 360,000 ($7,600)
Misc: You can't apply for undergraduate programmes if you're over 23 years old.
The Bottom Line: The biggest design school in India, it has cooperative agreements with international schools including RNIT, University of the Arts London, and Ryerson

http://www.nift.ac.in

ISRAEL

SHENKAR COLLEGE OF ENGINEERING AND DESIGN (RAMAT GAN)

Programmes: Fashion, Textile, and Jewellery Design
Number of Students: Total: 2,300
Fashion: 217
Tuition: 11,000 ILS ($3,000)
Misc: International students are accepted as 2nd or 3rd year students. You have to have completed a year of fashion school. Most classes taught in English, so not necessary to know Hebrew.
Famous Grads: Alber Elbaz, Kobi Halperin (CD Elie Tahari), Nili Lotan
The Bottom Line: Definitely off the beaten path and with a definite point of view, this well-kept secret has an amazing fashion design programme.

http://www.shenkar.ac.il

ITALY

ISTITUTO MARANGONI (MILAN; FURTHER CAMPUSES IN LONDON AND PARIS)

Programmes: Fashion Design, Fashion Business, Fashion Buying, Brand Management and Fashion Promotion
Number of Students: 2,000 (all 3 campuses)
Tuition: 13,900€ ($17,670) to 19,000€ ($24,550) depending on programme
Misc: Italian, French, and English are the official languages of the school
Famous Grads: Domenico Dolce, Franco Moschino
The Bottom Line: An Italian design school with campuses in three major fashion capitals is a plus, and a 90% placement rate after graduation.

http://www.istitutomarangoni.com/home/eng

POLIMODA (FLORENCE)

Programmes: Fashion Marketing, Design, Media & Communication, Fashion Styling
Tuition: €7500–16,000 ($9,900–$21,300) depending on course of study
Misc: Founded in 1986, it has ties with FIT in New York.
The Bottom Line: It's got a lot of high-tech equipment and an 87% placement rate after graduation. More well-known for careers other than design.

http://www.polimoda.com

KOEFIA (INTERNATIONAL ACADEMY OF HAUTE COUTURE AND ART OF COSTUME) (ROME)

Programmes: Fashion Design; Costume Design; Fashion Product Management
Fashion Students: 150
Tuition: €4,700 ($6,300)
Misc: They offer a modeling course.
The Bottom Line: Very Italian with some cross-cultural programmes offered through the Department of Humanities (like a project in Saudi Arabia).

http://www.koefia.com

JAPAN

BUNKA FASHION COLLEGE/ BUNKA WOMEN'S UNIVERSITY (TOKYO)

Programmes: Fashion Design, Fashion Creation & Technology, Marketing, Accessories & Textiles.
Number of Students: Total in both colleges: 8,000 Design: 4,000
Tuition: ¥1,045,000– 1,570,000 ($12,677– $19,030) depending on college and programme

Misc: You must have a good understanding of Japanese and have the financial means to live in Japan; part-time work is not allowed when you're a student.
Famous Grads: Kenzo Takada, Junya Watanabe, Yohji Yamamoto, Hiroko Koshino, Chisato Tsumori
The Bottom Line: Created in 1919, it's always been on the cutting edge of fashion. Bunka most notably came to prominence in the 1960s when its graduates starting showing in Paris. It's now synonymous with Japanese avant-garde design. The top-notch design is rounded out by marketing and technology programmes.

http://www.bunka-fc.ac.jp/en/index.html

MODE GAKUEN (TOKYO, OSAKA, NAGOUA)

Programmes: Fashion Design, Fashion Business, Styling, Hair/Makeup
Number of Students: 5,500 students
Misc: You must be able to speak and read Japanese.
The Bottom Line: A vocational school for various fashion professions.

http://www.mode.ac.jp/lang/english.html

NETHERLANDS
HOGESCHOOL VAN AMSTERDAM (AMFI AMSTERDAM FASHION INSTITIUE) (AMSTERDAM)

Programmes: Fashion and Design; Fashion and Management; Fashion and Branding
Number of Students: Total students: 30,000.

Fashion students: 845 in Dutch, 280 in English-taught programme (same content as Dutch)
Tuition: Non EU/EEA int'l students: €6,800 ($9,000)
Misc: Offers English-taught programmes, so Dutch fluency isn't necessary.
The Bottom Line: The tuition is heavily subsidized (read: cheap) and the education is classic with a modern spin. The school has lots of cool initiatives, like selling student wares in shops around Amsterdam, for lots of exposure and experience.

http://www.international.hva.nl

SINGAPORE
RAFFLES UNIVERSITY (SINGAPORE, PLUS SE ASIA, CHINA, INDIA)

Programmes: Fashion Design/Fashion Marketing
Number of Students: 9,000 students across Asia; 1,787 in Singapore
Tuition: SGD $79,200 ($60,690)
Misc: 38 colleges in 35 cities across 14 countries in Asia; the schools are taught in English
The Bottom Line: Another huge educational system, this time in Asia. They have produced many international award-winning students.

http://www.raffles-education-corporation.com

SOUTH AFRICA
TSHWANE UNIVERSITY OF TECHNOLOGY (PRETORIA)

Programmes: Fashion Design & Technology
Fashion Students: 180
Tuition: R 26,800 ($3,890)
The Bottom Line: The biggest design and technology school in Africa, combining European design principles with indigenous flair.

http://www.tut.ac.za

UK
CENTRAL SAINT MARTINS (LONDON)

Programmes: Fashion, Textile, and Jewellery Design
Number of students: 1,200 fashion students
Tuition: £9,500–12,700 ($14,900–$20,000)
Famous Grads: Stella McCartney, John Galliano, Alexander McQueen, Phoebe Philo, Christopher Kane, Hussein Chalayan, Zac Posen, Hamish Bowles, Paul Smith, Giles Deacon, Luella Bartley, Jenny Packham, Jonathan Saunders, Marios Schwab, Alice Temperley, Riccardo Tisci, Matthew Williamson
The Bottom Line: Currently CSM runway shows are archived on Style.com.

http://www.csm.arts.ac.uk

UNIVERSITY OF WESTMINSTER (LONDON)

Programmes: Fashion Design
Number of Students: Undergrads 3,000;
Fashion Students: 130
Tuition: £10,500 ($16,538)
Misc: You can choose a three or four-year course, and spend a year working in the fashion industry.
Famous Grads: Vivienne Westwood, Christopher Bailey, Michael Herz (formerly of Aquascutum now Bally), Stuart Vevers (Mulberry, Loewe), Katie Hillier, Sophie Dean (fashion editor at *Wallpaper*)
The Bottom Line: Don't overlook this London University that produces creative designers. In addition to the fashion program, they have a well-known journalism

programme.

http://www.westminsterfashion.com

ROYAL COLLEGE OF ART (LONDON)

Programmes: Fashion Design, Textiles
Number of Students: less than 100 fashion students
Misc: This is a post-graduate program only!
Famous Grads: Philip Treacy, Erdem Moralioglu, Christopher Bailey, Ossie Clark, Zandra Rhodes
The Bottom Line: A world-renowned graduate fashion design program to aspire to.

http://www.rca.ac.uk

LONDON COLLEGE OF FASHION (LONDON, ENGLAND)

Programmes: Fashion Design, Fashion Journalism, Marketing, Beauty, Buying and Merchandising
Number of Students: 2,547 first-year students
Tuition: £12,700 ($18,500)
Famous Grads: Jimmy Choo
The Bottom Line: The fashion journalism school here is the standout. It's not known as a design school, but there are many unique programmes that you won't find anywhere else: Beauty therapy, cosmetic science, fashion broadcast journalism, fashion curation and criticism, fashion business, footwear and accessories, makeup and image styling.

http://www.fashion.arts.ac.uk

UNIVERSITY OF BRIGHTON (BRIGHTON)

Programmes: Fashion Design; Fashion Business; Fashion & Dress History
Tuition: £11,580 ($18,200)
Famous Grads: Emma Cook
The Bottom Line: The fashion and textile programmes are world-renown, and design programmes are often combined with business studies.

http://www.brighton.ac.uk

KINGSTON UNIVERSITY (LONDON)

Programmes: Fashion Design
Number of Students: Undergrads in 3D Design: 400; Fashion: 200
Tuition: £10,650 ($16,720)
Famous Grads: Glenda Bailey
The Bottom Line: Another strong UK school, with a well-rounded programme.

http://www.kingston.ac.uk/undergraduate-course/fashion-2012

USA
PARSONS, THE NEW SCHOOL FOR DESIGN

Programmes: Fashion Design, Fashion Studies, Fashion Marketing
Number of students: Undergrads: 4,100; Graduate: 500; Fashion design: 1,400
Tuition: $36,800
Famous Grads: Donna Karan, Marc Jacobs, Tom Ford, Narciso Rodriguez, Alexander Wang, Anna Sui, Jason Wu, Jenna Lyons (J.Crew), Jack McCollough and Lazaro Hernandez (Proenza Schouler), Behnaz Serafpour, Doo Ri Chung, Sophie Buhai and Lisa Mayock (Vena Cava), Flora Gill and Alexa Adams (Ohne Titel), Prabal Gurung, Steven Meisel, Thakoon Panichgul, Carmen Marc Valvo

The Bottom Line: The school has partnered with many retailers and corporations (like LVMH) with the aim of getting student work seen and critiqued.

http://www.newschool.edu/parsons

FASHION INSTITUTE OF TECHNOLOGY (FIT)* (NEW YORK)

Programmes: design, business, marketing, illustration, styling, etc.
Number of Students: 10,000
Tuition: $2,584/semester (NYC/NYC residents); $6,775/semester for out-of-state residents
Misc: Very comprehensive programmes. Part of the SUNY
Famous Grads: Reem Acra, Francisco Costa, Nina Garcia, Carolina Herrera, Calvin Klein, Michael Kors, Nanette Lepore, Ralph Rucci
The Bottom Line: In addition to fashion design, FIT offers fashion marketing, business, textiles, visual arts, and countless other fashion-related degrees. The lecture series and FIT museum are exceptional. Valerie Steele, as Chief Curator of the Museum of FIT, gives this school a brainy credibility.

http://www.fitnyc.edu

KENT STATE UNIVERSITY (KENT)

Programmes: Fashion Design; Fashion Merchandising
Number of Students: Undergrads: 18,000
Fashion students: 200/year graduate from the school.
Tuition: Ohio resident: $9,030; Non-Ohio resident: $16,900
Misc: Has a garment center studio in NYC where 120 students/year go to study.

The Bottom Line: With study abroad programmes in Paris and Milan, a huge endowment for scholarships, and a high-profile program allowing you to complete a fashion-focused undergraduate and MBA in fashion-focused business in just five years, this school is one of the top American fashion schools and keeps getting better.

http://www.fashionschool.kent.edu

DREXEL UNIVERSITY (PHILADELPHIA)

Programmes: Fashion Design; Design & Merchandising
Number of Students: Undergrads: 11,500 Fashion: 120 Design and Merchandising: 240
Tuition: $33,000
The Bottom Line: Many students have won national and international awards, gone on to study at the Chambre Syndicale and nabbed huge jobs in France.

http://www.drexel.edu

OTIS COLLEGE OF ART AND DESIGN (LOS ANGELES)

Programmes: Fashion Design
Number of Students: Undergrads: 1,200 Fashion students: 180
Tuition: $32,900
Famous Grads: Rick Owens (didn't graduate – dropped out), Cynthia Vincent
The Bottom Line: One of the top US design programmes in the country.

http://www.otis.edu

SAVANNAH COLLEGE OF ART AND DESIGN (SAVANNAH)

Programmes: Fashion Design; Fashion Marketing & Management; Accessories Design
Number of Students: All programmes: 9,800. Fashion students: 540
Tuition: $31,510
Misc: Andre Leon Talley is on the Board of Directors and a Lifetime Achievement Award is given in his name every year.
The Bottom Line: The new-ish dean, Michael Fink, is turning this school into a fashion powerhouse, with lots of new industry connections and faculty hires.

http://www.scad.edu

RHODE ISLAND SCHOOL OF DESIGN (PROVIDENCE)

Programmes: Apparel Design; Jewellery and Metalsmithing; Textiles
Number of Students: Undergrads: 2,000; Fashion/apparel/textiles/jewellery: 220
Tuition: $39,000
Misc: You can cross-register at Brown University.
Famous Grads: Nicole Miller, Sari Gueron, Philip Crangi, Marcia Patmos, Sarah Welsh & Madeline Davy (formerly of Octopi)
The Bottom Line: One of the most respected design schools in the world, their profile as a fashion design school is only getting rosier.

http://www.risd.edu

COLUMBUS COLLEGE OF ART & DESIGN (COLUMBUS)

Programmes: Fashion Design
Number of Students: Undergrads: 1,350; Fashion: 130
Tuition: $24,864
The Bottom Line: Ohio for some reason has three fantastic fashion

design programmes, and this is one of them.

http://www.ccad.edu

UNIVERSITY OF CINCINNATI (CINCINNATI)

Programmes: Fashion Design (combined w/Product Development)
Number of Students: Undergrads: 24,000; Fashion Design: 180
Tuition: OH residents: $10,065; Out of state: $24,588
Famous Grads: Stan Herman (former CFDA president)
The Bottom Line: The Design program, in general, consistently ranks as one of the best in the nation.

http://www.uc.edu

ACADEMY OF ART UNIVERSITY (SAN FRANCISCO)

Programmes: Fashion Design, Knitwear Design, Textile Design, Fashion Journalism and Fashion Merchandising & Marketing
Number of Students: School: 17,000. Fashion students: 2,600
Tuition: $20,343
The Bottom Line: The only fashion school that shows at NY Fashion Week, and they have good fashion journalism, merchandising, and business programmes.

http://www.academyart.edu

PRATT (BROOKLYN)

Programmes: Fashion design
Number of Students: Total freshmen: 3,000; Fashion: 140
Tuition: $35,000
Misc: Part of a larger design school, so you can combine arts studies.
Famous Grads: Jeremy Scott, Betsey Johnson (didn't graduate from Pratt), Andy and Debb
The Bottom Line: Pratt has shed

its image as an up-and-coming fashion design program and become a force to be reckoned with. One of the few design programmes which offers electives in fashion editorial/magazine publishing.

http://www.pratt.edu

CALIFORNIA COLLEGE OF ARTS (SAN FRANCISCO AND OAKLAND)

Programmes: Fashion Design; Textiles; Jewellery Design
Number of Students: Undergrads: 1,640. Fashion students: 65
Tuition: $36,000
The Bottom Line: A CFDA-affiliated school, its students have won many industry awards and landed jobs with marquee-name labels and companies.

http://www.cca.edu

FASHION INSTITUTE OF DESIGN & MERCHANDISING (LOS ANGELES)

Programmes: Fashion Design, Footwear Design, Costume Design, Jewellery Design, Textile Design, Merchandising (Fashion & Beauty Programmes)
Number of Students: 7,500
Tuition: $27,000–$36,000 depending on area of study.
Misc: Most are Associate of Art degrees
Famous Grads: Monique Lhuillier, Pamela Skaist-Levy (Juicy Couture co-founder), Randolph Duke
The Bottom Line: A great vocational and design school for practical experience and they have an incredible career database for placement post-graduation.

http://fidm.edu

SCHOOL OF THE ART INSTITUTE OF CHICAGO (CHICAGO)

Programmes: Fashion Design
Number of Students: Undergrads: 2,500; Fashion students:120
Tuition: $18,000
Misc: Three year curriculum within a four year fine arts foundation.
Famous Grads: Cynthia Rowley, Maria Pinto, Halston, Matthew Ames
The Bottom Line: With a non-traditional fashion design program, Georgia O'Keefe's alma mater has a serious art and design pedigree.

http://www.saic.edu

MASSACHUSETTS COLLEGE OF ART (BOSTON)

Programmes: Fashion Design; Fibers; Jewellery
Number of Students: Undergrads: 1751. Fashion Design: 110
Tuition: MA resident: $9,000; New England resident: $15,700; Out-of-state: $25,400
The Bottom Line: An historic art college with a tidy fashion design programme.

http://www.massart.edu

UNIVERSITY OF MISSOURI (COLUMBIA)

Programmes: Textile and Apparel Management (no design!). Offers a concurrent journalism minor
Number of Students: 250 undergrads in Textile & Apparel Management
Tuition: MO residents: $8,500 Non-MO residents: $19,690
*The Bottom Line:*This is not a design school, but a very unique program offering insights into the production and business of fashion.

http://tam.missouri.edu

COLUMBIA COLLEGE (CHICAGO)

Programmes: Fashion Design, Fashion/Retail Management (the two programmes have just been combined as Fashion Studies)
Number of Students: Undergrads: 11,400 Art and Design: 1,800
Tuition: $20,190
The Bottom Line: A small programme in a big city at a cool arts programme. They have a great journalism programme too.

http://www.colum.edu

LIM COLLEGE (NEW YORK)

Programmes: Fashion Merchandising, Marketing, Management, Visual Merchandising. (No design.)
Number of Students: 1,500 Students
Tuition: $20,900
The Bottom Line: Will give you thorough preparation for the behind-the-scenes aspects of the fashion business.

http://www.limcollege.edu

CHAPTER 3

WORKING IN THE FASHION INDUSTRY AS A FASHION DESIGNER

This chapter digs into deeper detail about how to venture down your chosen career path. Having covered some of the different kinds of careers within the fashion industry and the benefits of work experience and how to get it in the previous chapter, it is now time to consider what work kind of work you want to do. What kind of designer do you want to be? What market would you like to work in? Who would you like to work for? It is time to get more specific and in this chapter these questions will be answered.

The core fashion markets are 'womenswear', 'menswear' and 'children's wear', within which fall certain categories such as 'knitwear', 'lingerie', 'bridal', 'streetwear', 'couture,' 'footwear' and 'accessories'. Depending on where your passion leads, you could end up designing men's tailor made suits, women's handbags or children's shoes. You could become a costume designer or discover a passion for textile design. Designers are typically based in a studio or workshop for their creative activities but depending on their role they may have the opportunity to travel and visit manufacturers (often overseas), trade shows such as Pure, Bread & Butter and MAGIC city, and fashion weeks around the globe. Instead of working for themselves many designers work for leading design houses or mass manufacturers whilst others work on a freelance basis. For those living under any illusions of grandeur, it would be wise to take heed now as fashion design is not initially a fantastically well-paid job, with salaries for some entry level fashion designers starting around £12,000 to £14,000. Salary of course depends on what you do and who you work for but in the UK you can earn up to £60,000+ and beyond as a Creative Director. In the USA the average salary is between $30,000 and $70,000. If you are entering the fashion industry with the primary motivation of getting rich quick, rethink. It is possible to work your way up to a high salary but this undoubtedly takes a great deal of time and hard work. If money is your main motivation, make sure you are realistic about your goals or you may end up feeling frustrated and like you're in the wrong business!

When we started we never thought about making money; a lot of creative people don't. We wanted to create beautiful things.[1]

Sarah-Jane Clarke, Co-Founder of fashion label Sass and Bide

The different types of designers

I remember the day that I found out the 'designer' I worked for actually outsourced the entire creative design process to a brilliant young design student in Japan and then simply approved final sketches, sample and colour swatches from her office in London and took the job title Creative Director. At the time I remember thinking that it was really wrong for her to take credit for someone else's work, but later on, as I gained experience, I began to understand about the different types of designers in the industry and that, in truth, not all of our favourite designers begin or stay 100% hands on. Even before the Stella McCartneys and Vera Wangs of the world reached the stage of being able to employ a design team, they had design strengths and weaknesses, and being successful involved identifying and working on them. I believe that the secret to being a good designer is knowing what those strengths and weaknesses are. It is a known fact that many designers do not sew, they create. There are different types of designers and each one plays a different part in the design process. I have created two simple descriptions to help to explain this concept further: visionary designer and making designer.

What skills do you need?

When you read about some of the most successful fashion designers in the business, you will see that their career paths have varied greatly. However, they share some common skills in addition to the genuine and unwavering passion for fashion design:

- Exceptional creative talent and ability;
- A keen eye for detail;
- Good fashion market understanding;
- Good verbal and visual communication skills; visual communication (written and illustration);
- An ability to work as part of a team;
- An understanding of fabrics and colours.

Visionary designers

'Visionary designers' are all about the creative vision when it comes to garment design. Their focus is coming up with ideas and creating new styles. In an established fashion house this can be a person in a junior or senior position. Their responsibilities can include coming up with ideas, developing a story for a collection, choosing the colours and fabrics and generally overseeing the whole creative process. In a more senior position a visionary designer might be called the Creative Director, and will be responsible for managing the design team and leading the development of concepts. These designers work to balance functional design with something that fits the aesthetic of the brand, taking into consideration where the clothing will be worn and for what occasion. Most visionary designers collate their ideas using a storyboard or a mood board. A storyboard tells the story of a collection and is used to showcase the designs in context, for example, the model is drawn wearing the design with accessories. The storyboard shows the illustrated design, sometimes with annotations and descriptions. A mood board is a collage of inspirational images created by designers to use as visual stimuli for their

designs. This is often a collection of colours, shapes and swatches of different textures.[2]

Visionary designers can have a very general or very thorough understanding of the technical design process but may not be as interested or passionate about making clothing as they are about designing it. As a result they will work with specialists in the fields of pattern-making, fabric cutting or garment manufacture to create the garment. They will create the idea and then work closely with manufacturers to get the clothing made to their requirements. Visionary designers who run their own clothing label may outsource manufacturing to allow themselves more time for other activities such as promoting the label, securing finance and attending networking events.

Making designers

Making designers are focused on the technical side of fashion design and have developed an understanding of the processes involved in garment manufacture such as sewing, pattern making, cutting, pinning and draping. Their preoccupation is with the physical act of making the clothing that has been designed. You could say that visionary designers are like the directors of the film and making designers are the actors.

All clothing labels have both visionary designers to create direction/vision and making designers (such as pattern cutters or machinists) to create the actual clothing. In some cases the same team or person carries out both tasks; in larger companies two separate departments exist who liaise continually. Making designers can work for a fashion house full time – referred to as 'in-house designers' – working

alone or as part of a team. They may also work as freelancers, creating designs to sell to fashion houses. Making designers who have their own clothing label are more likely to seek assistance with activities such as the promotion of their brand so that they can focus their time on producing clothing, since this is a hugely time-consuming element of fashion design.

What kind of designer are you?

These are very simplified definitions that aim to give you an overview of the different types of designers and to help you decide whether you have a strong preference for one over the other. As a designer, I know that I sit more towards the visionary end of the spectrum, as creating the visual and coming up with the ideas has always been of more interest to me than making the clothing. Having said that, I oversee the manufacture of my garments and can carry out some stages myself (such as cutting and draping). I also enjoy experimenting with different embellishment techniques, from basic hand embroidery and appliqué to beading. It takes time to understand the process of garment manufacture and there is nothing wrong with not knowing it all with respect to the bigger picture. A great quote from Christian Louboutin which exemplifies this point is, 'To be a good technician is only a help, but should never be a priority. Why? Because technique can shrink your creation, and creation is everything, and the rest should gravitate around this.'[3]

I am a huge fan of designers who bring a sense of their personalities to their designs. Every designer wants to be able to create something unique, and remembering what makes you unique can be part of your design story, giving you a creative edge. For example, my background as a British-born Ghanaian contributes to my design style and has definitely influenced my design aesthetic. I believe that I design with a curvier woman in mind in order to celebrate the Ghanaian ideal of beauty but I combine this with a very British, innovative approach. For example, for my dresses I often lean towards a more cinched in waist and flattering cut. What part of 'you' can you bring to your designs?

You define

I asked some friends from a variety of backgrounds and industries to give me their definitions of a fashion designer. I was intrigued to discover how designers are seen by people inside and outside of the fashion industry. Their ideas and feedback was both interesting and amusing!

A fashion designer...

...is the soul of fashion

– Marco, photographer

...is an individual, a creative spirit, one that communicates through materials, textures, cuts, finishes, colours, and linings; their skills are far reaching and touch every element of human life and allow style to blossom

– Jono, business development director

...is someone who likes to make others look good

– Manike, graphic designer

...is usually a diva!

– Laura, garment technologist

...is someone who creates something new from a piece of fabric or a knitted swatch

– Kate, head of design

...has the vision, creativity and imagination to give people belief in their story

– Aneeqa, wholesale merchandiser

...is someone who creates designs that people love

– Alis, fashion merchandiser

...is a peacock of style and creativity and most importantly revolts against conventionality!

– Sarah, senior garment technologist

...is an artist for the people, because it is through his creations that man can express himself

– Lamia, PR

is ... a sculptor, bringing his/her vision to life for everyone to see, feel and love

– Alex, photographer

...is someone who maintains a creative view on how to make a product desirable to the consumer

– Emily, assistant designer

...is a practical creative visionary, able to translate their view of the future into something material within the present. They have great potential power to effect change and progress human evolution through communicative expression, broadening the mind and awaking individual self awareness to inspiration and empowerment by using accessible forms of art with far reaching effects to all parts of society

– Melanie, business consultant

Dior Couture Spring/Summer 1997,
photograph by Niall McInerney,
Bloomsbury Fashion Photography Archive

Haute couture

Haute couture is credited to English designer Charles Frederick Worth (1826–95) for his work designing bespoke pieces for rich, fashion-loving Parisian socialites and actresses.[4] In France, the use of the term is exclusive to certain brands, as to be able to describe itself as haute couture a fashion house must meet certain well-defined standards, set by the Chambre de commerce et d'industrie de Paris (Paris Chamber of Commerce). These include having an atelier in Paris; employing at least fifteen people full-time; creating made-to-order pieces for private clients with more than one fitting.[5] Well-known haute couture designers are Christian Dior and Elie Saab design. Chanel SA (the French fashion house founded by the couturier Gabrielle 'Coco' Chanel) owns Chanel, Eres and seven ateliers who specialise in haute couture techniques including Les Broderies Lesage (one of the most famous embroiderers in the world). When Chanel acquired these ateliers in 2002 they said it was to ensure that the ateliers in France – and the techniques they used – did not disappear (for example, much embroidery is done in India now, rather than France).[6]

A true trendsetter in this market and a popular name in the couture world was Yves Saint Laurent, whose self-named brand was considered to be the first luxury ready-to-wear brand.[7] Yves Saint Laurent was one of the few designers who made the concept of ready-to-wear luxury more tangible. At his last show in 2002 his grand finale dress was made in black and white, and customers were able to select the colours they wanted and have it made up at Saint Laurent Couture, complete with fittings. The Algerian-born French designer left an undeniable legacy in the world of haute couture, a world that some fear will shrink into obscurity unless the younger generation is trained up in the art. According to the late illustrator Joe Eula, 'It's a shame the top designers like Yves and Givenchy didn't train people to take over as Balenciaga did. With Balenciaga, you had Ungaro, Courreges and Givenchy himself. Dior produced Saint Laurent. But nobody came out of Saint Laurent and Givenchy, and this is the pity of today's couture.'[8]

Fashion markets

The main markets for fashion are haute couture, high street and ready-to-wear.

The excitement of haute couture

Haute couture for womenswear, referred to as 'bespoke' for menswear, is the style of fashion design which some say allows for the most creativity and extravagant design features. Haute couture is high quality, expensive, detailed, exclusive and hand-crafted. Pieces are one-off, ususaly for the catwalk or made to measure for a specific customer. Designers in this area are not always inspired by practical fashion or motivated by commercial success. By one definition haute couture fuses fashion – *'the modern entity that combines novelty and synergy with personal and social needs'* – with costume – *'the arts of dressmaking, tailoring, and crafts constituent to apparel and accessories.'*[9]

Above: High street fashion is known for being easily accessible, constantly on trend and the source of a great deal of 'fast fashion'; Below left: Ready-to-wear fashion, or Prêt-à-Porter, is clothing you can buy 'off the rack' without requiring significant alteration..

The evolution of high street fashion and ready-to-wear

After the invention of the measuring tape in 1820 and the sewing machine in 1846 by Elias Howe,[10] followed by Isaac Singer's electric sewing machine in 1889,[11] the possibilities of manufacturing standardised clothing en masse became more technically practical and affordable. The rise of department stores, such as Le Bon Marché, opened in Paris in 1838, made ready-to-wear fashion accessible and convenient, particularly for those who did not have the time or funds to purchase bespoke clothing.

HIGH STREET FASHION

Nowadays high street fashion is the home of mass retailers such as Zara, H&M, Topshop, America Apparel and Forever 21 where clothing is manufactured in large numbers and in standard sizes on a quick turnaround. Design for the high street is heavily steered by popular culture, media and celebrities; it is affordable, on-trend fashion which is accessible to all. It is not about exclusive expensive fashion design, rather interpreting popular trends for the high street shopper. High street fashion brands such as H&M or American Apparel tend to have a collective of designers working for them rather than one main designer, who create large collections of many pieces.

High street brands have recently started to bring celebrities and well-known designers on board to create new lines and maintain a buzz. Examples of these collaborations are Giles Deacon for New Look, and the Designers at Debenhams range or more recently in 2012, Lana Del Rey for H&M, showing that the link between designer and retail fashion has become closer over time, with high fashion designers adding credibility to high street fashion. An entrepreneur known for this kind of activity is Topshop CEO Sir Philip Green who brought supermodel Kate Moss on board in 2007 as a designer for Topshop. High street fashion has a quick turnaround when it comes to manufacturing and maintains a close relationship with media and celebrity.

READY-TO-WEAR

Ready-to-wear, or prêt-à-porter, is a sector of fashion design where smaller collections are created by designers and tend to be manufactured on a much smaller scale than high street. It comes in standardised sizes and is not cheap or made for the mass market. Ready-to-wear sometimes imitates couture style but at a lower cost and greater 'wearability'. Popular designers such as Diane von Furstenberg, Philip Lim and Alexander Wang fit into this category. It is more expensive than high street but can steer the direction of high street fashion. Ready-to-wear is a wise choice for an emerging designer as it presents an opportunity to present a manageable-sized collection that can be made in affordable quantities, creating a specific look for a targeted customer. When you are a new designer trying to find your place in the market the best way forward (given that you are likely to have limited resources) is to start small and develop quality pieces, building up quantity over time. Donna Karan's first collection consisted of just 7 pieces yet it was an instant success.

Trends

Trends are most commonly defined as 'any form of behaviour that develops among a large population and is collectively followed with enthusiasm for [a] period, generally [because] the behaviour [is] perceived as novel in some way.'[12] Fashion trends develop in the accessories, menswear, womenswear and childrenswear markets, and in colours, textiles, cut, and style. Trends work in two ways – from the top down, i.e. from the catwalk into mainstream fashion, or from the bottom up, where fashionable individuals influence industry direction. An example of this bottom-up direction was seen during the early to mid 1990s, when high street trends such as the hip-hop B-Boy style influenced Karl Lagerfeld with his 1991 Chanel collection where Lagerfeld showed piles of gold jewellery on models. Trends aren't always easily attributed to any one group, there can be a number of influencers including celebrities and key industry movers and shakers. Nowadays designers pay an increasing amount of attention to high-profile consumers such as fashion industry influencers and celebrities, who are known to be able to raise the profile of a designer by association and have long held influence on trends. This was seen as far back as the Audrey Hepburn and Hubert de Givenchy wardrobe collaboration for Hepburn's 1954 movie *Sabrina* which influenced a key trend of the time, for feminine, yet very simple, and beautifully tailored womenswear.[13]

After a trend begins there is no guarantee it will last. It can be said that once a trend is out there in the public domain, it is the consumer who ultimately decides whether it will be picked up or not. The usual flow of a trend starts with what the American Marketing Association[14] refers to as the 'distinctiveness' part of the cycle, where an 'it' style is born/spotted. For example, it may be spotted in an influential street style blog such as The Sartorialist (http://thesartorialist.blogspot.com) or on the red carpet. It then becomes increasingly sought after, with the key industry players, magazines and celebrities getting first access via exclusive designer collections, and members of the public creating the look for themselves. The style is spotted in magazines, on TV and through other media platforms and so follows the gradual flow of the trend until it is eventually manufactured for mass-market consumption. Somewhere within that process, the 'bandwagon effect' occurs where the probability of any individual adopting the style increases with the proportion of people who have done so already.

Years ago it used to take quite some time for a fashion trend to filter down to the mass market but nowadays because of the Internet, fashion magazines, celebrity exposure and faster and cheaper manufacturing capabilities, a trend from the catwalks of Paris can appear in low cost retail stores in a few days. What starts out as an exclusive trend in exclusive circles becomes more and more accessible to the masses and hence loses its appeal, which is why some trends have relatively short lives and can change at a moments notice. So if you bought into a trend in its early stages then you may have a good few seasons left of wear (a year or maybe more depending on the trend; trends which tend to last longer are the ones which are less 'edgy' and 'far out'). Conversely, if you purchased it

A designer needs to be experimental yet sensitive of the world around them to be sought after now and referenced in the future.[15]

Nigel Barker, former *America's Next Top Model* Presenter

during the height of mass adoption, you may only have a few months of 'in trend' wear left.

Designers create fashion five or six months ahead of season therefore the ability to create, spot and develop trends is an important part of being a fashion designer. The success or failure of a fashion brand greatly depends on the buying public's opinion as well as what other designers are producing. One of a fashion designer's strengths lies in knowing how to watch trends but also initiate them which is tricky as it is often easier to become more of a follower than a setter.

Putting together your collection: the creative process

We have covered the theoretical side of being a fashion designer including the different types of fashion designers and the different markets; it is now time to look at the practical side of making your clothing.

The end goal for all designers when creating a clothing collection is to create one which is consistent with the clothing label's image and one which will sell; your clothing line should be both 'c's – creative and commercial. For a designer working for a fashion house, the clothing is developed to guidelines set by the Creative Director, Head Designer or senior designers so that it fits the fashion houses' particular design brief. However, a self-employed designer will make these decisions for themselves. Outlined below are some guidelines that can be applied when preparing your own collection.

Less is more

The best advice for any emerging fashion designer when developing their first few collections, is to start small. As tempting as it is to step out, all guns blazing, with a 30-piece collection, keep it small and strong. Editing your collection with a critical eye is one of the most important things you must do. Ten amazing pieces will have more impact than a 30-piece collection with only seven strong pieces. The other bonus about focusing on a smaller collection is that you are able to invest in better quality fabrics as you are making fewer pieces, whereas with a bigger collection you may have to compromise the quality of the fabric or find other ways to cut corners to make it affordable. With a small collection you can invest in quality and deliver your strongest work.

The design brief

When a designer starts to create a piece of clothing they typically start with a design brief. This is information about the clothing to be designed such as design style, cut or fabrics, all of which are decided with a specific target customer in mind. Clothing labels will have these briefs to ensure that their collections reflect a consistent image (a style they are known for) whilst trying to design clothing, which is unique to them. A designer working for a clothing label or a freelance designer will have this brief set for them by their employer or client; a self-employed designer will set this for themselves.

The most successful brands maintain a consistent design story within their collections. For example, take a household name such as Calvin Klein. Calvin Klein is known as a classic American brand that presents fashion which is accessible, simple, clean, elegant, and iconic, and it has been known for this design story for over 50 years. As such Calvin Klein would not have a design brief to create collections using diamante, appliqué and sequins, because this would not be consistent with what customers expect from the brand.

Create a theme

The first stage of the creative process (after creating a design brief) is idea generation, brainstorming and getting inspired. Using this inspiration you should start to sketch out design ideas, and as the ideas begin to flow, a theme is created that shapes your design. This is commonly known as your 'story' and allows the pieces you design to form part of a collection that works well together. All the pieces in your collection should complement each other and form members of a family. When flicking through a rail of your designs a customer should be able to see all the pieces as part of the same collection. You should not try to throw everything at one collection, overdoing it with the use of different fabrics, styles, cuts and techniques. Instead aim to keep it strong but simple, and allow your different design techniques to be seen through your story into your collection.

Each collection begins with clothing samples. Making samples is a costly part of the design process and one that rarely goes exactly according to plan with regards to time or budget. Maybe the fabric does not behave how you expect it to and it takes several attempts until you get your style right. In addition materials are expensive so getting feedback on your designs at the sample stage before you make more than one of each style is priceless. A simple way for an emerging designer to get feedback is by presenting the designs to a focus group, which could be a group of friends or people you know who represent your target audience.

How do visionary and making designers develop the garment?

Every designer works differently to develop the garment, with some creating storyboards on paper which are then developed into a piece of clothing, whereas others can take an idea and start to realise it in physical form by draping fabric on a mannequin, finding the right style through trial and error. This part of the creative process is about transferring a set of ideas from the mind into a physical form. Most designs begin with a sketched idea.

Sketching

The concept of sketching designs was established around the late 1800s, when design houses would hire artists to draw designs to be shown to clients (in this case individuals/customers). The design houses would work from the artists' sketch to make clothing the client liked.[16] This process saved money in the long run by introducing designs through illustration instead of showing a completed garment on a model to customers first.

Every designer's creative process is different and some are not particularly good at sketching but they can still get their message across. Those who prefer traditional sketching methods can choose between chalk, charcoal, pastels, watercolours, acrylic, gouache, markers, coloured pencils and ink. For those who like working digitally, software such as CAD is quite popular (see box above) because it

Popular fashion design software:

- CAD (computer assisted design) software – allows you to create virtual representations of your different designs using models. Two popular programs are:

  OptTex, which includes a 3D runway designer feature that enables you to construct a virtual fashion show;

  and **Fashion Toolbox**, which is similar to CAD and allows you to sketch realistic pictures of your designs in addition to storyboard.

- Pattern-making software – usually used by beginner designers who want to test their patterns against varying designs and materials. This software is easier to use than CAD.

- Product development management (PDM) software – used to develop a clothing line, it includes both design features and tools as well as promotion, sales and marketing elements.

- Software for embroidery design – used for producing special patterns such as monograms.

enables designers to produce an accurate technical drawing and see a virtual model of their garment in different colours, textures and sizes. Many software solutions come with clip art and storyboard samples that show how designs will look when actually made, which can be helpful for decision making. Drawing using vector-based tools for symmetrical drawing and editing is taught in fashion drawing classes.

Fashion illustration

Fashion illustration is used by fashion designers as well as fashion publishers and retail outlets. Illustrators use painting, collage, drawing, stencilling and imaging

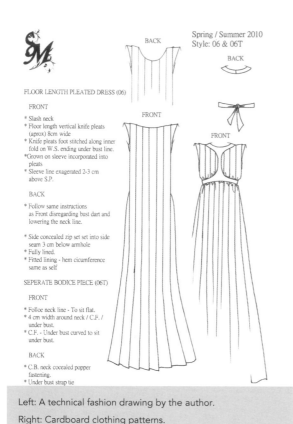

SM

Spring / Summer 2010
Style: 06 & 06T

BACK

BACK

FLOOR LENGTH PLEATED DRESS (06)

FRONT

FRONT

FRONT

* Slash neck
* Floor length vertical knife pleats
  (aprox) 8cm wide
* Knife pleats foot stitched along inner
  fold on W.S. ending under bust line.
* Grown on sleeve incorporated into
  pleats
* Sleeve line exagerated 2-3 cm
  above S.P.

BACK

* Follow same instructions
  as Front disregarding bust dart and
  lowering the neck line.

* Side concealed zip set into side
  seam 3 cm below armhole
* Fully lined.
* Fitted lining - hem cicumference
  same as self

SEPERATE BODICE PIECE (06T)

FRONT

* Folloe neck line - To sit flat.
* 4 cm width around neck / C.F. /
  under bust.
* C.F. - Under bust curved to sit
  under bust.

BACK

* C.B. neck cocealed popper
  fastening.
* Under bust strap tie

Left: A technical fashion drawing by the author.

Right: Cardboard clothing patterns.

software such as CAD to create images that are used across a range of platforms. The work may be commissioned by PR agencies, fashion magazines or design consultants and used for advertising and promoting fashion designers or fashion retailers. Talented illustrators of the past include Andy Warhol, Antonio Lopez, Joe Eula (who skilfully captured Christian Dior's revolutionary New Look) and Cecil Beaton; well-known present-day illustrators include Francois Berthoud, David Downton and Julie Verhoven. When describing his favourite fashion illustrators, René Gruau and Eric Rene, David Downton says, '… I don't believe there is a frivolous subject for art (although there are undoubtedly frivolous artists) and these superb draftsmen were masters of the fluid, reductive line that I loved and tried so hard to emulate. They told not just "the story of the dress", but also the story around the dress, describing the time, the place and the woman with an economy and flair that photography, however striking, could never match.'[17]

Creating a pattern

By combining the sketch or illustration with information about the design dimensions, a pattern can be made by a pattern maker, usually from cardboard. Some designers are able to make their own patterns, whereas others may choose to employ someone to do this for them.

A pattern maker, working from either a sketch or the draped fabric (often muslin), uses paper, card or CAD software to create the pattern for a garment, which is then graded (duplicated and scaled) into different sizes. For example, a pattern is made in a size 10 and then graded into alternative sizes such as 6, 8, 12 and 14. Alternatively fabric can be draped onto a dress form and the pattern created from this by using a paper pattern for example. The fabric is draped in the required style, pinned into place and marked.[18] These markings are traced onto a paper to create a pattern, which is in turn used to create a final piece.

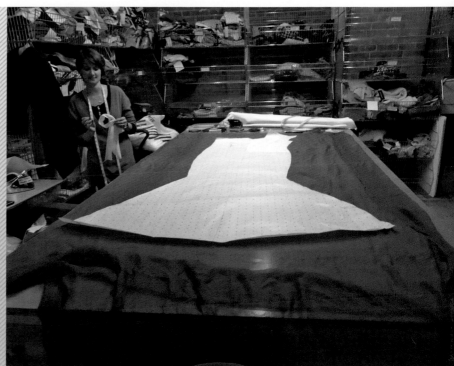

A pattern placed on fabric, about to be cut.

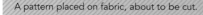

Pattern making is extremely technical and relies on the pattern maker's accuracy and technical skill; the best pattern makers have over ten years' experience. If this is a particular area of interest for you it is worth taking a professional pattern making course. For example, making a pattern involves learning how to create shapes and silhouettes for different styles, constructing hem, collar and sleeve variations. Pattern cutting classes give instruction on dart manipulation, pivoting and slashing, grain lines and balance marks. (These words may not make sense right now but as you see more and more patterns they will become an understandable part of your vocabulary!) Pattern making can be a complex and time consuming process hence why many emerging (and established) designers employ experienced pattern makers. This can be expensive but is worth the cost; the pattern is one of the most important parts of clothing design so it is important to get it right. Experienced pattern makers will work with you to help you understand the limitations and possibilities of your design. For example, pattern makers have an understanding of fabrics and how these different fabrics will interact with the pattern.

They will help you understand what the fabric you have chosen will not allow for and what elements can be built into your pattern to give you the desired style. For instance, a stretch fabric will need different allowances in the pattern measurements than a more rigid fabric with less 'give'. For a less intricate design, such as a simple T-shirt, it may take just one attempt to make the right pattern, whereas a more complex style, such as a pleated evening gown, may require several attempts and multiple changes. In this case every change made to the toile must be reflected in the pattern. For example, if the toile dress (a rough version of the design; see picture on p.78) is made but the designer decides that the style should be a little longer, or the waist taken in, then these changes to the hem and waist measurements need to be reflected in the final pattern. Patterns are always, therefore, thoroughly checked before they are graded and put into final production, to ensure that they are accurate and that all modifications have been incorporated into the final pattern before the pattern is finally used. If you are able to master pattern making then you will definitely have a useful and cost-saving skill, however, if this is not your forte

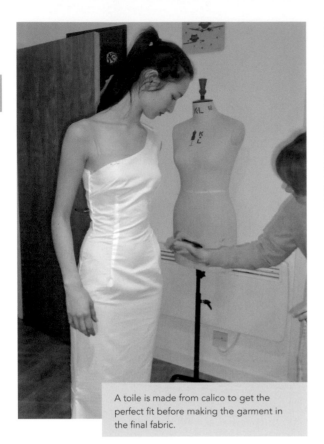

A toile is made from calico to get the perfect fit before making the garment in the final fabric.

Definition: draping

Draping is a procedure where you use muslin or a fabric similar to the one intended for the final garment and drape it on a mannequin, allowing it to lie in the way you want your design to look on the body.

Samples are made for lots of reasons:

- to have a physical piece to approve and get feedback on;
- to present styles and colour way options to buyers/stockists;
- to take photos for look books and stylebooks;
- to use for promotional reasons and PR;
- to sell as part of a collection.

then it is better to hire an expert to develop your patterns for you, or you could end up paying for your inexperience later by having to re-do designs and wasting much-needed money.

Pattern making is one of the elements of fashion design that I have personally always found quite difficult. I remember trying to teach myself the basics of pattern making. I went to a department store to buy a pattern for a simple pair of trousers. I opened the packet, played around with the pattern paper and re-read the notes and descriptions several times. I set about trying to understand the pattern and what the lines, circles, triangles and annotations actually meant but eventually came to the conclusion that I may not ever master them. However, in my view the most important thing is to try constantly to gain as much understanding as you can. I spend time with my pattern maker to learn how he works – sometimes he uses draping (see box above) and other times he goes straight into making the pattern from flat card. It is always fascinating to watch.

From the pattern, a toile is made from calico or muslin; a step towards the completed piece. Calico or muslin fabric is used because it is cheap and malleable enough to be draped and hung properly, and it comes in different weights. The toile is then fitted on a model or mannequin and adjusted until it is perfect. Once the toile has been adjusted to perfection these changes are incorporated into the pattern and the garment can be made from the chosen fabric and then fitted on to a model. Any final adjustments are made in the final fitting and the garment is tidied up (i.e. loose threads cut, it is checked thoroughly for stains) and steamed. The selection of material, trimming and details will impact upon the care instruction for the pieces, for example, if the garment is made from a fine luxury fabric which can not be cleaned at home in a washing machine it will need a 'Dry clean only' label sewn into the garment.

Designers' rights

After you have taken the trouble to create a collection you will want to protect it from being copied. Designers are now sharing more content more freely as a result of blogs and social media platforms such as Facebook but when your ideas are your creative 'currency' it is important to be cautious. It is very difficult to prove that your design rights have been infringed, so I prefer to focus on protecting my work rather than worrying about how someone might copy it.

You should also remember that whilst creating you are often referring to other people's designs as a source of inspiration. It is a tough pill to swallow but it's very hard to have a completely unique idea, although who doesn't want to think they can create something original? Not many of us. In 2011 Yves Saint Laurent responded to accusations that it copied Christian Louboutin's signature red soles, by asserting that the shoe designer did not own the colour red and issued this statement,

> 'Red outsoles are a commonly-used ornamental design feature in footwear, dating as far back as the red shoes worn by King Louis XIV in the 1600s and the ruby red shoes that carried Dorothy home in The Wizard of Oz, court papers filed by YSL read. '[19]

What are your thoughts on this? After all, what is the first thing you think of when you think red outsoles? In an interview with the French newspaper Libération, Louboutin responded that he wasn't trying to copyright a colour, but the issue was more complicated:

> 'I understand that, but it is a red in a specific context [in the way that], there is Ferrari red [and] Hermès orange. Even in the food industry, Cadbury recently won a lawsuit against Nestlé for using purple packaging. All this proves that the colours play a part in a brand's identity. I'm not saying that red usually belongs to me – I repeat that this is about a precise red, used in a precise location.'[20]

Fashion law is an emerging and important specialty. It encompasses legal issues around the life cycle of a garment (from conception through to sale), brand protection, consumer advertising, commercial contracts and third party collaborations. The rise of e-commerce, social media sites, digital fashion magazines, and blogs and celebrity endorsements adds another layer of legal issues. Whether you're a stylist, designer or fashion house; you need to be equipped with the finest legal knowledge in order to benefit your brand, ideas, and business.[21]

Beverley Dei, Legal Executive, Calvin Klein Europe

Tips for protecting your designs

- Draw all of your designs out and annotate them with details (don't keep them in your head);
- Send them to yourself by recorded delivery and do not open;
- Consider sending your designs to a third party like ACID or a solicitor for safekeeping;
- Make a note of anyone who has access to your designs who could potentially use them;
- Be careful about who you share your designs with;
- Keep a record of your design process and the dates you created your work;
- Put the copyright symbol on each page of your designs and sign and date them.

How can I protect my designs?

The most important step to ensure your designs are protected is to commit designs to paper so that they do not just exist in your head. This is where the copyright process begins. The drawing does not need to be perfect but annotate it and take a picture of a sample if you have one. Sending it recorded delivery to yourself is a popular way of protecting designs, as the time-stamp on the envelope formally records a date from which you can stake a claim to your design's existence, if the envelope can be proven not to have been interfered with. However, sending designs to yourself has never been used as evidence in court. It is therefore safest to ensure that a third party holds copies of your designs, such as a bank, solicitor or an organisation like ACID (which has a Design Databank for Members' designs).

In the UK, drawings count as two-dimensional works and therefore qualify for protection under Copyright Law. Copyright lasts for 70 years plus the life of the originator, although this may be reduced to 25 years if the copyright work is produced commercially in large quantities. Prototypes or three-dimensional pieces are protected by unregistered Design Right.

I would suggest joining an organisation like ACID (Anti-Copying in Design; www.acid.uk.com). ACID helps its members to understand what rights they have and how to protect, commercialise and maximise their designs potential, and its logo is recognised as a strong symbol of deterrence.[22]

What if my designs have been stolen?

If you see a design that looks exactly like one of yours and find that it was designed after yours then you need to prove that the designer of the piece had access to your design, e.g. a shared pattern-maker or manufacturer. In actuality it can be hard to prove a link and deliberate copying even with suspicious circumstances. For this reason many designers just dismiss the situation as bad luck. A designer may pursue the legal route when the similarity and link between the designer accused of copying and the 'original' designer is simply too strong to ignore, i.e. the two worked side by

Copyright organisations

Most countries have an Intellectual Property Office or a government department which provides information about patents and trademarks. In addition to contacting your local government patent office, the following organisations are useful.

IDEAS21

ideas21 is an innovation network and specialises in the successful exploitation of ideas and intellectual property. It provides networking events, workshops, seminars and one-to-one advice.

http://www.ideas21.co.uk

INTELLECTUAL PROPERTY OFFICE

In the UK the Intellectual Property Office is responsible for patents, designs, trademarks and for copyright.

http://www.ipo.gov.uk

WHATISCOPYRIGHT.ORG

WhatisCopyright.org is a non-profit web site that contains basic and general copyright information provided for educational purposes.

http://www.whatiscopyright.org

CREATIVE COMMONS

Creative Commons develops infrastructure that maximizes digital creativity, sharing, and innovation. They assist with the protection of creative work by providing copyright licenses.

http://www.creativecommons.org.uk

THE WORLD INTELLECTUAL PROPERTY ORGANISATION (WIPO)

The World Intellectual Property Organisation (WIPO) is a specialised agency of the United Nations dedicated to developing an accessible international intellectual property (IP) system. WIPO administers 23 international treaties dealing with different aspects of IP protection.

http://www.wipo.int

side. If this situation arises you should get in touch with a copyright lawyer or anti-copying organisation for advice about the best steps to take.

The best advice I have ever been given is to concentrate on my talent and on getting my best work out into the public eye. A stunning design is of no use to anyone, including its designer, if left on a piece of paper in a locked drawer. Take solace in the fact that being creative and talented means that design ideas come to you a dime a dozen, and they will keep coming to you. Many argue that no design is truly original in the sense that everything has been designed before in one way or another. In addition, in the world of 'fashion karma', imitations make high-fashion affordable for the high street. For example, it is very easy for any one of us to pick up a runway imitation from Topshop, ZARA or H&M and many of us do. However, knowing about copyright and protecting your work will also help you if you are ever accused of copying yourself!

NOTES

1. Sarah-Jane Clarke quoted in Adele Horin, 'Young Creative Types the New Mega Rich', *Sydney Morning Herald* (11 December 2006); available at http://www.businesslists.com.au/business-lists-articles/2006/12/11/young-creative-types-the-new-megarich/, accessed 5 November 2012

2. For an interesting discussion on mood boards, see http://forums.thefashionspot.com/f90/storyboards-5152.html#ixzz1hy4llsjk.

3. Quoted in Mary Gehlhar, *The Fashion Designer Survival Guide* (New York: Kaplan Publishing, 2008)

4. Harold Koda, and Richard Martin. 'Haute Couture', in Heilbrunn Timeline of Art History (New York: The Metropolitan Museum of Art, 2004), http://www.metmuseum.org/toah/hd/haut/hd_haut.htm; accessed 18 October 2012

5. Wikipedia, 'Haute Couture', http://en.wikipedia.org/wiki/Haute_couture; accessed 18 October 2012

6. Alexandra Suhner Isenberg, 'Fashion 101: Who Owns What', Searching for Style website, http://searchingforstyle.com/archives/11048/ (November 2010); accessed 18 October 2012

7. Alexandra Suhner Isenberg, 'Fashion 101: How Haute Couture Works', Searching for Style website, http://searchingforstyle.com/archives/4972/ (April 2010); accessed 18 October 2012

8. Joe Eula, 'Au Revoir, Yves', *New York Times* website, http://www.nytimes.com/slideshow/2002/03/31/magazine/31style.slideshow.ready_13.html (2002); accessed 18 October 2012

9. Harold Koda and Richard Martin. 'Haute Couture', in *Heilbrunn Timeline of Art History* (New York: The Metropolitan Museum of Art, 2004), http://www.metmuseum.org/toah/hd/haut/hd_haut.htm; accessed 18 October 2012

10. Graham Forsdyke, 'A Brief History of the Sewing Machine', The International Sewing Machine Collectors' Society website, http://www.ismacs.net/sewing_machine_history.html; accessed 18 October 2012

11. Wikipedia, 'Sewing Machine', http://en.wikipedia.org/wiki/Sewing_machine#History_and_development; accessed 18 October 2012

12. Wikipedia, 'Fad', http://en.wikipedia.org/wiki/Fads_and_trends; accessed 17 October 2012

13. Famous Women and Beauty website, 'Hubert de Givenchy and Audrey Hepburn', http://www.famous-women-and-beauty.com/hubert-de-givenchy.html; accessed 17 October 2012

14. American Marketing Association, Marketing Power website, http://www.marketingpower.com; accessed 17 October 2012

15. Nigel Barker in conversation with author

16. David Downton, *Masters of Illustration* (London: Laurence King, 2010)

17. David Downton, *Masters of Illustration* (London: Laurence King, 2010)

18. For a good explanation of creating a pattern from a design sketch, see http://bcatthreads.com/n-1157-step-3-in-fashion-design-create-first-pattern-flat-pattern-or-drape.html

19. Lauren Milligan, 'Save Our Soles', *British Vogue* website (24 May 2011), http://www.vogue.co.uk/news/daily/110524-yves-saint-laurent-on-christian-lou.aspx; accessed 18 October 2012

20. Ella Alexander, 'YSL Closes Louboutin Court Case', *British Vogue* website (16 October 2012), http://www.vogue.co.uk/news/2011/04/20/christian-louboutin-sues-yves-saint-laurent-for-red-sole-shoes; accessed 5 November 2012

21. Beverley Dei, in conversation with the author. For Beverley's blog see www.tildasbulb.com.

22. Jane Stephenson, Membership Development Manager of ACID (Anti Copying In Design), in conversation with author.

CHAPTER 4

FINDING YOUR FEET

Being yourself in the fashion industry

■ ■

In order to be irreplaceable, one must always be different.

Coco Chanel

Designers in the fashion industry want to stand out and make a name for themselves, but whilst striving to be unique many people find themselves losing sense of who they really are, or at times pretending to be someone they are not. There is no norm for who you should be, the industry is full of eccentric characters. I remember being in the hallways at the London College of Fashion and hearing a girl walk past in a group and she said 'I just seem to be so different from everyone else here,' and I thought to myself 'That's a good thing'; I wonder if she knew how lucky she was! It is always better to be yourself, even if that means not being who others expect you to be. Success within the fashion industry is often linked to the relationships that you manage to build for yourself so yes, it is important that you make

a positive impression on the people you interact with, but it also needs to be true representation of yourself. I once heard about a manager who had tested an intern by mentioning a fictional non-existent designer to them; the intern then gushed positively about the designer's amazing work only to be told later that this designer did not exist. Lesson learned? Do not pretend to know things you don't or to be someone you aren't as people may decide to find out how genuine you really are.

■ ■

The fashion industry is full of creative individuals who are comfortable expressing their personal style, such as this reveller at Vivienne Westwood's London store during 'Fashion's Night Out' 2011.

83

Etiquette within the fashion industry

It is difficult to know what you should and should not do to work your way around this industry because there is no golden handbook, but some things go without saying. Here are a few useful starting points.

◆ Appearance matters because first impressions count. It is crucial that you think about how you present yourself and make an effort with your appearance. Following trends and being fashion forward does show a keen interest in the industry but most importantly staying true to yourself and your personal style is the best way forward.

◆ Dress for success! A former boss once told me that the way you dress for a meeting shows the level of respect you have for the person you are going to see. This has stayed with me; dress appropriately depending on who you are going to meet. Some people may be offended if you turn up to meet them wearing jeans when they have made an effort to meet you in a suit. Even if you are dressed formally it is still possible to inject your creativity into your clothes whilst looking professional.

◆ It goes without saying that you should not be rude to or dismissive to anyone. The fashion industry is very small so being polite to everyone is important. Wherever you are on the industry ladder, your behaviour can help or hinder you. Treat everyone you meet with respect, not only because that is how you would like to be treated, but also because you never know who you are speaking to. Your reputation takes years to build but can be destroyed in minutes so work hard to protect it.

◆ Don't be two-faced in your dealings with others – it will catch up with you. If you disagree with someone, be honest about it.

◆ Don't think that the fashion world should revolve around you, simply because you are talented. Be humble and modest so that the people who come into contact with you have positive things to say about their experience.

◆ Don't believe your own hype or get so caught up in the glamour of the industry that you forget to focus on your product. Focus on delivering excellent work above all else.

◆ Return all calls and follow up with actions when you say you will. For example, if you take someone's business card, email or call them as soon as possible afterwards. It is always important to follow up as soon as you can, in case you forget who the person is and what they do. Jot down something easy to remember the person on the card, for instance their hair colour, or memorable remarks.

◆ Know when to leave the party if you want to make a professional impression. In an industry where a great deal of networking is done in glamorous and exciting settings – for example at a fashion show or launch event – it is easy to get swept away by it all and forget that you are surrounded by future colleagues, business contacts and peers. One of the exciting things about working in fashion is the events you get to attend, so getting the correct balance between enjoying yourself and behaving in a professional manner is important.

Finding your network

Being the kind of person who can easily strike up a conversation is helpful when it comes to building a network. I'm not shy to ask a stranger where they got an amazing coat from, or if they could they advise me where to go for a decent quality beaded fabric, and so far I am lucky that I have never had any unfriendly reactions. This aspect of my personality has helped me to connect with people and get information and recommendations. An aimless conversation with a lady on a London bus led to me being introduced to one of my favourite go-to places for fabric, Southall,

Finding a crowd you feel comfortable with is part of finding your feet in the industry. You will have to put yourself 'out there' to connect with people, but it is well worth the effort.

and an exchange with a man in a bright purple coat outside Topshop in Oxford Circus, London, introduced me to the Portobello Business Centre. Finding a group of like-minded people is easier than you may think. It starts with conversations followed by actions, and slowly your social circle starts to grow. Once I had located the various fabric hotspots in London and logged into the right blogs and websites I started going to fashion shows, boutiques and networking events. I met other designers, models, photographers, entrepreneurs and fellow creatives, and found that one relationship often leads to another. Sometimes I found out about an event I wanted to go to but had to go on my own. Although this may sound intimidating, people are actually more likely to approach you if you are alone. This is a small industry, and after a while you will recognise faces and others will recognise you. As your confidence grows it will become easier to go to more events. All that is left is for you to make conversation.

Volunteer work can expand your network too and is a more natural way to build up your contacts. Volunteering to help out at friends' photoshoots and fashion shows will help to get you into conversations with other designers, models, photographers and like-minded people. Building a good circle of friends begins with the 'like factor' (those you connect and get on with), so apart from finding like-minded people who share you interests, you want to find people who you genuinely like and enjoy spending time with. (For more reasons to volunteer see p.173!)

Networking and relationship building

Networking seems to be an intimidating and forced concept for most people. You may shudder at the thought of attending an event on your own; I know many designers who cringe at the thought of it because it seems so daunting and unnatural. Going to events and looking around a room, trying to decide who you think will be worth talking to is the wrong way to approach networking – this is not a natural way to think and operate. The truth is that we actually network every day of our lives without thinking about it – for example, when we connect with new people with shared and common interests. So, if you can apply the same confidence (real or false) you use when it comes to making new friends to making a network of contacts, you will be half way there. Even if you are shy, consider the reasons why networking is important and you may feel encouraged to come out of your shell a little.

Networking is important for many reasons

- Building a support system;
- Getting advice and information;
- Exchanging ideas;
- Building up confidence by taking yourself out of your comfort zone

The steps I take to build relationships depend on where I am going and why. Most of the events I attend in order to connect with new people are not specifically networking events so I try to research them beforehand to get a rough idea of what to expect, the purpose of the occasion and to get a feel

From top to bottom, the author meeting: Hilary Alexander, the Fashion Director of the *Daily Telegraph*; model Janice Dickinson; Harold Tillman, former Chairman of the British Fashion Council; Christian Louboutin and Film Director Eva Ionesco.

for the crowd who may be there. When you attend a fashion industry event your aim should not be to get as many business cards as possible or to talk to as many people in the room as you can, but to make genuine connections. Remember that everyone is there to enjoy themselves and to connect with people they can help and who can support them in return. Knowing the other people in the room are all looking for help with something too should help you relax. I have outlined some useful advice I was given about the subject of networking below.

Just talk

Talking allows you to find out information and see where opportunities may lie. Having natural conversations without agendas ('what can I get out of this') is one of the best ways to find out information and build relationships. One of my favourite sayings when it comes to networking is 'If you are somewhere, be completely present there'. Don't be texting on your phone in the corner of the room, or forget to focus because you are looking around for someone 'better' to talk to. Make an effort. In order to get help and advice you need to be willing to talk and share. It is the only way you are going to make connections with anyone.

Know your message

Get your 'blurb' together so that you can describe what you do concisely in no more than a few sentences. If it takes you more than ten minutes to describe what you do you will soon suffer in the networking arena because you may lose the interest of those around you. You should be able to get a punchy message across about who you are, what you do (perhaps with an example of a key achievement) and what you are looking for, and to be able to convey it all with passion. For example you may say 'I am a menswear designer and right now I am looking to build relationships that will help me to grow and develop my brand. I am at the sampling stage with a new collection and would really benefit from an investment'. In the business world this is described as the elevator pitch, '…. an extremely concise

presentation of an entrepreneur's idea, business model, company solution, marketing strategy, and competition delivered to potential investors. This should not last more than a few minutes or the duration of an elevator ride.'[1] After you have introduced yourself take the time to listen to what is said in reply. There is nothing wrong with picking up tips from the elevator pitches you hear and applying the techniques you found interesting and engaging to your own pitch in the future.

Be proactive

By following up with the people you meet, sending 'touch-base' emails (a general email to see how the person is doing with no set agenda) and frequently attending industry events, you can build relationships and form a network. You will have to do a lot of work in the beginning to become a recognized face on the scene so consistency is important. Sometimes people will forget you, not because you did not matter but because they became busy – maybe they were snowed under with emails and although they had been meaning to get in touch with you the time was never available. Being proactive means trying to keep yourself in the forefront of others' minds so that if an opportunity to meet, connect and share information or advice, or even work together, arises you will be remembered. Being proactive also means going out and trying to create your own 'luck' – don't wait for opportunities to come to you but go actively looking for them.

Be organised

Being organised makes a world of difference and encompasses everything from getting back to people on time to wearing your own designs at the right occasion. Little things like entering information from business cards into your address book as soon as you can or sending an email right after you meet someone can help to start and maintain relationships. Being organised also means looking the part and bringing examples of your craft with you when you can – by wearing your own design, for example, or carrying images of your work on your phone.

Finding local networking groups

You can find a comprehensive list of meetup and networking groups in your area by searching online platforms such as http://www.meetup.com and www.linkedin.com by location. Some examples of such groups are below:

THE INDUSTRY

The Industry is a private members club, created on the basis of bringing bright-minded, fashion professionals together six times a year to listen, learn and do business together in London.

http://www.theindustrylondon.com

FASHION 2.0

Fashion 2.0 is a group of people who work in the fashion industry in New York, primarily online, including fashion bloggers, new media publishers, entrepreneurs, industry insiders, fashion PR reps, and web trendsetters. To be able to join you should be a professional within the fashion industry and have an online presence.

www.meetup.com/fashion20

FASHION GROUP INTERNATIONAL

Fashion Group International is a global, non-profit, professional organisation with members in the fashion industry including apparel, accessories, beauty and home.

The Fashion Group offers a range of benefits and programs to a growing membership of more than 6000 men and women across the globe from Paris to Sydney and Toronto to Seoul.

http://www.fgila.org

THE HONG KONG DESIGNERS ASSOCIATION

With support from the industry and fellow designers in the past 26 years, the Hong Kong Designers Association has evolved into a key platform to share ideas and experiences through organising fashion events such as catwalk shows, seminars, interviews and group discussions.

www.hkfda.org

There are networking groups across the globe that give you the opportunity to meet like-minded people.

Use your network and look outside it

Always use your network. This may mean starting with family and friends. You may be surprised by the connections and contacts that your immediate circle turns up. Your network always consists of two parts: the first is your existing network such as friends and family, colleagues, mentors, peers and fashion industry contacts; the second is the network you are one step away from connecting with. Relying on your existing network means sitting in the comfort zone but in order to grow and work through the fashion industry it is important to step out of this zone and start contacting new people.

Respect the network you are introduced to

Respect any network you are introduced into. If someone has connected you with a contact of theirs, then in many ways they are vouching for you. Therefore when you follow it up it is crucial to not only be polite and gracious but also to acknowledge the introduction by communicating with both parties on the first occasion of contact (if sending an email, copy both in for example). Some people prefer to be left out of the loop completely once they have introduced you to someone, but it is always worth finding this out first.

Keep good company

It is very important to keep positive people around you, people who encourage you and give you confidence in your abilities. One of my mentors frequently tells me that to be the best, you need to study and move around with the best too; being around hard working and self-starting people can help you to become a self-starter too. I try to work and keep company with a mixture of positive people who are either striving to reach their dreams (inside or outside the fashion industry) or are happy with

Author with buyer Aneeqa Flynn and stylist Anne Look at a Richard Nicoll event at Liberty store, London.

their accomplishments, as they encourage a feeling of contentment within me. Both elements can keep you motivated and ensure you remain appreciative of any progress you do make. Being around negative people in an already tough and competitive industry is a sure way to make your life even more difficult. It is hard enough remaining driven and focused without adding the burden of negative people slowing you down or making you question yourself. Self-belief is hugely important and you should hold onto it.

What kind of people should you have in your network

Coach, strategist and speaker Tai Goodwin offers a great perspective on the top ten people you should have in your network, each one playing a critical and useful role.[2]

2

THE COACH

This is someone who comes in at different times in your life. They help with critical decisions and transitions, and offer an objective perspective with no strings attached.

5

THE CONNECTOR

This is a person who has access to people, resources and information. As soon as they come across something related to you, they send you an email or pick up the phone. Connectors are great at uncovering unique ways to make connections, finding resources and opportunities that most people would overlook.

1

THE MENTOR

This is the person who has reached the level of success you aspire to. You can learn from their success as well as their mistakes. Heed their wisdom and experience. This relationship offers a unique perspective because they have known you through several peaks and valleys in your life and watched you evolve.

4

THE TRENDSETTER

This is someone outside of your chosen industry who always has the latest buzz. It may be on any topic that you find interesting. The goal in having this person in your network is to look for those connections that spark innovation via the unconventional. It will also help you keep your conversations interesting.

3

THE INDUSTRY INSIDER

This is someone in your chosen field who has an expert level of information or access to it. This person will keep you informed of what's happening now and what the next big thing is. Invite them to be a sounding board for your next innovative idea.

7

THE REALIST

On the flip side you still need a person who will help you keep it real. This is the person who will give you the raised eyebrow when your expectations exceed your effort. These are not people who knock down your dreams rather they challenge you to actively make your dream happen.

10

THE WANNA-BE

This is someone you can serve as mentor to. Someone you can help shape and guide based on your experiences. One of the best ways to tell that you understand something is to be able to explain it to someone else. And sometimes, one of the best motivations for pushing past obstacles and hardship is knowing that someone is watching.

6

THE IDEALIST

This is the person in your network you can dream with. No matter how 'out there' your latest idea is, this is the person who will help you brainstorm ways to make it happen. Without judgment, they are focused on helping you flush out your dreams in high definition, even if you don't have a solid plan yet on how to make it happen.

8

THE VISIONARY

Visionary people inspire you by their journey and path through life. They are similar to the idealist, but the visionary can help you envision an actual plan to reach your goal. One personal encounter with this type of person can powerfully change the direction of your thinking and life.

9

THE PARTNER

You need to have someone who is in a similar place and on a similar path to share with. In fact, partners do a lot of sharing. This is a person you can share the highs and lows with. Partners will also share resources, opportunities and information.

NOTES

1. Wikipedia, 'Elevator Pitch', http://en.wikipedia.org/wiki/Elevator_pitch; accessed 18 October 2012

2. Tai Goodwin, 'Top Ten People You Must Have in Your Network', Careerealism website (January 2012), http://www.careerealism.com/top-10-people-you-must-have-in-your-network/; accessed 18 October 2012 and reproduced with permission

THE BUSINESS OF BEING A FASHION ENTREPRENEUR

So, you've been inspired to start a clothing label? Then now is the time to put your thoughts and ideas onto paper, to find out whether your idea can take off. Making a business plan is not the most exciting part of sticking your flag on the global fashion map but it is crucial. After the idea and inspiration comes the business plan. This section covers key parts of planning, finance and manufacturing.

Writing a good business plan

Although many start-up clothing labels have been set up without a written business plan it is widely advised that you do write one, to help you take first steps in the right direction. You can write your plan on your own or ask someone to do it for you, but I think that it is important that you develop your plan (i.e. do the research) yourself. Writing it yourself will ensure you think about every aspect, research and develop your ideas and completely understand your business idea inside out. Ask someone to look over your plan once it is written to get feedback, insight and a different perspective (e.g. a business owner who works outside the fashion industry). This will help you to spot any gaps. A good business plan can be used as a reference point once your clothing label has launched to guide you as you move forward.

It takes time to put together a business plan. You may end up taking a month, three months or even longer to write it. It took me a few months to research and write mine and it was 16 pages long (the rough guide being no more than 20 pages). It can be a daunting prospect so remember that the aim is not to agonise over it so much that the state of play has changed by the time you have finally finished it – but to make sure it is a thoroughly researched and relevant document, which will help you.

Some emerging designers find the process slightly confusing, as some of the information required is based on your future sales – data that you do not know yet. This includes an assumption that your clothing

Definition

'A business plan is a formal statement of a set of business goals, the reasons why they are believed attainable, and the plan for reaching those goals. It may also contain background information about the organisation or team attempting to reach those goals.'[1]

will be well received and liked, but the fact is that the fashion industry is unpredictable – designers are faced with short product life cycles, varying demand, and tough and inflexible supply processes. The customer is king and personal taste can be very difficult to predict with a high degree of certainty, even with industry intelligence such as trend forecasts. But if you're worried about it, fear not! It is almost impossible for your business plan to be 100 per cent accurate, instead, it acts like a guideline.

If you are a clothing designer who is primarily focused on the creative side of fashion, the business plan might seem boring and mundane, but remember that a good business plan puts exciting

ideas into perspective, drawing your attention to the critical things that you will need to do. It is like a cold shower of reality, but very useful.

Calculating your finances

When writing your business plan you need to calculate your finances for the first year of operation. You should also calculate finances for three to five years to get a more realistic picture of the costs required to get your business off the ground. On average it takes three to five years for a business to break even, so only calculating for one year may give you a limited (and depressing) overview. Many emerging fashion designers or entrepreneurs seek assistance and guidance from business advisors, online resources or friends and family because getting accurate information for this section is difficult, but very important.

Defining your product

Your product can be defined by the benefit or value it gives to the customer, that is, the benefit the wearer gets from your clothing. For example, this can be physical (it feels better on their skin, the silk is soft and of a high quality etc.) or it can be psychological (the jacket makes the wearer feel confident). In fashion, your product is the most important piece of the puzzle. Getting your clothing right is crucial because even if you tick every other box, without a strong product you will not have longevity within the fashion industry. It is important to think very carefully about the kind of product you will be making. You will be spending so much time with it, your clothing needs to be something you will enjoy spending hours and hours working on. Design fashion you really love! I believe that your passion for the clothing you are designing is sewn into the pieces you make; this may sound a little kooky but when you are not designing something you like, I believe there is a difference in the end product.

What type of product do I want to make?

To help you think through what kind of product you want to make consider the following. What is your

What is the purpose of a business plan?

Your business plan has many functions, from securing external funding to measuring success within your business; bear in mind that the main person that your business plan helps is you. It needs to:

- Describe your business;
- Structure your objectives and strategy;
- Set short- and long-term goals;
- Find out exactly how much money you will need;
- Raise any red flags or potential problems;
- Help you analyse the market and competitors;
- Outline the funding required;
- Make sure that in the end it is all about the customer and the product.

What should I include in my plan?

Each business plan varies but here is a list of core elements it should include.

EXECUTIVE SUMMARY

Introductory text that summarises your plan and highlights the key points and objectives. Make this section as interesting and engaging as you can as it will be the first thing that anyone you show it to will read.
Example: Amira Designs Ltd is a high fashion clothing label based in London, UK, specialising in the production of womenswear described as 'unique fashion, affordable luxury'. Amira Designs was founded by British designer Lucy Smith, who has over 5 years experience working within the fashion industry as a clothing designer. In 2010 Amira identified a niche within the market for unique high fashion design of high quality yet at affordable cost. With this in mind she set up Amira Designs targeting women in the 20–30 year old demographic who seek well-designed fashion which sits in an affordable price range.

COMPANY BACKGROUND

How the company came into being or 'the birth of the idea'.
Example: 'Lucy Smith worked as a fashion designer for womenswear brand Amira Designs for 13 years and spotted a gap in the market for organic clothing'.

COMPANY OVERVIEW

An explanation of the company and its products.

MISSION AND OBJECTIVES

What is your purpose?
Example: to supply womenswear to a niche market, to address the needs of customers seeking a luxury high fashion brand.

NAME, ADDRESS, TYPE OF COMPANY

Example of types: limited or sole trader

DESCRIPTION OF THE STRUCTURE OF THE BUSINESS

How many members of staff the company has and what is the company structure? For instance, will you be the Company Director and own all of the shares, or will shares be distributed between other people, shareholders?

PREMISES AND EQUIPMENT OWNED OR NEEDED

Example: sewing machine, cutting desk, mannequins.

DIRECTORS AND TEAM

CVs of key personnel including details of their key skills such as small business management, project management, leadership and technical skills.

DESCRIPTION OF PRODUCTS AND SERVICES

Example: luxury high fashion womenswear consisting of ready-to-wear and contemporary dresses made from quality fabrics such as chiffon, satin, silk jersey and silk.
There is more information about defining your product opposite (on p.94).

PRICING

How much will your clothing sell for? Is there a strategy behind your pricing? To get your pricing right you need to do market research to determine your target market and competitors. You can then decide what is the most appropriate pricing for your garments. Setting your prices high could imply quality, luxury and exclusivity to your target customers but if the price is too high your customers may not actually be able to afford your product. On the other hand, too low a price could take away that exclusive appeal.

PRODUCT'S UNIQUE SELLING POINTS

What makes your product unique and special? Where does your advantage lie over your competitors? Why would your product be special?
Example: Manufacturing – Dresses made in Great Britain with handwoven design.

DESCRIPTION OF CORE CUSTOMER

Focus on answering key questions about your customer such as who is your target audience?
Example: My customer sits in the 18 – 30 year old age demographic. She is a woman who is a fashion lover, investing in the clothing she buys and who tends to see her choice of clothing as a strong expression of who she is.

SALES STRATEGY

How will you sell your product? Online? In-store? Where will you sell your goods? Nationally? Internationally? Through which channels will you sell? Who will sell your products to distributors?

THE MARKET

An overview of the market you are entering into with key facts and figures that define your target market. What is the size of this market? How much is spent on your product in this market? Use industry intelligence – facts and figures.
Example: The UK womenswear market in particular has been responsible for the rise in sales that the UK apparel industry has seen and despite the slowing growth for 20XX (estimated to be X% year on year) as luxury womenswear is a growing market.

SWOT ANALYSIS

Describe the Strengths, Weaknesses, Opportunities and Threats facing your company.
Examples: Strength – unique positioning of the brand through unique product design at affordable cost; Weakness – lack of historic retail presence; Opportunity – customers growing interest in durable quality designs; Threats – strong brand awareness (longer established) of competitors' products amongst customers.

MARKETING OBJECTIVE

What is the point of your marketing?
Example: The marketing objective is to increase awareness of the Amira brand and to build sales through a targeted advertising and online marketing campaign.

ANALYSIS OF MARKET COMPETITION

Who are your competitors? Why are they your competitors? How do they operate? Who are their customers and how do they serve them? What are the strengths, weaknesses, opportunities and threats of your competitors?

MARKETING AND BRANDING

What will your approach be to marketing your product? How will your company be branded?
Example: Amira Designs will endeavour to create product awareness through a targeted online marketing strategy. The brand will do this by creating and building brand awareness through existing relationships with leading online fashion websites such as InStyle and Vogue, ongoing promotions offered through social media, celebrity endorsement and product placement at key events such as London Fashion Week.

FINANCE

How much finance will you need? What for? How will you manage the finances? This section will require you to list all of the money that will be going into and out of your business on a monthly basis with a year-end summary. This includes everything from the cost of fabrics to sampling, travel and clothing production costs, photo shoots, model fees, transport, and any employees you will have on the payroll. Some figures can be calculated based on money you have spent, other figures will be estimates. In areas where you are unsure, seek guidance from a business advisor (I spoke to my local bank manager to get pointed in the direction of useful resources).

Profit and loss statements are included in this section to show profits over a specific period. These show your operating costs, expenses and income (through sales and other sources), including income and expense you have not received or paid yet. Here you will enter accrued transactions for that accounting period. This section will also have a cash flow statement showing a detailed list of your financial investments and operating costs, which shows the money required to run your clothing label on a day to day basis. This gives you an accurate picture of how much cash you will have coming in, as only the cash spent and received will be entered.

FINANCIAL AIMS

Example: Amira Designs aims to reach profitability in year 2.

SOURCES OF FINANCE

Where will you get your finance from?
Example: Bank Loan and Private Investor.

design style going to be? Glamorous? Pretty? Practical? Cool? Urban? Classic? Striking? Fashion forward? Understated? Timeless? Will your designs be practical and casual or intricate and sophisticated? Formal and classy or trendy and inexpensive? Luxury or high street? Make a list of the words you would (and would not) like to be associated with your designs so that when you make important decisions about your brand, from creative to operational, you can have these in mind.

As your career develops you will find a 'signature style', a style that is unique to you and will be associated with your clothing. 'Your "signature style" is your unique personal brand, communicating your mood, attitude, status and personality.'[2] For example, when you look at Italian fashion house Versace's womenswear you will see a chic, dramatic, glamorous and sexy aesthetic which is consistent whether the brand creates dresses, skirts or tops. This is further enhanced by the recruitment of women whose style complements this image as models for the brand, such as celebrities like Jennifer Lopez or Halle Berry, who have both been used as brand ambassadors for Versace.

Defining your customer

To be able to reach your customers in a targeted way you first need to know who your customer is. When you design you will have an image in mind of your ideal customer, but also consider who your customers aspire to be like, or the lifestyle they aspire to live, not just who they already are. If you can successfully inspire your customer to connect with your brand 'role model' then you are taking a step in the right direction. You should give your target customer characteristics and a personality, for example, 'a carefree, easy-going woman who likes to look and feel effortlessly stylish'. Your target customer should be able to identify with that person in some way and feel that she has the same attitude to life and way of being. Avoid simply defining your customer with very broad generic classifications such as their age group. Ask more specific questions such as what is their income? What do they do? What brands do they buy? What influences their buying decisions? What is their personal style?

Think about your design style. What is it going to be?

'A truly, great, talented and successful fashion designer who knows their craft should be able to have the ability to know what designs are commercial and affordable to produce which will therefore save money and time. A fashion designer who is top of their game and who wants to achieve longevity in this industry, from high end to high street, should be able to understand which customers their collection will be suitable for, i.e. who will be wearing their designs and creations, what is their lifestyle, what is their job, where do they shop, what do they look like, what are their favourite brands, what is their style, and lastly how do you want them to feel when they are wearing your creations?'
Aneeqa Flynn, Wholesale Account Manager[3]

Pricing

As a designer you must make something that is both creative and sellable, as unless you are simply creating clothing for your own personal enjoyment, this will be the source of your livelihood. If you want to run a successful clothing label the trick is to create fashion that gets the cameras flashing and gets you column inches, but which at the same time also keeps the tills busy. To achieve this

SAMATA

LUXURY EVENING AND OCCASION WOMENSWEAR

The price you set is ultimately determined by your costs. The first criteria that the price you set needs to fulfil is that it must cover your costs. If you set this too low you will lose money from the outset and if you set it too high then you run the risk of not selling anything! Although this information is not going to predict exactly how much customers will be willing to pay, it is key that your pricing allows you to make money from your work. You need to factor in both the direct and indirect costs of the goods you have made, which includes everything from fabric to cutting, assembling, finishing, and packaging. Don't forget the cost of your trips to and from suppliers, and all the other time and expense spent preparing your goods. You should also take into consideration the money you have spent on promotion. This will help you to set a justified cost which is sustainable.

When you have added up your costs you can then think about pricing, which as a rough guide can be calculated by multiplying your costs by two, or even up to three times for luxury goods. The price has an implied meaning about the value of the goods. A good way to get an idea of the value perceived by the customer is to look at products from other brands that are similar in style and quality to yours and use those prices as a starting point. Also, seek advice. If you are planning to sell to a store then you have to take their price mark-up into consideration. For example, if you want your brand to retail within the price range of £200–£400, then you cannot sell your products to a store for that same price range. The store will need to mark up the price so that they can make a profit, so your clothing could end up selling for £600–£1200! Pricing is a tricky area to fully understand and navigate but with careful calculation and time, and by constantly looking at ways to reduce your costs, you can price your clothing to make a healthy profit.

your collection needs to be commercially viable, particularly in this day and age where consumers are really seeking to justify their purchases. If it looks great but is uncomfortable to wear, or if it is such a bold and statement look that it can only be worn once and comes with a very hefty price tag, it becomes a less justifiable purchase.

Setting a wise price means setting a price customers will be willing to pay for your product without feeling that they have been over- or under-charged. At the perfect price a customer will think, 'That is worth every penny and is an amount I am willing to pay'. The price of your product may vary according to your packaging and delivery methods, where your clothing will be sold and the prices of your competitors. Bear in mind that pricing communicates a message about the value of your product.

Research resources

You can source market information for your business plan through a range of online and offline platforms. Use a search engine such as Google and try searching by key words such as 'business plan advice', 'sample business plan', or through an online search such as the Microsoft small business start-up toolkit or the SME toolkit: http://www.microsoft.com/smallbusiness/startup-toolkit; http://www.smetoolkit.org/smetoolkit/en.

Sample business plans are easy to find online and very useful as a reference point for the structure and content of your own plan. You may also need templates for the numerical requirements of a business plan such as sales projections and financial statements. Other starting points are market research firms such as Mintel, who provides global market intelligence, information, analysis and recommendations.

Another useful website, MPDClick.com, is an online subscription trend forecasting service which provides business reports on global fashion and trends in addition to consumer intelligence and industry news. http://www.mpdclick.com.

You should also use resources such as your local business library. You can conduct market research in other ways, for example, I ran a simple survey through a holding page on my website asking online visitors to tell me their favourite colour for an evening dress, which fabrics they loved and which they hated. The answers helped me to get feedback that I then incorporated into my end product. Understanding what your market research is telling you is important (although it is tempting to ignore the results when it does not point to the conclusions you want!), as is incorporating what you find into what you do next. For example, if you have researched online retail as an important part of your sale strategy, and discovered useful pointers about building a great e-commerce site, then these findings should be fully incorporated into your company website. If you are researching fabrics for an urban menswear brand, for example, then it goes without saying that you should incorporate your findings into the product design. It is important to find out how the trends you have researched relate to your product.

After writing your plan you should be able to ascertain your competitive advantage – why is your brand unique and special? How will you best serve your customers with the best product? After you have finished it, you may decide to go back to the drawing board and come up with a better plan or to abandon ship all together! But at least you would have saved yourself making any costly mistakes.

Fashion entrepreneurs

When discussing the business side of the fashion industry it is impossible to ignore the fashion entrepreneur – a role that is becoming increasingly significant on the global fashion scene. An increasing number of emerging designers are now starting up their own business, rather than choosing to work for a fashion brand. These designers need to be well informed, have entrepreneurial skills and business experience to succeed. In response to this need it has become more common for fashion schools and academies to provide training and tailored courses. For example, in the UK, the London College of Fashion has a specific division for developing the entrepreneurial skills of its creative student base called LCF Enterprise which was set up, amongst other reasons, to support students by ensuring that they are well equipped to match their skills, personalities and aspirations to the needs of businesses.[4] This type of department is popular in modern fashion colleges as it is widely believed that in order to be successful in any facet of fashion, students need to have an understanding of both the business side and the creative side of the industry.

What is a fashion entrepreneur? I define it as a fashion creative who sets up and runs their own venture, managing or understanding both the business and creative sides of their label in the knowledge that both parts are important in order to be successful. In short, a fashion entrepreneur creates, organises and manages their fashion business. When I speak of fashion entrepreneurs I do not refer only to fashion designers but also other fashion-based businesses such as someone running a profitable fashion blog or setting up a business in fashion illustration. Anyone willing to set up an innovative fashion venture that combines creativity and business acumen is a fashion entrepreneur. However, I will focus on a fashion designer to help contextualise the example I want to give. I have always been in favour of describing fashion designers who set up fashion brands as fashion entrepreneurs (rather than fashion designers) because running a clothing label (even if you do not look after every side of the business) involves so much more than just designing clothing. In their day to day interactions fashion entrepreneurs may liaise with a range of people from buyers to journalists to stylists, negotiating with fabric manufacturers, keeping up to date with the latest industry trends and news, networking, looking after PR, marketing, sales, financing and other aspects of the clothing label. That is part of the reason why I am glad that more and more people are embracing the term. Although not all designers who set up their own brands look after the business side, I believe it is still important for them to have an understanding of what running a fashion label entails. Working with a business partner is a great idea but every fashion designer should still aim to have a basic understanding of business. The ability to micro- and macro-manage key business elements is a valuable skill to possess.

A crucial skill entrepreneurs have to have is the ability to spot unique opportunities. Entrepreneurs are important to any industry because, with their innovative and creative way of thinking, they hold the key to economic growth. The June 2010 OECD report stated that 'Economic growth must … come from … productivity growth [and] innovation holds the key to boosting productivity',[5] and according to Doug Richard in his book *The Rise of the Entrepreneurial Class*, '…most innovation comes from the creatively destructive efforts of start-ups. In short, we are looking to one set of companies for both of the key engines of growth. And one set of individuals to set it alight: Entrepreneurs.'[6]

I would describe a fashion entrepreneur as someone willing to take the necessary risks to build a business

As in any desirable industry, the fashion industry is notoriously difficult to break into – especially in today's current economic climate and if you're operating on a limited budget. However, with sheer belief and relentless determination it can be achieved. It's important to understand the cycle of how a garment comes to be created and then comes to be worn. Without embracing this 360 degree process you cannot be successful: finance, design, production, merchandising, sales, distribution, marketing, press, logistics, credit collection: all aspects of the cycle are fundamental. To make it, you need to be a master of them all![7]

Simon Whitehouse, Worldwide Sales Director at Diesel Black Gold

and innovate an industry, whether that is through designs, projects, ideas, or even through introducing structural changes to that industry. Fashion entrepreneurs do not only work on their own ventures, they can also work within other organisations (as intrapreneurs) bringing their entrepreneurial passion and innovation to the table. This energy definitely helps companies remain creative and competitive. In truth, fashion entrepreneurs have always been present working within organisations, inspiring and innovating, but often went unnoticed.

SOME EXAMPLES

Some notable and inspirational entrepreneurs, past, present and future include: Ralph Lauren, Levi Strauss, Louis Vuitton, Rene Lacoste, Stella McCartney, Harold Tillman, Sir Philip Green and Nicole Fahri. My personal favourite is Gabrielle Bonheur Chanel, commonly known as Coco Chanel, and after watching the film *Coco before Chanel* I fell in love with her story even more. The film covers her earlier years of struggle, and all that took place before her brand, 'Chanel', took flight. Starting off as a musician and performer she began her career as a fashion designer in an area she is less known for: hats. Chanel became a licensed modiste (hat maker) and in 1910 she opened a boutique at 21 Rue Cambon, Paris, named Chanel Modes.[8] She then settled into designing luxe casual clothing for women. Her signature design style was elegant and versatile, and her determination and creativity led her to become one of the world's most influential fashion designers, and the only couturier to be included in the *Time* magazine 'The Most Important People of the Century'.[9,10] Diana Vreeland, (former editor-in-chief of *Vogue*, 1963–71), described Coco Chanel as '… passionate, focused and fiercely independent … a virtual tour de force'[11] Chanel's signature pieces are recognised globally, from the iconic Chanel suit to the gilt bag to a simple string of pearls. What made Coco Chanel a true entrepreneur in my opinion was her ability to innovate; she embarked on new ventures, from hat designing to clothing, and through networking she created opportunities for herself. Her career path demonstrates her extraordinary level of determination. She was a woman who understood manufacturing, networking, PR, finance and other key elements of the fashion industry.

Getting support

Although some people believe that entrepreneurs are special and unique, born and not bred, there are many who believe that there are great benefits in teaching the principles of entrepreneurship thereby encouraging people to be ambitious and helping them to understand risk and reward. Fashion designers trying to establish themselves in the industry need support and direction in order to successfully navigate it without feeling overwhelmed, and the most important element must be the willingness to learn. Over the past ten years organisations and institutions have been created and developed to serve the various needs of hopeful, emerging and established designers, some of which are listed opposite.

Common characteristics of entrepreneurs and key skills

- Confidence in ability and talent;
- Determination to work, push and drive beyond your expectations;
- Passion, energy and stamina;
- Genuine love for craft;
- Focus and ability to tune out the noise/disturbances;
- Great communication skills to be able to build relationships and communicate vision;
- Enthusiasm to sell yourself, your products and vision to others, getting others to buy into your vision;
- Leadership to be able to bring together the people and resources needed to pursue opportunities;
- Organisation to keep on top of micro and macro tasks;
- Fearless nature to take unprecedented risks;
- Ability to identify a new opportunity and determine needs;
- Generation of unique ideas;
- Good management of time, project and risk;
- The ability to be tenacious and assertive.

The importance of a mentor

One of the most useful things that a clothing designer can have is a mentor – someone who has experience in the fashion industry specifically, or even another industry, and can provide advice, moral support, perspective, access to resources, encouragement and occasionally a necessary reality check. This could involve a simple task such as looking over your CV. Some designers start out with one mentor but over time build relationships with a few people and form a supportive mentor network. Of course having a mentor is great but finding one is not an easy ride and as anyone who has tried to find one knows, they rarely come to you! Start out by listing what you are looking for, such as personal attributes or specific experience you would like your mentor to help you to gain. Good starting points are the usual suspects, such as introductions from friends and family, networking events and through school or college or work. Another option, if you are in urgent need, is to pay for one. You can look for a consultant although this route is not cheap.

Getting it right with a mentor is not about requesting hours and hours of their time, which is unfair and unrealistic, it is about building trust slowly through open and honest communication whilst being discerning with your requests. In some cases, a mentor and student have become business partners later on. In order to manage and preserve this relationship it is important that you do what you say you will do, when you say you will do it. Paying attention to the way you conduct yourself with your mentor is important because your behaviour will influence their decision about the introductions they give you and the networks they help you to access. If your mentor introduces you to a contact, they need to feel confident that you will make a positive impression that reflects well on both of you.

Money, money, money

To be able to launch and grow your fashion design business you need money. Fact. There are a large number of designers sitting on plans to launch a clothing label because they do not have enough money to do it. And it is a very frustrating position to be in when you have a truckload of great design ideas or demand for your products but not enough capital to do anything about it. Designers who find the cost of starting up a clothing label is just too high can be deterred from setting up on their own, instead choosing to work for other brands where this financial pressure does not exist and their focus can be on the creative side of things. For those who are not deterred there are a number of questions to be answered in order to determine the immediate, unforeseen and ongoing costs involved in starting a clothing label started.

How much do you need?

To be honest, there is no set answer to this question as it simply depends on a number of factors. If you will be starting from scratch completely and need to buy equipment, where you will be based, the quantity of clothing you want to produce and the type – will you be manufacturing on a large or small scale, will you be designing jeans or evening dresses? If you are designing T-shirts, jeans and not high fashion evening dresses the cost of the fabrics alone would be a great deal lower. In addition if you start selling quickly and need to fulfil increasing orders then to be able to grow, earn a salary and manage the costs of a growing business, more finance will be required quickly. If your aim will be to show every season you will constantly be spending money, finalising orders for one collection whilst sourcing materials for the sampling of the next.

Useful schemes and initiatives for designers

To be eligible for support various criteria may apply, but typically include the length of time a designer has been in business, where they obtained their qualifications or the stage they are at with their business. Visit the organisations' websites to check your eligibility. Some organisations work closely with businesses and can lead to training placements, internships and sponsorship. It is worth researching all of these schemes thoroughly yourself. Examples of useful organisations in the UK and the type of support you can get can be found below.

Somerset House, London, home to the British Fashion Council.

THE FASHION RETAIL ACADEMY

Fashion East is an initiative that receives sponsorship funding from Topshop, TOPMAN and The London Development Agency. It supports emerging designers and gives them the opportunity to present a catwalk collection to press and buyers attending London Fashion Week. Selected designers receive a bursary, catwalk show, mentoring and in-house PR.

www.fashioneast.co.uk

THE CENTRE FOR FASHION ENTERPRISE

The Centre for Fashion Enterprise programme provides intensive support to London's fashion talent to help nurture new business in London. It does this by providing specialist mentoring, grant funding, access to incubator/studio facilities and specialist equipment. It has helped launched the careers of Peter Pilotto, Marios Schwab and Richard Nicholl.

www.fashion-enterprise.com

BRITISH FASHION COUNCIL INITIATIVES

The BFC/*ELLE* Talent Launch Pad offers PR and marketing opportunities for emerging designers to help them develop their businesses and relationships with British retailers. Other perks include access to the industry's top stylists, photographers and creative directors alongside editorial and promotional support.

The BFC/*Vogue* Designer Fashion Fund is supported by key fashion brands and retailers such as Burberry, Harrods, House of Fraser, Marks & Spencer, and Paul Smith. The selected British-based designer is provided with £200,000 and access to high level mentoring to help them to develop creative business transition into a global brand.

www.britishfashioncouncil.com/
talentlaunchpadapplication
www.londonfashionweek.co.uk/
designerfashionfund

NEWGEN

New Generation (NEWGEN) was the world's first scheme to support emerging designer talent and is supported by Topshop. Fashion designers receive £5000–£10,000 towards their show costs, sponsored exhibition space, use of the BFC Catwalk Show Space and mentoring. This support can be awarded for four seasons. Previous winners include Matthew Williamson and Christopher Kane.

www.britishfashioncouncil.com/
NEWGEN

FASHION FORWARD

The Fashion Forward scheme provides funding to talented emerging British designers enabling them to show and develop their businesses in London by providing the opportunity to showcase during London Fashion Week. Previous winners of this award include Christopher Kane, Erdem and Jonathan Saunders.

www.britishfashioncouncil.com/
fashionforward

You must also factor in there are the expensive early design stage costs of patterns, toiling, fabrics and trim, and final sample production, which always costs more than expected. Manufacturing is also expensive, although some of these costs go down the more you produce, (i.e. the cost price of producing clothing declines after the initial sample so although it may cost you £150 for the sample, the cost of production for 50 of these items could be £120).

A clothing designer can start up with £5,000, £10,000 or £50,000 and successfully launch a first collection. Calvin Klein launched his business with under $10,000,[12] which may be surprising as it hardly seems a realistic figure with which to launch a brand. What Klein cleverly did was to start small, using a loan to rent a small showroom where he could exhibit a small line of samples. In the first few years of manufacturing, designers can feel overwhelmed as any money they may make in the first year needs to be pumped back into the business to build up sales and reputation. In addition you have no guarantee your products will sell.

There are many ways to keep your costs low. For example, designers often work from home instead of trying to rent or buy a studio space. Other tips are to start out with smaller collections, wait before you take on members of staff, and be selective about the orders you agree to fulfil. Of course it is very exciting if you have three department stores knocking on your door to stock your brand, but if you do not have the finance to deliver them one way of managing is to prioritise your orders and say yes only to the best option, or say yes to a few but ask for the sizes of the orders to be reduced. You could have a fixed strategy for your payment terms, for example, asking for a deposit or requiring that you are paid in full when all of the clothing is delivered to a buyer and not 60 days later.

Why is getting funding so difficult?

Most fashion designers struggle to make a living because securing much-needed finance is so difficult. Terms of business in the industry are not favourable towards young start-ups. One of the problems seems to be that fashion is perceived by potential investors to be a risky business, dependent (as it is) on too many variables, such as

fashion trends, which are outside the designer's control. The information a lender/investor requires when considering designers for an investment may not actually be available if the designer has not started trading. Therefore data about what might sell and hard facts such as cash flow, profit and loss calculations, or cash forecasts simply aren't deemed accurate enough by some lending institutions. Some start-ups find it hard to calculate and present the data requested. As it is difficult to get credit from buyers and suppliers designers often have to pay for materials and services up front entirely or a large healthy percentage of it, but in turn do not get paid until the goods are delivered to the customer.

What is the investor's perspective?

Successful designers look at things from an investor's perspective because from this vantage point they are better equipped to figure out what an investor is looking for. An investor is often looking for an opportunity to make money – they want a return and to know that you have an understanding of what you are doing. They need to be confident that sending money in your direction will not be a wasted resource. Investors want to back a winning horse and in most cases to know their money will be coming back to them. With fashion projects they can become nervous and understandably so. An investor wants reassurance that you will be able to pay them back, so even if you cannot show a long sales history at the very least proof of interest such as a pre-order is useful. But be warned In some cases, even a purchase order from a shop will not guarantee financing, as once the goods have been made the shop could reject the order if the pieces do not meet their quality standards.

Securing finance is definitely difficult, but it is not impossible, and a good way to understand the lender's perspective is to imagine the questions that you may have to answer or information you may need to provide. Here are some examples of these questions.

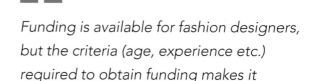

Funding is available for fashion designers, but the criteria (age, experience etc.) required to obtain funding makes it difficult for an individual to qualify.[13]

Sombo Dakowah, Show Coordinator for the Festival of Youth Arts

◆ Does the business have an established client base? For example, are there enough clients to sustain the business?

Evidence: weekly or monthly sales/diary.

◆ Does the designer have premises for the business? Are they suitable?

Evidence: working from home/market stall (license to be produced), evidence of rent/lease. Are they essential? Adequate? Not excessive?

◆ Does the designer have basic business experience and skills? Do they have product or market knowledge within the relevant industry?

Evidence: CV and evidence of any formal or informal training.

◆ Did the designer start the business with their own/family/friends money?

Evidence: bank statements.

◆ Does the designer have previous employment history?

Evidence: is this mentioned in the CV?

◆ Does the designer have a satisfactory credit search?

Evidence: Equifax or Experian credit search.

When trying to secure finance you should leverage everything that you have going for you including your industry references, mentors and anyone who can help you build up your profile in the lender's eyes. Be ready to produce the following if asked: accounts, business insurance, invoices, list of suppliers, web site, business cards, appointment book.

Looking for funding

According to fashion entrepreneur Dr Neri Karra,[14] there are three types of investors:

◆ Emotional investors: family, friends and investors attracted by fashion itself

◆ Strategic investors: typically equity investors, business angels or venture capitalists.

◆ Debt financiers: banks, loan and insurance schemes.

Before approaching banks or other lenders I would advise that you talk to your friends and family first. See if anyone would be willing to support you and rather than approaching one person for a large sum, you can try speaking to a few people for smaller amounts, which may be more feasible. Remember that they can invest in you by providing equipment such as an old sewing machine or printer and not just money. If you believe in your idea then you should have the confidence to share it with your friends and family in a carefully thought through and clear way. The benefit of getting financial help from friends

and family is that they bring a level of flexibility, understanding and extra support.

The important thing when dealing with friends and family is to have something formally written up so that there is transparency and it is clear how and when the funds will be repaid. The worst situation would be for you to owe money to a family member and for that to put a strain on your relationship. Another danger may be that your friend or family member feels that they should have a say in your business, wanting their opinion to be heard and actioned. Try to keep investments from friends and family small, think wisely before spending them and make sure communication is understood, particularly in the early stages.

If family and friends are not an option start looking at other alternatives. This can be done through online research, contacting local business authorities, attending conferences, researching investor groups, referrals and online networking. Do your own research to find the right bank, business angel or venture capitalist for you. These investors vary in a range of ways from if and how the money will be repaid, the expected return and the agreed terms of trade; for example, you may be required to pay the amount back with either a variable interest rate[15] or a fixed interest rate;[16] to what the ownership structure will be and how company shares will be divided, if at all.

EQUITY INVESTORS

Equity investors put cash into your business in return for a share of the business itself. They expect to recoup their investment amount plus interest from their share of the business profits or, more commonly, their share of the proceeds when the business is sold. Therefore these investors tend to invest in companies with a substantial track record and revenue.[17]

Sometimes these investors offer their expertise and skills in addition to investment. However, they tend to typically request less control over the day to day running of the business and are more risk averse. The main expectation that they have is for a return on their investment.

BUSINESS ANGELS

Business Angels are affluent individuals who invest their own funds in business start-ups, usually in exchange for convertible debt or ownership equity.[18] Angel investors tend to be successful entrepreneurs themselves who want to make profitable investments and help others who are just starting out. They invest smaller amounts than venture capitalists but more capital than friends and family.[19]

VENTURE CAPITALISTS

Venture capitalists provide financial capital to early-stage, high-potential, high risk startup companies. The venture capital fund makes money by owning equity in the companies it invests in.[20] Much like equity investors, venture capitalists may provide expertise alongside investment and take an active interest in supporting a startup company through its first years of trading. The end goal is for the venture capitalist to exit the company within 3–7 years, with a return on investment.

BANKS

Commercial loans from banks are available to most small businesses and start-ups, subject to a set of varying requirements (all banks differ slightly in these requirements). As with a personal loan, your business will borrow money and repay it over a pre-agreed number of months or years, at a fixed or variable interest rate. Securing a loan from a bank can be difficult for a fashion design business for several reasons: their assets are harder to tangibly define, sales are tricky to predict with any degree of certainty and intellectual property (i.e. innovative design) is difficult to protect and uniquely own. For these reasons, coupled with high interest rates on loans and overdrafts, it is hard, but not impossible, for emerging designers to get funded via the 'traditional' route of borrowing from a bank.

Be prepared

The information required to secure investment varies according to the lender/investor; listed below are some of the standard requirements:

- Bank statements for the last six months;
- Copy of passport, official identification document, evidence of residency/work permit;
- Copy of a recent utility bill;
- Business plan;
- Records of current orders in progress;
- If you are a registered company, a copy of your Certificate of Incorporation;
- Credit search on each party.

Additional information you may be asked to supply includes:

- Catalogue of your achievements to date;
- Receipts/proof of money invested so far, e.g. personal bank statements, business bank statements, invoices.

Alternative forms of investment

CROWD FUNDING

Crowd funding describes the collective cooperation, attention and trust by people who network and pool their money and other resources together, usually via the Internet, to support efforts initiated by other people or organisations.[21] This form of investment is exciting for designers because it comes from supporters who like the product and want to help support their ideas and fashion business. Crowd-funding is not a new concept. As far back as the 1800s, French and American organisations part-crowd-funded the construction of the Statue of Liberty. Donors were offered miniature models of various sizes depending on the amount they donated.

In November 2011, the House of Representatives in the USA passed 'The Entrepreneur Access to Capital' bill, which, according to its sponsors, 'allows small businesses to raise capital without burdensome regulation and thus promote job growth'.[22] The bill allows individuals to invest up to the greater sum of $100,000 or 10% of their income into young companies in exchange for a share of the business. It will also remove the limit on the number of shareholders a private company can have.

Websites for crowd funding

- Kickstarter.com
- Crowdfunder.co.uk
- Crowdcube.com

FACTORING

Factoring is a financial transaction whereby a business sells its accounts receivable (i.e. invoices) to a third party (called a factor) at a discount – in exchange for immediate money which they can put back in to finance continued business.[23] For example, if a start-up fashion designer receives an order from a department store, they can take this invoice and use it as collateral by selling it to a third party (i.e. a lending institution/financier) at a discount in exchange for money. Agreements of this kind are typically sought by growing fashion businesses due to the long period of time that passes between orders being placed, the goods being made and delivered to the store and the designer finally being paid. Emerging fashion designers can struggle when they have to wait a few months to receive payment for the clothing they have financed and then sold. If you only have a few clients, how you deal with outstanding invoices can make or break your business. Factors provide a percentage of this money when your clothing is shipped and the rest when complete payment is received from your buyer, taking a fee for their services. However, finding the right financier with whom to enter into a factoring agreement is important.[24]

Some designers are not comfortable with the factor taking over the collection of their sales. Yet others are not yet large enough companies to be of interest to factors, or they do not feel confident enough in this area. In addition, the factor may want to pre-approve customers, which means there may be constraints on who you can do business with. If you are interested in this path a good starting point is to look online for factoring companies and read up about the services offered. It is worth asking your bank for advice on what to look for. Most banks have a knowledge centre or a business forum that can help you.

GOVERNMENT GRANTS

Applying for a government grant is another option. The size of the grant you are eligible for can be directly linked to the size of your business; the purpose of the grant and your eligibility is linked to criteria such as location or number of years you have been trading. Some grants must be paid back if you sell your business in the future. These options are best researched online and locally, for instance, through your local business authority.

GET ADVICE BEFORE YOU SIGN

According to Crowdcube,[25] a business finance crowd-funding platform for businesses to raise equity finance, these are the typical amounts raised via these routes:

Source	Typical investment
Banks	£10,000–250,000
Business Angels	£25,000–500,000
Crowd funding	£10,000–150,000
Grants	£500–100,000
Venture Capital (VC)	Over £250,000

If you do get the go ahead for any of the forms of investment described above it is important not just to say yes to the first person or institution agreeing to finance you but to look around and compare your options. Desperation can cause some start-up designers to agree to unfavourable terms and hastily sign a contract, putting forward more than they can vouch for. Before accepting any form of investment it is advisable to seek guidance from an expert on the type of investment you are agreeing to – for example, you can contact a local business authority with any questions you may have and go over the terms of the agreement. For example, if you are being offered £10,000 but in return for that you will need to give up 60% equity in your business, you must stop and think if the deal is worth it. As much as you want to get your brand up and running, you do not want to put yourself in a position a potential investor is taking advantage of you.

Many designers would like to find finance and a business partner at the same time. They may chose to do this because they do not want to oversee the business side completely or lack the relevant skills to (even though they possess an understanding of the business industry). They could also want someone on board who understands the kind of investment the business needs and has a vested interest in doing things the right way for their brand. Beneficial partnerships can be formed when the funding has come from an investor who has a good understanding of the fashion industry and a strong network. For this kind of arrangement an investor may seek equity, i.e. shares in the business as mentioned above. Some designers feel nervous about sharing equity in their business because they feel that it means relinquishing control over their company and having less of a say in the decisions made, or even not having the right to make major decisions without consulting the investor first. This all depends on the investor and the relationship that you manage to develop with them. For those who understand your ambitions and genuinely believe in your product, it can be a very successful relationship. If that understanding is not there, designers can end up regretting the decision to team up and feeling like they have signed away their creative freedom. In some extreme cases designers have even lost the right to use their name, such as in the case of British designer Amanda Wakeley. Despite starting her company from scratch in 1990 and building up a reputation for designing luxury womenswear, she became a victim of a corporate takeover of her own fashion company and was forced to resign from it. In 2009 she finally regained control of the Amanda Wakeley name having paid an undisclosed amount for it in 2008.[26, 27]

Managing money and being resourceful

However much investment you manage to get you will still need to be able to make it stretch. Outlined below are some examples of ways to look at saving money.

TEAM WORK

Never underestimate the value of teamwork when it comes to making ends meet. One example is using team work such as – getting involved in organised shows with other designers. Not only does it save the costs of doing your own solo show (such as venue hire and promotional material), but it also means you get increased exposure and networking opportunities.

GET HELP FROM CLOSER TO HOME

Do not forget to get help when and where you can from your immediate friends and family. They may be keen to help you and have your best interests at heart, even if they do not have industry experience. Even if their knowledge does not extend to the fashion industry there are other ways they can support you and offer advice, which can help you save money or make it.

NEGOTIATE WHEN YOU CAN

As most start-up businesses do not have a huge budget it is important to be able to negotiate and essentially 'haggle', so think about what you have to exchange. Starting out you could save money by working with graduates on photo shoots such as graduate makeup artists, photographers and stylists. You can still get good quality work. Try to shoot your collection for a reduced fee by fully crediting those involved for their work and covering expenses. Creatives who are getting started are more likely to be happy to do this than established artists. Even if you cannot afford a great deal, pay what you can and do not take advantage of people – this shows respect for the time of others. Crediting, for example, can mean allowing those involved to use the images in their portfolio or sharing website links for all collaborators' work. Throughout your careers you can continue to support each other; your talents will grow together. There are some photographers I have known for years and as I have got better at what I do, so have they.

BUY BULK AT THE RIGHT TIME

A good example of this is when it comes to buying fabric. Buying fabric is an expensive part of the business and at sampling stage you will be paying more per metre for the small amount of fabric you need to create your sample. For example, a fabric may cost £4.50 per metre but at 30 metres the cost will go down to £3.90. One money-saving tip is to buy the fabrics you will have a constant need for, such as lining and muslin, in bulk, but also learn to buy good quality as this saves money in the long run.

If you do not need extra, do not purchase excess just for the sake of it as that is a waste of money and resource. Instead, you can either try your best to negotiate a better price or simply buy the quantity needed at the sample price and accept that this is the most cost effective way to do it.

The ability to negotiate and find favourable terms requires you to develop and nurture good relationships

GO THE EXTRA MILE

Be prepared to travel a little further out of your comfort zone to access cheaper services and resources. For example, in Central London, Soho, the Old Brompton Road and Liberty are particularly good for fabric but you can definitely get good quality fabric for less than West End prices, if you are prepared to travel a little further out of Central London to places such as Brick Lane, Southall and the Goldhawk Road. Where ever you are based, it is worth seeing what you can find further away. If you can afford to go abroad then places such as India and Thailand are fantastic for fabrics.

WORK

I have found that the most common way for designers to approach raising money for their clothing label is to get an additional job. Although working two jobs is very tiring it enables designers to raise funds for their venture whilst juggling the costs of living, especially when, in many cases, they have moved to a fashion capital to get their foot in the door. Living in a fashion capital such as New York or Paris can provide access to opportunities and to network but it is often very expensive, so having a 'day job' allows designers to make ends meet whilst funding their own fashion lines. The job could be full or part time and could be, within the fashion industry providing the opportunity to raise money and gain experience at the same time, or it could also be in a completely unrelated field. I worked as a PA for a telecommunications company whilst saving funds as I found it easier to be anonymous at work and not have my every moment filled with fashion. In a way, it was like my down time.

Useful start-up resources

Although securing funding is difficult, designers have more options than they did five years ago and can be better informed about those options due to the accessibly of information through the Internet. Listed below are a few useful organisations and resources to be aware of.

CFDA/*VOGUE* FASHION FUND

The Council of Fashion Designers of America and *Vogue* magazine have created an endowment to support the next generation of American fashion designers. The CFDA/*Vogue* Fashion Fund has been established to provide significant financial awards to one or more designers and provide business mentoring. Award recipients are selected by a committee of industry experts, based on the talent they have already demonstrated in fashion design and their capacity for future growth in the fashion industry.

http://www.cfda.com/cfdavogue-fashion-fund

COMMUNITY DEVELOPMENT FINANCE ASSOCIATION (CDFA)

The CDFA represents the Community Development Finance Institutions (CDFI) who provide loans and support to people who have difficulty accessing finance from the commercial banks.

http://www.cdfa.org.uk/about-cdfis

STARTUP BRITAIN

StartUp Britain is a national campaign run by entrepreneurs for entrepreneurs with support such as discounts on business insurance, free Start Up Guides, training on business and marketing activities and other useful resources such as a business directory and a platform for start-ups and growing businesses to search enterprise hubs, co-working spaces and other start-up friendly office providers in the UK.

www.startupbritain.co

PROSPER.COM

Prosper is the world's largest peer-to-peer lending marketplace, with more than 1,130,000 members and over $255,000,000 in funded loans. It allows people to invest in each other.

www.prosper.com

INDEPENDENT FASHION BLOGGERS

A community of fashion design bloggers and industry pros sharing ideas and growing their businesses.

http://heartifb.com

FASHION-ENTER

Fashion Enter is a member's only site offering advice from experts on key areas of the industry including legal, accounts, production, design and intellectual property.

www.fashion-enter.com

YOUNGENTREPRENEUR.COM

YoungEntrepreneur.com is an online forum community for entrepreneurs worldwide. It is a resource for start-up CEOs, founders, aspiring entrepreneurs, mentors and investors worldwide. It showcases Marketing, Online Business Strategies and several features, and offers support to assist small business owners in relation to starting, managing and growing successful business ventures.

http://www.youngentrepreneur.com

THE CENTRE FOR FASHION ENTREPRISE (CFE)

The CFE in the UK identifies fashion designers in the start-up stage and acts as an incubator by assisting with funding, managing and developing business by providing access to an experienced industry team and high level industry intelligence.

www.fashion-enterprise.com

LONDON APPAREL RESOURCE CENTRE

The LARC is a centre providing designers, manufacturers and retailers with facilities and support for fashion business and clothing manufacture

www.londonapparel.com

PORTOBELLO BUSINESS CENTRE

The PBC helps small businesses raise capital and assists with growth, finance, IT services, expertise and training courses

www.pbc.co.uk

Registering your company

Depending on your business structure and where you set your business up you will need to take a key step – registering your business. The authority to register your company with varies according to country. For example, in the UK, if you work as a sole trader you must register with HM Revenue & Customs for tax and National Insurance purposes. In the US certain types of business owners are required to register their business through state government. However, if you establish your business as a sole trader (a type of business that is owned and run by one person and where there is no legal distinction between the owner and the business) you won't need to register your business at the state level.

To help you make the right decisions and understand the information fully you should seek professional legal advice to help you better determine the right legal structure for your brand. This advice is freely available online or you can arrange a meeting with a company advisor, solicitor or accountant.

The registration steps you need to take will vary according to the structure of your business i.e.

self-employed, partnership, limited partnership, limited liability partnership, limited company or social enterprise. These different business types can be researched online for you to decide the best structure for your business. Typically start-up designers register as a sole trader, partnerships (where two or more people own and run a profit-making business together) or a limited company (companies owned by shareholders and are limited by shares). It is vital to get advice before you submit any paperwork as the different structures have different implications on your company. For example, a limited company has its liability limited to the share capital, which is the money invested in a company by the shareholders ('an individual or institution…that legally owns any part of a share of stock in a public or private corporation').[28]

Getting things made
Manufacturing

We discussed making designers earlier in this book (see p.68). In this section, manufacturing specifically refers to the stage when you are ready to manufacture your designs for retail. Some start-up designers are able to pull a team together so that their production can be handled in-house, under one roof and overseen by themselves. This is expensive but has the obvious advantage that they are able to oversee and manage all elements of the process from design to manufacture, as well as being able to keep track of the inventory and ensure that money is saved wherever possible. For example, when it comes to cutting fabrics, with an in-house production team you are able to ensure that any unused fabric is kept and used again if possible, to save money. However, not many start-ups can afford to do manufacturing in house as it involves a continual running cost – but fortunately there are other ways! One way around this expense is to get a CMT (Cut, Make and Trim) unit to manufacture their goods. This is the most common name for production units, but they can also be referred to as a factory or manufacturer.

Case Study

Manufacturing overview of the UK

The UK has different speciality areas for production: Scotland is known for wool and knitwear and has a strong textile industry; there is also a strong textile base in West Yorkshire. Thirty per cent of UK fashion manufacturing jobs are based in the East Midlands with a focus on lingerie and footwear, the latter of which is manufactured in areas such as Northampton.[29] Over the past 10–15 years UK manufacturing has declined because of competition with emerging markets such as those in China who offer cheaper manufacturing due to lower labour costs. Some brands, however, have rooted their manufacturing loyalty to the UK, e.g. Mulberry, Aquascutum and Burberry. Some of the brands that have kept their manufacturing in the UK are those who specialise in niche areas, and/or produce high end, luxury products with a focus on quality over quantity. In response to the difficulties faced by designers trying to manufacture in the UK the Manufacturing Alliance was set up. This comprises of the British Fashion Council, the Centre for Fashion Enterprise, the London Manufacturing Advisory Service, Skillset and the UK Fashion and Textile Association.[30] Through the Fashion Alliance designers can search for manufacturers and explain their needs to production units using resources such as the Fashion Toolkit.

www.fashionalliance.co.uk

A textile mill in Lancashire. The textile industry has historically been important in Lancashire, and after many decades of decline it is now experiencing a revival.[31]

Production capitals – choosing your CMT (Cut, Make and Trim unit)

For any clothing designer manufacturing costs are a huge consideration. I think that it works in your favour if you can afford to produce where you are based due to ease of access, ability to communicate quickly and get progress reports. Knowing what is going on with your production is very important: if you are an emerging designer you may not be able to travel extensively to check on things but neither can you afford a huge production mistake. In addition you can try to ensure that your clothing is being made in a socially responsible way.

A Cut, Make and Trim is a production unit that does not supply any of the components required to make the clothing, apart from thread and bag, and only manufactures the clothing with the materials supplied. When selecting a CMT unit, try to take into consideration the following factors:

◆ Production price and minimum quantities: are these feasible for you?

◆ Turnaround time: how soon would you need your clothing delivered after placing an order? Are you factoring in distance for delivery?

◆ Manufacturer relationship: do you need to call every day or will you need to work with limited contact/via email? Can you use various forms of communication to check progress?

◆ Support: do you have anyone who will be checking the progress of your order or will you be the main contact?

◆ Will you need to trade off quality to get the prices you want from manufacturers?

◆ Can you get references from other people about the factory?

◆ Will the CMT agree to make a sample first so you can judge the quality?

◆ Will they sign a working contract or agree to adhere to a code of practice?

◆ What is the CMT's area of speciality? What equipment do they have?

◆ What are the health and safety standards for the CMT like?

The CMT unit you choose to manufacture your clothing can be determined by a number of factors such as the type of clothing you are having made and the quantity of clothing you are ordering. Factories have different expertise and capabilities – one factory may specialise in the production of men's jackets whereas another may specialise in T-shirts, without the capability to make any other items. A designer may find a suitable CMT unit that has a minimum order quantity for 50 pieces when the designer can only afford to get 15 pieces made. Some CMTs will agree to a smaller quantity, and if the work is successful the first time around, repeat it and build up quantities slowly. These kinds of terms are built on trust on both sides. Other times the designer can try to negotiate, agreeing to place a larger order if the first order sells well, although for the CMT this offers no guarantee of repeat business. Negotiation can be a tricky and it is crucial to be very clear up front.

Some designers may require the expertise, raw materials and skills that can only be sourced abroad but this really depends on what you want to get made, how much you can afford to pay and if you can travel a great deal or not at all. Other factors to take into consideration when choosing your factory are their list of current clients and whether this list includes any of your competitors. A popular factory indicates high quality work but at the same time could mean you end up being pushed to the bottom of the priority list if a larger order comes in from another company. In some cases it is much better to go with a small manufacturing unit who will be able to give your work their full attention. I also think it is important to consider factory working conditions. If a factory quotes you an unbelievably low price to manufacture your pieces, you should ask yourself how they could afford to offer this price. I think that it is important for designers try to visit the prospective CMT unit working on their designs if possible, to see what it looks like, what the working conditions are for staff, and how organised and tidy it is. These considerations can, in turn, indicate if the factory will be able to stay on top of orders or lose track of things.

The only way to be sure you get it right is to thoroughly research your potential CMT unit, which includes meeting the owners. In some cases you may have to resort to trial and error in order to find a CMT unit who suits your budget and is flexible enough for your requirements. It is worth taking your time to find the right production unit for you, as in my experience the right one will do more for you than you expect, whether that is pointing you in the right direction of fabric suppliers or providing favourable terms of trade. The best way to find a CMT unit is through word-of-mouth, industry organisations such as the Manufacturing Alliance and Internet searches. After several searches you should be able to turn up some websites with a full directory of manufacturers. For example, UK website FashionCapital.co.uk offers an online manufacturing showroom for CMT, manufacturing units and small runs. Designers struggling to contact manufacturers can access a cross section of CMTs and manufacturers in the UK through the Internet so online searches are a great place to start.

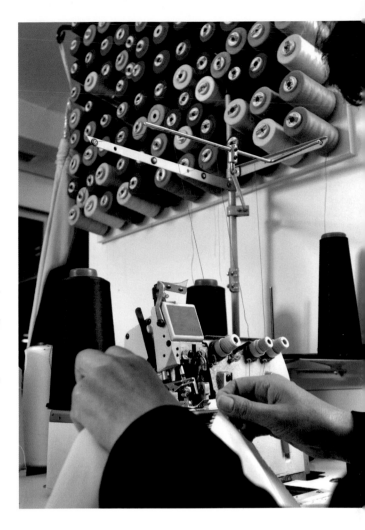

Fabric

Fabric is a key resource for your collection, and it is important for fashion entrepreneurs to keep up to date with the latest unique and innovative fabrics. I am a huge fan of designers who spend time playing around with fabrics to get the best understanding of how they behave and which ones should be used for their designs. When I moved to London I visited some of the popular fabric spots, bought their off-cuts and pieces from the bargain bins and played around at home with draping and pinning. This was how I started to develop an understanding of how certain fabrics fell and moved and which ones I liked working with. I would also ask the fabric suppliers I was buying from questions such as how the material would react when washed or where it was sourced

Trade shows are great places to go to discover new fabrics and suppliers.

and how it was coloured. I wanted to understand why some materials were so much more expensive than others despite having a similar feel or look, and which countries were best for different types of fabrics. By building up a relationship with fabric suppliers and giving them a picture of my preferences, they were able to alert me when certain fabrics came into stock or when they had new deliveries that they thought I would like.

Some of the simple lessons I learnt when it came to fabric revolved around buying quality and negotiating on quantity. I learnt early on that it was much smarter to invest in a higher quality fabric and then try to cut costs in other ways, than to try to cut costs by using cheap fabrics. The overall effect of cheap fabrics on a beautiful design is detrimental but at the same time some fabrics are worth investing more in; for example, using a standard lining for a skirt will not take away from the design as much as using cheap chiffon to make an entire evening dress would.

FINDING FABRICS

I found out about fabric shops through fabric trade shows (where suppliers gave me contact details for UK offices), word-of-mouth and using the Internet. Good fabric destinations depend on your location, for example, in New York the Garment District is mostly on 39th and 40th Streets, between 7th and 8th Avenues; in London, try Soho (around Berwick Street), Southall and Goldhawk Road; and in Beijing the Muxiyuan Market is a great starting point for fabrics.

Recommended resource

ApartmentTherapy.com has put together a list of designer fabric and textile shops which is very useful. See www. apartmenttherapy.com/ top-10-designer-textile-stores-140731

Trade shows are also a good way to discover new fabrics. Textile trade shows include the Florence Pitti Filati Yarn Show, the Frankfurt Interstoff Fabric Show, the Paris Première Vision Fabric Show and Paris Expofil.

Depending on where you are based it is quite easy to research online to find good starting points for the type of fabric you are looking for. Design Sponge (http://www.designsponge.com) has put together a list of fabric resources, ranging from inexpensive and vintage designs to higher-end trade studios.[32] Two other great websites for sourcing fabric are www.fabric.com and www.source4style.com.

Once you have found a fabric manufacturer, you may find that they only tend to work as wholesalers, with customers who buy in bulk. See if you can make some sort of deal if you think the fabric is worth paying a little extra for. If the fabric manufacturer is not interested you can take a sample and see if any of your usual fabric suppliers can source the fabric on your behalf, but you must be prepared to pay a little extra for this.

Some designers choose to source their fabrics from overseas for a number of reasons such as the lower cost or the better quality of fabrics. (For example, I love chiffon and silk and have been told by fabric suppliers from both within the UK and outside the UK the best places for these fabrics are countries like France, India or Thailand. It is also known that Italy produces some of the finest cashmere wool.) You can source your fabrics yourself or sometimes your CMT may be able to source fabrics for you (through their relationships with fabric suppliers). In this case the factory may negotiate with the supplier for minimum quantity, discuss terms of payment and make sure that the materials received match the order. This can give you a more integrated and efficient manufacturing process. For many, this option takes away the stress and saves time. Some manufacturers will not be able to source fabrics but may still be able to recommend good companies for labelling and packing accessories which they have worked with before and trust. With these set-ups it is important for the designer to check that the material has been sourced before the clothing goes

The warehouse of a fashion clothing factory in Italy.

into production as this kind of set up is not without problems. When I had some dresses manufactured in India I sent over my patterns and swatches of fabrics (which I had sourced in London) to a CMT unit which was then going to source and match the fabrics for me. This was done perfectly for the sample dress but when I received my actual order the fabric and manufacturing quality was not the same. If I had a) sourced the fabric myself and b) been there to oversee manufacturing this may not have happened. Sourcing your fabric overseas is also not without its problems as communicating with a factory on the other side of the world over colour swatches, changes, problems or delays can be very difficult. This is made easier if your fabric supplier is in the same country as you.

When it comes to both manufacturing and sourcing fabrics overseas it is important to be aware of local holidays and festivals, which may influence your schedule, for example, factories and mills are closed in China during the Chinese New Year and European mills tend to be closed in August.

Dealing with your CMT unit

Contract manufacturing is where a designer makes a contract with a manufacturer to produce their designs – to cut material, make the garment and trim it. The designer will supply the fabric and other components such as a pattern, labelling, packaging accessories such as zips and buttons, size labels and brand labels. To start with you should discuss the style, the fabrics to be used, the labels to be sewn in, any hanging labels, cost and quantities. You should also discuss time frames and establish these clearly allowing some additional leeway for tweaks and changes out of your control, for example if a fabric becomes unavailable.

You should also try to minimise any complications and delays caused by poor communication, for example, I prefer dealing with that person and keeping one person fully updated so that changes and tweaks do not get lost in the chain of communication.

PURCHASE ORDERS

A purchase order is a written sales contract between buyer and services to be rendered from a single vendor.[33] When preparing your purchase order you will need to put together a clear specification sheet for your styles (which lets your CMT unit know exactly how the garment is to be made) and a production docket. The production docket is a document that gives the factory important information about your garments, the styles, quantities and sizes, what they need to use (zips, type of threads etc.). It features an illustration of the design and outlines the delivery date and the agreed prices. You can prioritise your designs in order for the CMT unit – so they know which ones to start working on first – by numbering your work sequentially. You may prefer to get the most technical ones done first and out of the way so that you can get the tough styles finished as soon as possible. Complications late on could really impact your deadlines. You can provide this information on your docket. Once your CMT unit has everything confirmed with the production docket details work can begin.

How long will manufacturing take? Lead times

A crucial consideration during the production process is lead time, which is the time between the start or sign off for work to begin and when the garments are completed and ready to be delivered to you. For the materials you source and order you have to factor the lead time into your production schedule, which can vary and be anything from three weeks up to two months. You should also factor in the time it takes to transport the fabric and check it to ensure it is up to scratch for use. Your lead time is likely to be high if the fabric you using is hard to source, far away from your CMT unit or needs to be specially treated or prepared for you. To avoid huge delays in your lead time, source your material as soon as possible. Ideally, you should try to deliver all the fabrics and

production elements to the factory at the same time to help your CMT unit work more efficiently. In some cases your unit will not even start production unless patterns, fabrics, trim and details are all delivered together.

Quality control

Quality control means ensuring that the garments you are getting manufactured reach a satisfactory standard for your end customer. If the garments are not up to your requirements your retailer may reject them. Clear communication with your CMT can help you to ensure the quality of your garments is up to scratch. When it comes to quality control the main person responsible is you – the designer – and no one else.

Although you should not hound your CMT unit you should try to be around or available for questions at crucial times, i.e. when the fabric is going to be cut. Providing your CMT unit with specification sheets and check lists helps to ensure that details can be checked and are more likely to meet the quality

continued on p.122

Good communication with your CMT unit will help avoid any misunderstandings.

Communication with your CMT unit

Although communication can be difficult, especially when you are on a learning curve, there are ways to make things run smoothly.

1

Be really clear and open about what you are expecting. A physical, perfect sample is the ideal way to show what it is you are expecting from your CMT unit, as well as agreeing a list of key specifications/checkpoints. It is equally important not to keep changing your mind about what you want as this will delay the process and frustrate your manufacturer.

2

Be clear about what is included in the price and what is not. In this way you will avoid any unexpected costs when the work has been completed. Also be clear about when payment is expected and under what terms.

3

Allow a reasonable time frame for your work to be completed. If you can manage your time frames well and give a fair amount of time, work will not be hurried through and you will not need to put the manufacturer under undue pressure. Demanding inspections too frequently is not advisable but consistent communication and visits in person are essential. It is for you to judge the best way to do this whilst allowing the manufacturer room to work on your garments. With this in mind it is better to start your manufacturing as early as you can so that if your deadlines get moved forward you are not unduly rushed. If there is an end buyer involved let them know as soon as possible if there may be delays with delivery.

4

Inspect the work early and before it is delivered to you. If you are having fabric delivered to your CMT check the fabric thoroughly for any imperfections, colour changes and so on when you get it so if there are any problems or faults you notice them sooner rather than later. If your fabric has been delivered either to your CMT unit directly or they have sourced it for you, you may need to go there to check it for yourself. If there is a problem, act quickly. Depending on the fault, you may need to change the fabric, or if the problem is minimal – a slight colour difference for example – you may be able to agree on a discount. You can demand a refund if the fabric has too many flaws which you could not possibly cut around. It is always easier if something can be done about the problem without having to re-order the fabric as this will further delay your production schedule.

5

Make sure your payment terms allow you to inspect/approve the final garments before they are fully paid for or shipped. If this is not possible, discuss how you can ensure you are happy with the quality before full payment and shipping so there are no complications at the last moment.

6

Be kind. When you visit the manufacturer, be polite to all the workers, talk to the owner and make an effort to develop a friendly relationship. Even if you are not happy with something do not yell and stomp your feet. The problems may have arisen due to poor communication so try again and listen to their suggestions on how to solve the problem, working together for a mutually beneficial outcome. Remember, you are not likely to be the only client your CMT unit has.

7

Honour your word. Pay on time and as agreed. If you are struggling with your finances, be honest and communicate this as soon as possible: word spreads quickly if you do not keep to the terms you have agreed and you can end up being blacklisted by a network of manufacturers. Contracts are important to build trust, develop a working relationship and to protect both parties, they outline a professional set of standards that you should both adhere to. A great sample of a contract outlining code of practice is available from the official website for the Fashion Alliance.[34] This includes content about what information the designer will provide, such as the order details, specification sheets and measurement charts. In addition it covers the factory's obligations with sample contract wording such as:

I, the factory, in agreeing to make the designer's orders, will ensure that:
- All technical issues arising that affect make, delivery date, sizing, price or quantity will be communicated in writing to you as soon as we become aware of them.
- All fabric and trimmings remain your property. Any unused fabrics and trimmings will be returned to you in their entirety.

you want; for example, on a specification sheet you may indicate key measurements, the type of zip to be used, seam type and allowance, and other descriptive details. The specification sheet will also have fabric swatches attached and samples of trim. As production units are in such fierce competition with each other they often take on a great deal of work at the lowest competitive price they can charge, meaning they often need to rush production due to time constraints. Being able to visit in order to ensure your work still gets the time and quality it deserves is the designer's responsibility, as is being able to manage the balance between quality and costs.

Touching base with your production unit and seeing how things are progressing is preferable, but this is not always easy if your CMT unit is far away or outside the UK. When a CMT unit is far away it makes quality control more difficult but not impossible, you may just have to send samples to and fro and email photographs until things are right. As demand for your garments increases and your quantities rise, you need to be super organised and able to keep an eye on costs, managing your relationship with the CMT unit, making sure fabrics are available when needed and providing feedback when needed. This may mean flying out to your production unit if it is based overseas to keep a handle on things.

Managing your production

It can be very stressful trying to juggle everything when working to deliver and pay in accordance to the terms you have with your buyer(s) and manufacturer. Make it easier for yourself and have a process set up that you will follow from the point of securing the order from buyer to placing an order with your factory, all the way through to delivery to the buyer. Designers handle this in various ways. Some use database tools such as Access or Order Management Software which guides users through the order workflow process enabling them to track customer payments and credits, calculate sales and report to Excel.

Whichever method you use this is an area where you need to keep an eye on money, deadlines and resources, and ensure clear communication at all times between yourself and anyone you are working with from day one.

Getting your clothes

Check, check, check! The sooner you spot any problems the better. The longer you leave it the more you are reducing the likelihood of the CMT unit accepting responsibility for any mistakes or being willing to do anything to correct the problem – if you delay getting back to them they may have started work for another customer. Check quantity first – the number of garments and the sizes, and then check thoroughly for quality. Think about it this way: check it as thoroughly as your customer might! Do this at the factory before the goods are sent to you if you can. If you have any problems discuss these with the factory clearly and work together towards a solution. Once you are happy then the garments can be dispatched. Your clothing should be treated with the utmost care so it is not damaged in transit.

If things go wrong

The worst-case scenario is that things really do not go according to plan and your relationship with your CMT unit breaks down for whatever reason. This is a time when most designers will panic, as they will commonly have invested money (which was not easy to come by) and time. Being faced with the prospect of production being delayed or stopped is extremely distressing. If this happens to you, talk to the CMT unit and try to reach a compromise to salvage the situation. If this isn't possible, you could take legal action if you feel blame can be assigned to your CMT unit and if you have the resources to do it. Having a signed contract makes a world of difference if you reach this stage. Alternatively, depending on the extent of the loss

and who was to blame (and this is a tough decision to make), forget about it – regard it as a costly lesson learnt and begin all over again, selling what you can of the goods. Manufacturing your garments is an exciting stage to reach and a huge learning curve. If you work hard at your relationship with your CMT unit and remain organised, you can get into a successful of cycle producing garments that both you and your CMT are happy with and proud of.

NOTES

1. Wikipedia, 'Business Plan', http://en.wikipedia.org/wiki/Business_plan; accessed 30 October 2012

2. Definition of signature style by the London College of Fashion, http://www.hotcourses.com/uk-courses/Signature-style-courses/page_pls_user_course_details/16180339/0/w/53970454/page.htm

3. Aneeqa Flynn, in conversation with the author

4. For more information about the LCF Enterprise see http://www.fashion.arts.ac.uk/enterprise/

5. OECD, 'The OECD Innovation Strategy: Getting a Head Start on Tomorrow' (June 2010); available at: www.oecd.org

6. Doug Richard, 'The Rise of the Entreneuripal Class', (25 October 2010); available at: http://www.schoolforstartups.co.uk/the-rise-of-the-entreprenurial-class/

7. Simon Whitehouse, in conversation with the author

8. Wikipedia, 'Coco Chanel', http://en.wikipedia.org/wiki/Coco_Chanel; accessed 30 October 2012

9. *Time Magazine* website, 'All-TIME 100 Fashion Icons', http://www.time.com/time/specials/packages/0,28757,2110513,00.html; accessed 6 November 2012

10. Ros Horton, and Sally Simmons, *Women Who Changed the World* (London: Quercus, 2007)

11. Hal Vaughan, *Sleeping With The Enemy: Coco Chanel's Secret War* (New York: Alfred A. Knopf, 2011)

12. Voguepedia website, 'Calvin Klein (Brand)', http://www.vogue.com/voguepedia/Calvin_Klein_%28Brand%29; accessed 30 October 2012

13. Sombo Dakowah, in conversation with the author

14. Neri Karra, *The UK Designer Fashion Economy Value relationships – identifying barriers and creating opportunities for business growth* (December 2008); available online.

15. An interest rate that moves up and down based on the changes of an underlying interest rate index.

16. An interest rate that, once established, does not vary according to fluctuations in the prime lending rate.

17. Business Funding.co.uk website, 'Equity Investment', http://www.businessfunding.co.uk/sources/equity-investment/; accessed 6 November 2012

18. Wikipedia, 'Angel Investor', http://en.wikipedia.org/wiki/Angel_investor; accessed 30 October 2012

19. Guy Kawasaki, 'Guy Kawasaki on Angel Investors', http://www.inc.com/articles/2000/12/21310.html; accessed 6 November 2012

20. Wikipedia, 'Venture Capital', http://en.wikipedia.org/wiki/Venture_capital; accessed 30 October 2012

21. Wikipedia, 'Crowd Funding', http://en.wikipedia.org/wiki/Crowd_funding; accessed 30 October 2012

22. Securities Law Prof Blog, 'Crowdfunding Legistlation: An Answer to Enrepreneurs' Prayers or Nightmare for Small Investors?' (November 2011); http://lawprofessors.typepad.com/securities/2011/11/crowdfunding-legislation-answer-to-entrepreneurs-prayers-or-nightmare-for-small-investors.html, accessed 6 November 2012

23. Wikipedia, 'Factoring', http://en.wikipedia.org/wiki/Factoring_(finance); accessed 6 November 2012

24. HSBC bank has some useful guidelines at: http://www.knowledge.hsbc.co.uk/run/finances/control+your+cashflow/factoring+and+invoice+discounting

25. www.crowdcube.com

26. Telegraph.co.uk, 'British designer Amanda Wakeley leaves her label' (11 December 2008), http://fashion.telegraph.co.uk/news-features/TMG3708735/British-designer-Amanda-Wakeley-leaves-her-label.html; accessed 6 November 2012

27. Lauren Milligan, 'In Her Wake', British *Vogue* website (30 January 2009), http://www.vogue.co.uk/news/2009/01/30/amanda-wakeley-back-in-charge-of-her-own-business; accessed 6 November 2012

28. Wikipedia, 'Shareholder', http://en.wikipedia.org/wiki/Shareholder; accessed 6 November 2012

29. British Fashion Council report, 'Regional analysis of the UK Fashion Industry: The Value of the UK Fashion Industry', available at www.britishfashioncouncil.com

30. http://www.fashionalliance.co.uk/about_alliance.php

31. Peter Day, 'Lancashire leads new British textile manufacturing revival', BBC Business website, http://www.bbc.co.uk/news/business-17827741; accessed 6 November 2012

32. For Design Sponge's list of fabric resources go to http://www.designsponge.com/2010/09/top-20-fabric-resources.html

33. retail.about.com/od/glossary/g/purchase_order.htm

34. NESTA, *Code of Practice*, available to download at http://www.nesta.org.uk/areas_of_work/creative_economy/fashiontoolkit/designers_edition/assets/documents/fashion_toolkit_-_code_of_practice

SHOWCASING YOUR WORK

Designers showcase their work in a range of different ways. For some designers a small presentation to buyers is the best route to take as it saves time and gets the desired result – the collection is bought – without the additional expense of a runway show or trade show participation. In fact, despite the popularity of fashion weeks, catwalk shows and trade shows, designers are constantly looking for new ways to showcase their collections. In 2011 I attended the Film *InStyle* launch in London. For this event, *InStyle* magazine had invited luxury brands such as Roberto Cavalli and Mulberry to collaborate with film directors to create a series of short films, each exploring 'the meaning of style'. This event is an example of the growing interest amongst fashion designers in exhibiting their work through different platforms. More and more designers are using video to create small presentations for buyers and other more cost-effective platforms to showcase their work. Economically, fashion films make sense for designers. According to Uduak Oduok, an attorney, former journalist and fashion model:

> *Producing a fashion show can be rather expensive. Shooting a fashion film video, on the other hand, is much cheaper. As a marketing tool, it is great for promotions. If your video is [strong], it can have a viral effect, especially if you distribute it online via YouTube, Facebook and Twitter. A site like YouTube can do for you what it did for Justin Bieber [provided] your video is great and shows your excellent work as a designer. If you are an established designer like Tom Ford, fashion films keep you relevant...[1]*

Trade shows

Fashion trade shows are exhibitions for clothing companies within the fashion industry to showcase new ranges, services and other related products such as textiles. These shows are not usually open to the public and you must be registered to gain entry. Typically registration is done through the official website for the event. Trade shows are for buyers and sellers mainly, but also for the press. Designers take part in trade shows because it is a route to generate sales and meet new buyers. The presentation areas are broken up into dedicated areas, for example, menswear, womenswear and childrenswear – these may be further divided into luxury and high street. Some trade shows distinguish the areas yet further by placing 'new' companies or start-up brands together. These areas are great locations for emerging fashion designers, as buyers visiting these areas will be looking to buy new, fresh and emerging brands. By showcasing next to other designers in the 'emerging designer' section, for example, you are increasing your chances of meeting and attracting the attention of a buyer looking for new start-up brands.

Renting a space to exhibit at a trade show can range from a few hundred to a few thousand pounds or dollars depending on the trade show, its size, and the kind of space you want. A large, customised space (10 x 10 m) with electricity, carpet, railings,

Designer Ekhaterina Kukhareva exhibiting at Vauxhall Fashion Scout, London.

Some global trade shows for fashion and textiles

- Bread and Butter, Barcelona
- Bread and Butter, Berlin
- Capsule New York Womens, New York
- Copenhagen International Fashion Fair, Copenhagen
- CPH Vision & Terminal-2, Copenhagen
- CurveNY, New York
- MAGIC Marketplace, Las Vegas
- Mi Milano Prêt-à-Porter, Milan
- Premiere Vision, Paris
- Prêt-à-Porter, Paris
- Pure, London
- Stitch, London
- West Coast Trend Show, Los Angeles
- World Boutique, Hong Kong
- WSA Show, Las Vegas

cupboards etc., will cost more than a smaller one with minimum accessories (3 x 3 m). You can find out information about trade shows from forums, online searches or through industry trade directories such as the Apparel Search Trade Show Directory (http://www.apparelsearch.com). Some brands prefer trade shows to fashion shows and others only showcase their brand at fashion shows. The most suitable platform for your brand is best determined by research, looking through and analysing the potential pros and cons for each option, things that might affect your decision including cost, location and brand exposure.

If you chose to exhibit at a trade show you should be prepared. These are some things to consider when exhibiting your collection:

- Alongside buyers also invite potential financial investors to your stand and use this as an opportunity to market your brand;

- Make sure you have business cards and look books (images of your collection) available but give these out sparingly;

- Make your stand as appealing as possible! Sweets in a bowl and small details count. Also consider having a model at your stand during the busiest period of the day for an hour or so to showcase your clothing;

- Have a guestbook for visitors to sign and include a section to get their contact details. Use this to put together a database of contacts to keep in touch with;

- If a buyer expresses interest never just give a fixed bottom-line price, ask about the proposed quantity first as your selling price should vary according to this.

Runway shows

Fashion weeks are another way to showcase your collection to the fashion audience of buyers, editors, press, industry influencers and celebrities. By doing a runway show during fashion week you have the opportunity to promote your brand, but timing is key. Right from the beginning you should be asking yourself Is this the right time to show my brand? Am I ready for this as a business? Do I have the resources to fulfil orders? If after answering these questions you still feel that a fashion show is for you, then go for it.

Almost every designer in the world dreams of having their own fashion show. It is the 'show and prove' moment in front of an audience of your peers, buyers and media, and it takes planning, organisation and of course money! You cannot decide to do a fashion show just because of the flashing lights; in reality shows are expensive and pointless if you do not have the finance or infrastructure to support them properly. Yes, runway shows can get you great exposure and press but, at the early stages of your career, when you calculate the cost (of models, hair, make-up, guests, food, drink, venue, lighting and sound for example) it may not be the most feasible way to go.

If a runway show is for you

If you decide to have a fashion show then in order to participated in a registered fashion week event (such as New York Fashion Week or Vauxhall Fashion Scout, London) you will need to meet certain criteria, such as having been in business for a set period of time or having a certain type of stockist for a set period of time. These criteria do vary so visit the website for your respective fashion week/event to find out more. If you do not initially meet the criteria to showcase at your chosen event, do some further research as you may be eligible for an alternative platform or for assistance from an industry support body to help you to qualify.

A model walks the runway for designer Nova Chiu, showing her S/S 2013 collection at London Fashion Week.

Joining an organised fashion show before going it alone

The best start up advice I can offer is to take your time and try to get involved in fashion shows with other designers instead of splashing out on your own solo show. Organised fashion shows, staged by fashion organisations such as those mentioned on the previous page mean a large amount of the leg work is done for you (venue, models, makeup team). Most group fashion shows require you to pay to be included (especially the larger and more established events) but some smaller ones, such as those that are part of festival or charity productions, can be free. Group shows can showcase anything from three designers to ten or more. The shows I got involved in when I was starting out in London around 2005–2007 were mostly arranged by art colleges or boutiques (the latter often then stocking the pieces from the show afterwards). I found out about them through word-of-mouth, fashion networking websites and by visiting locations such as art colleges, community halls and museums. Group shows are a good starting point because participating in events with others takes the pressure off but still gives you a behind-the-scenes glimpse of the volume of work and team involved in such an event. This includes models, make-up artists, press and photographers, as well as all the planning, marketing and promotion that goes on. By participating you will also learn about the material you need to promote a show, including your biography, your logo, and images. Seeing how much money, time and energy goes into pulling off a 20-minute runway production may surprise you and even initially scare you off doing it on your own. Instead, getting involved in shared fashion shows saves you money and is a great introduction to how things are done.

Having your own show

If and when you go on to do a solo show, you will have a better level of experience and feel more prepared if you have previously been part of an organised show; you will have a better idea of how much rehearsal time is needed, how many models and so on.

You can organise your own fashion show as soon as you have your first collection if you choose to (which can range in size from as few as eight to as many as

40 pieces). You will need:

- a venue with a catwalk and seating;
- models;
- clothing;
- make-up and hair team;
- photographer, videographer and sound team;
- lighting;
- assistance for front of house;
- insurance for your garments in case of damage or loss.

FINDING SPONSORS

Getting sponsors on board to finance your show will help you with its costs, allowing you to direct more of your money to areas such as paying your hair and makeup team. Sponsors can be secured by preparing and sending out a proposal that outlines the purpose of the show, who will be attending, what press and coverage the show will get. A proposal should also suggest how a sponsor may get involved and explain what the benefits would be for them. For example, a sponsor could be involved through goodie bag placement, a stand selling their product at your fashion show, or by you featuring their logo on all the outgoing material about your show, such as flyers and brochures. Good companies to contact would be make-up and beauty brands.

FINDING MAKE-UP AND HAIR ARTISTS

Make-up artists and hair stylists for the show can be sourced from online forums, art colleges and by word-of-mouth; if you attend a fashion show and like the hair and makeup, ask the organisers for contact details. Make-up and hair stylists tend to be flexible with designers who are starting out and will understand your financial restraints; they may also be keen to build up their product portfolio and relationships within the industry. If you do not have a huge budget be honest and negotiate so that instead of having to pay money for everything you can pay by favour for some things. Paying by favour could mean including their business cards in your goody bags and on the seats or by paying travel and other expenses.

A model walking down the runway showcasing designs by Erdem Moralioglu at the Audi Fashion Festival 2011 Erdem Show on 14 May 2011 in Singapore.

WHEN TO SCHEDULE YOUR SHOW

Time your show so that it happens around – but not necessarily during – the busier times of the fashion calendar. You need to ensure you present your clothes during busy buying seasons (January–March and August–October for Autumn/Winter and Spring/ Summer) and preferably before the main fashion weeks rather than after them (for a list of fashion weeks see pp.30–1). If you go in early and make an impression the press and buyers may either buy your collection early before attending the main fashion weeks or remember you after the main fashion weeks and place an order with you. It is better to have your show early in the season rather than late, when budgets have been spent. Before the fashion weeks buyers have not spent their full budget but towards the end of and after the fashion weeks they will be closing their books. If you hold your show on the same day and at the same time as some of the larger and more popular brands you may struggle with attendance and coverage because the buyers and press you are after will probably have their full attention on the established brands. However, most will send representatives to cover other emerging designers they are interested in.

GETTING PRESS COVERAGE

Solo shows are costly when all the expenses are taken into account, so try to build up press by word of mouth through your network and by using online marketing (social media is a free and extremely effective). Drum up press interest as early as possible, listing news about your event on as many fashion forums and websites as you can to create a buzz. This means you need to send out a press release which really talks your event up. It goes without saying that you should send information about your show through all of your social media platforms such as Facebook and Twitter to get people talking about it.

If you can afford it, consider spending some money on advertising. An ad in a local newspaper or a banner online can be affordable if you find the right platform and very effective.

It is important to secure press and promote your show as otherwise you could put together a wonderful show which no one knew about and have rows of empty seats, which would be a huge shame. People need to know when your show is happening.

HIRING PR

If you do not have a PR agent but can afford one, now would be the time to appoint someone because to really make the most of your runway show you need as much press coverage as possible and PR will help you with this. You also need to attract buyers and this is where early conversation with them pays dividends; don't just start calling a month before your show to invite them, start as soon as possible so that you can build up the relationship and increase the likelihood of their attendance.

INVITING GUESTS

Speak to your friends in the fashion industry and see who you can get to come to your show. Celebrities and known-faces are always great to see but ultimately it is about the fashion so although a celeb on your front row might get the blogs buzzing the most important person you want at your fashion show is your buyer. A packed fashion show full of press and fashionistas will be of no benefit if you have put bums on seats but not sold a single piece or spoken to a single buyer at the end of the season. The aim is to have an amazing show which gets a buyer who is interested in your collection over to your showroom (a room used to display your collection) or an invitation to present the collection for closer inspection. (Most emerging designers cannot afford a showroom straight away, I know designers who have hired a hotel room and used that as a base to invite buyers in to view their collections. Empty showrooms are listed with estate agents and in online directories.) Keep the number of people you invite to your show to a reasonable size. There is no set size but most of the fashion shows I have attended have had a maximum of around 200 guests, although at global fashion weeks up to 400 or more people may be seated.

KEEPING COSTS UNDER CONTROL

Save money wherever possible. For example, you do not need to hire a huge hall or to print out fancy invitations for all of the guests if you do not have a large budget. Instead, try contacting your college or a local theatre and see if you can negotiate something for an evening when the space is not in use and make it look beautiful. You could design and create something online which is effective and interactive, with the option to RSVP by email. You can still send a handful of printed and lush invitations to the key buyers you would like to see, particularly the press and buyers. To cover costs some designers sell tickets for their shows, but if you try this do not set an unrealistic ticket price and remember you will have to make the evening entertaining so that people feel that they are getting value for money.

Models

Your model may become someone who inspires you, your muse, so choose carefully. Your model can give you feedback about your designs when they are wearing them, playing both a functional and creative role to help you understand and reach your target audience. Some designers choose a model they feel a connection with or whose look appeals, others choose a model to make a statement to and about the industry, for example, the frequent use of 80-year-old Carmen Dell'Orefice on the runway by the London College of Fashion defies the stereotype that only teen models can sell clothes. Some do not want their models to deflect attention from the clothes and hence may go for a less 'stand out' look.

Fashion designers will work with high fashion, fashion, fit, commercial and parts models. High fashion/fashion models do runway shows, for example, during fashion weeks, and are used for editorial shoots and campaigns for fashion magazines such as *Vogue* and *Dazed and Confused*. Fit models are used in the sampling process to fit garments and to give feedback on the styles, for example, how the style feels and, moves, and to check how the piece will look on a person instead of on a mannequin. In this way they are an important part of the design process. They may also be used in showrooms to show garments to buyers. Commercial models are the largest group within the fashion industry, appearing in adverts and on branding and packaging for a whole range of products and services, from drinks to gyms. Commercial models may be described as 'model beautiful' but they can also look like a regular person from the street. Both high fashion/ fashion and commercial models can be supermodels. A supermodel is defined as being a 'highly-paid fashion model [who] usually has a worldwide reputation and often a background in haute couture and commercial modelling' such as Naomi Campbell and Miranda Kerr.[2] Parts models can also do commercial or high fashion work and focus on a body part such as the hands, for

a brand like Tiffany's or feet for a brand such as Jimmy Choo. Other models include mature, child, petite (5' 2" to 5' 6"), plus size (size 10 and up), and glamour. Female models tend to be between 15 and 23 years old, although they can be found either side of this age bracket; male models can be older, ranging from 18–25. The minimum height is 5' 8" for women and 5' 11" for men; an exception to the rule is Kate Moss who is supposedly 5' 7". You can find good models on websites such as ModelMayhem who may not be signed to agencies but are still good nonetheless. To book a model through a modelling agency will require a bigger budget – from a few hundred to thousands of pounds or dollars – and start-ups can rarely afford it. However, if you do your research you can come across good agencies with decent models on their books who you can book at an affordable cost. Even if you do not have a great amount in your budget you should still cover travel and food for the model(s) on the day of the shoot or show.

Working with your model

The following set of guidelines is based on my experience and is worth following to ensure you maintain a harmonious and respectful working relationship with your model(s). It is based on observations I have made whilst working backstage at fashion shows and on photo shoots, but also from the perspective of a designer who dresses models in the moments of backstage madness!

Communication – models are actors in the sense that they take up and play a character in order to convey a message about the product they are showing. Therefore it is important that you give them clear advice and guidance so that they can deliver what you are seeking. Never talk down to or patronise your models; they are working for you and should be treated with respect and professionalism. This should go without saying but unfortunately rudeness happens all the time. When working with models before a shoot or runway show I sit down and go through images and concepts with them about exactly what I want. Far too often the concept behind a shoot simply doesn't work because the model cannot bring up the mood or expressions the designer and photographer are expecting to see and sometimes this is down to poor communication. Some models work best seeing a desired look rather than having it explained to them in words so as a visual aide show them photographs from a magazine. Planning enough time for your shoot also means that you do not end up rushing through a shoot or getting unnecessarily stressed out with your model.

Privacy – allow some privacy for your models to change and get undressed, even if this means roping off an area and hanging up a sheet; some of your models may be as young as 15 years old. I also try not to let men backstage if it is a womenswear show so that the models feel completely comfortable and the same in reverse.

Nutrition – feed your models! It should be obvious, but I have been to a photoshoot where there has been nothing provided to eat or drink, not even water. Bearing in mind that shoots can take anything from two to six hours or more, this is not acceptable. A spread of fruit, sandwiches and juices is not a big ask.

Cosmetics – Try putting yourself in your models' shoes. We all know that everyone's skin reacts differently to different products and typically we have our 'go-to' skin brand. Show your model consideration regarding the skin and hair products you expect them to wear. Ask if they have a skin allergy or react to certain products before the shoot. Finding out which products they use to remove makeup is another example of the consideration you can show. Makeup artists normally have makeup remover with them, but if you know they will not, bring some of your own.

Fashion show checklist

Your team

A good fashion show needs a great amount of team work and effort! Some of the first fashion shows I got involved in used students and graduates in the hair and make-up team. Most emerging fashion designers cannot afford to pay for a team so this is where your network of friends and industry contacts really becomes useful. Ask for help and be honest about what you can give in return. Contact local fashion colleges, modelling agencies and industry contacts as well as doing open calls on Facebook and through your blog or website. Some people will be happy to help you or be involved for the photos and coverage they may get in return. In some cases if you are willing to cover travel and provide food you will have a good team for the show, especially if it is your first show as people are more understanding and flexible. You will need a photographer and a videographer to capture your show – both of which are worth investing in so that you have quality images and footage that you can use for the post-event promotion blitz you will be doing. You will need assistance, someone to oversee backstage, making sure nothing gets lost or damaged, looking after models and helping you produce the show. You should ensure that every member of your team is fully credited for their work and as you grow and develop you should start paying people when you can afford to.

A designer working out the running order for her runway show.

Allow enough time

Allow plenty of time for your show. It will take at least two months or more from planning to the actual event; this should give you enough time to cast and fit models, run rehearsals and organise a professional show. A perfectly executed fashion show is magic to watch, a disorganised one is cringe-worthy. Enough time for rehearsals is especially important because the models need to be confident and happy about the running order, walking in your clothing and in the case of womenswear, walking in the high heels! You also need to allow enough time on the day for the hair and make-up to be done and for one dress rehearsal if possible. You can not realistically know if the music for your show will be long enough or how much time you will need between outfit changeovers if you have not done at least one walk through. There is no set guideline for the order in which your designs should walk out but typically your strongest look should be revealed last.

Don't forget:

- Have a clear and well organised area for models, hair and make-up;
- Give your models a clear brief;
- Make sure your models have a private area to get changed (even if it is just a sheet hung in the corner), and keep backstage access limited to those who definitely need to be there;
- To maintain order in all the mayhem put up photos of the models in the correct running order by the exit to the runway so that the models know they are lined up in the right order and the right looks;
- Make sure you have plenty of clothing rails, hangers and steamers
- Take lots of safety pins;
- Have backstage helpers to assist the models when changing and look after clothing so that nothing goes missing or gets damaged;
- Make sure you provide food and drink for the models and team; it can be a long wait from doing hair and makeup to hitting the runway – anything from three to eight hours!

Seating

Seating is crucial and it is important to have your seating plan made up before your event. Print several copies and give them out to the people responsible for seating guests so that everyone knows who should be seated where. Your key attendees such as buyers and press should always be given pride of place and it is often easier to group people in sections such as buyers; friends and family; press and others. Typically, information about the brand and the collection and contact details for the designer/designer's PR are printed up on a piece of paper and placed on each seat.

NOTES

1. Fashionentlaw website, 'Tom Ford Spring 2011 Collection', (January 2011), http://fashionentlaw.com/fashion-law/tom-ford-spring-2011-collection-fashion-film-agreements-contracts/; accessed 18 October 2012

2. Wikipedia, 'Supermodel', http://en.wikipedia.org/wiki/Supermodel; accessed 18 October 2012. The term supermodel was actually coined by model Janice Dickinson in 1979 and is a compound of 'Superman' and 'model'. I met Janice during London Fashion Week in September 2010 and she was every inch the supermodel!

Case Study

Alex Leonhardt Creative Director, Viktoria Modesta.
Stylist, Lloyd Scott Tyler Clothing; Rhiannon Jones
Hair, Roy Hayward.

Working with photographers

Advice from photographer
Alex Leonhardt

Most start-up designers cannot
afford to pay a professional
fashion photographer, but there
are some very talented semi-
pro photographers who might
be keen on doing the shoot for
free to update their own books.
Here is some advice from former
photographer Alex Leonhardt
about how to get the best out of
working with your photographer.

• Not every photographer will
be right for your style of photo
shoot – be very picky about
which photographer you hire and
you'll get a good selection of
professional photographs.

• Discuss who owns the
copyright of the images up front,
typically the designer pays the
photographer for the rights
to the photographs (for more
information see http://www.
copyrightservice.co.uk/protect/
p16_photography_copyright).

• Find out whether the cost of
retouching of a set of pictures
(say 30 images) is included in his/
her offer to avoid underestimating
the total cost of the shoot (though
it may well be worth considering
a professional retoucher to get
perfect results).

• Discuss down to the very
last detail what the final results
should look like and put together
a selection of images (a mood
board) that reflects the final
outcome that you want.

• Where possible select a model
with some experience and the

right 'look' for the shoot; there
are many good models working
for free or at affordable rates to
fill up their books.

• When booking a model for
a photoshoot ask the model/
agency for Polaroids/snapshots
to get a real idea of how the
model looks without their hair
and make-up done so that your
photographer knows what they
are really working with ahead of
the photoshoot.

SELLING YOUR BRAND

Public relations

Before we look at public relations (PR) it is important to remember the importance of having a sellable product. Make sure that you can deliver a good quality, professionally manufactured product through an efficient supply chain before going public.

Start-ups and emerging designers need PR in order to communicate their brand's products and image to customers. Some designers do their own PR, undertaking responsibilities such as writing press releases, attending key industry events, answering media requests and using industry contacts to secure opportunities for their brand. This can be done through online and offline platforms, and in person by the designer themselves. Many designers are willing and able to do their own PR, at least during their early days of business. I enjoy writing press releases and at the beginning of my career I spoke to PR friends who gave me great advice in this area (such as loading them with buzz-words and noteworthy information, including a few strong images, and keeping them short and succinct). I was advised never to let my press releases go over one and half pages. However, not all designers are comfortable managing this area for themselves, and at some stage, whether at start-up or as their business grows, a designer may decide to appoint a PR company to handle public relations. This can happen for a number of reasons, for example, when PR starts to take up too much time, or if it is an area that is not really of interest to the designer. In other cases a designer may feel that they do not have enough contacts or experience to really be effective in this area.

Finding a good PR company

Start by asking any friends you have within the fashion industry for recommendations, then read

Definition

Public relations (PR) is the practice of managing the flow of information between an individual or an organisation and the public.[1] Public relations provides an organisation or individual exposure to their audiences using topics of public interest and news items that do not require direct payment.[2]

Journalists need new designers to write about, and new designers need the exposure. Designers need to make sure they have the proper tools to compete in the PR game: professional press release, impeccable image, and infallible persistence.[3]

Courtney Blackman, Managing Director, Forward PR

trade publications and do your own research to compile a list of reputable PR companies. Word-of-mouth referrals are great and nothing beats feedback from someone's first-hand experience but there are other ways to get information. A good indication of a company's level of professionalism is their corporate website – it should be informative, user friendly and well designed with a comprehensive list of some or all of their existing and past clients. Most PR companies have a company biography and information about their clients on their website so you can find out how long they have been in business and their success to date. Some PR agencies also have active Twitter and Facebook accounts and for more information you can ask for references from previous or existing clients. As a courtesy, I would definitely recommend that you call the company first to see if they are happy for you to do this. There's a chance they will be reluctant, in which case, take note. Although they may not be prepared to share information about clients for legitimate reasons, it's worth paying attention to their willingness to provide information as this can be an indicator of their success. On the whole most PR agents will not mind asking existing clients for a referral if there is a good working relationship. The client always has the option of saying no.

A good fashion PR agent has a wealth of contacts within the industry and will use this network to secure

opportunities for your brand. You should also bear in mind that the number of clients a PR company has may affect the work they can do for you. You may opt for a smaller PR company with fewer clients if you feel that you will get more attention from them than a larger company with a long list of clients. Of course, it is not as simple as finding a PR company you would like to work with, they must also want or be able to work with you. This decision is based on a number of factors: if the PR company sees your brand as a good fit for their current portfolio; if you have budget for their services; and if they consider your targets and goals to be achievable. It has to work for both of you, but if everything aligns then there's every chance they will take you on.

What should your PR do for you?

Your PR's responsibilities could include any or all of the following:

- putting together a top quality press kit;
- creating press releases and running PR campaigns;
- using industry contacts to create opportunities such as interviews and product placements;
- promoting new product launches and (where relevant) sending samples to key industry contacts;
- answering media requests and dealing with sponsorship proposals;
- advising on brand strategy and presentation;
- facilitating attendance or inclusion in key industry events (such fashion weeks and trade shows)

Your PR should understand your product, your short- and long-term goals and your market. However, the only way for them to get this information is for you to communicate it. By providing your PR with all the relevant information right at the beginning of your working relationship (and going forwards) you will be enabling them to do their job more efficiently. Let your PR agency know your goals – such as the media platforms you are keen to gain or build exposure through, the magazines you are interested in, the celebrities you would love to dress – and listen to their feedback. They may not agree with all of your targets but you should listen to their advice and feedback. Through discussions with your agent you can decide on the right PR strategy for you.

How much should you pay for PR?

A good PR agency can cost anything from a few hundred to a few thousand pounds or dollars a month. In some cases the more you can afford to pay, the more you can get out of your PR campaigns. However, this does not mean that the largest and most expensive company will be the most effective for you. To save costs you can secure PR for specific events such a collection launch as opposed to hiring them full time, which will mean they are an ongoing cost every month. A smaller company or a freelance agent can be just as effective depending on their level of experience and attitude towards your project. Find out if you will have a junior team working on your campaign (who may be very dedicated and enthusiastic) or an experienced manager, and what guarantees you will be given that your brand will not disappear into a sea of other clients. Larger PR companies tend to look after big, established brands so do not be put off if they cannot work your brand in its early stages, you may work better together at a later date. In some cases it is actually best for a start-up label to go with a smaller, less expensive company that is closer in size to your own. This option may be more affordable and the company better able (depending on their number of clients) to give you the time and attention you require. If you do your research you could end up paying a small, experienced company a set amount for a year rather than the same amount monthly to a huge PR company.

Being a good client

The relationship you have with your PR is important and there are many ways you can ensure it is maintained. Be as cooperative and responsive to your PR representative as you can. To do their job properly they need to know every bit of news about your label as soon as possible. You should also be prepared to supply information quickly, for example, a speedy response can mean the difference between securing a magazine interview or not. Unless you are working with a very small company with no other fashion clients, you are unlikely to be their only client in need of public relations opportunities. Sometimes it is the client who gets back to the company the quickest and has the best relationship with them who gets considered or looked after more, however unintentional this may be on the part of the PR agent. It is not your PR's job to do everything for you. Their job is to sell your brand but this cannot be done without your passionate and consistent involvement. You still need to keep control of the other elements of running your brand so that if, for example, your PR requests a sample from you, you are able to deliver. It is also useful for you to keep track of publicity about yourself – Google your clothing brand and see what articles comes up, share your finds with your PR and see if you can leverage any opportunities from whatever you find.

Sponsorship as a route to PR your brand

Sponsorship is a route to securing exposure for your brand. This usually involves a designer paying a certain amount of money or providing a product for placement, at an event such as a gala or awards show – a good example of this would be an accessories designer using a goodie bag opportunity to promote their brand by donating earrings for each bag. Or a designer paying money and providing products in exchange for press coverage and visibility at an event. Choosing the right sponsorship can be tricky for an emerging designer, as if the wrong event is chosen you may get the wrong kind of visibility for your brand. For example, gifting earrings for a sports event for men may not benefit your brand as much as a fund raising gala for women. It can be hard to measure the direct result of what you have paid for, but the right event can help you to gain access to press, influencers and future customers in a targeted way.

Paths to exposure: reaching celebrities and magazines

The effectiveness of celebrity endorsement is undeniable. Charles Worth, creator of Parisian haute couture, was an early adopter of celebrity-linked PR. He sought the patronage of a high society lady, Princess Von Metternich (wife of the Austria ambassador to France and a close friend of Napoleon's wife Empress Eugenie), in order to promote his couture house, La Maison Worth[4] (also see p.70).

The bottom line is that magazine editors want to be on top of the latest exciting style trends and celebrities want to look stylish and fashion forward. You should be full of confidence when it comes to introducing your creations to them as you may have the exact kind of designs they are looking for!

The main area where designers struggle is when it comes to making contact with the right people. Magazine editors and stylists drown in emails on a daily basis so cutting through is hard but persistence is key. Magazines such as *Vogue*, *InStyle* and *Tatler* can only devote so many column inches to emerging designers because they also have an obligation to the established brands who pay for space. They need to keep the latter happy and this directly impacts on the magazine's selected features. Remember that you are not alone in your attempts to get coverage, other new and emerging brands are also competing for attention, so you may hear a few 'no's before you get a 'yes'! Don't let this deter you, it is all part of the journey.

What are editors and stylists looking for?

Dressing a celebrity for the red carpet is a dream come true for any designer because it brings such fantastic exposure to their brand through magazines and TV. Imagine being able to dress Halle Berry for the Oscars or Mila Kunis for the front cover of *Vogue*. In this area, good relationships with stylists and fashion editors are invaluable.

Contacting editors and stylists

I'm always looking out for new talent, it's what drives me. But to make the grade, young designers have to have a fresh perspective, pay attention to every detail and construction and present their collection to the press in a professional manner, including creating lookbook images and a press release. It's not about spending a lot of money, but it is about having real skill and understanding how the industry works.[5]

Helen Jennings, Editor of *Arise* magazine

Helen Jennings backstage at the ARISE NYFW show with AMFW (*Arise* Magazine Fashion Week) womenswear designer of the year, Tsemaye Binitie.

A stylist looks for something that will be stunning on and off camera – something that looks unique and doesn't swamp the star wearing it – remember it's the celebrity wearing the clothes not the clothes wearing the celebrity! I look for something that will make a statement in a good way![6]

Nick Ede, Celebrity Stylist and *Project Catwalk* judge

Magazines have a good online presence and contact details can sometimes be found on their website. Finding contact details for celebrities is much harder, but not impossible. Start by creating a list of targets you would like to contact, these could be magazines, celebrities, bloggers or press. Good starting points for industry contacts – in addition to business networking site LinkedIn – are:

◆ Le Book (www.lebook.com) An online directory for industry contact details including fashion designers, art directors and stylists.

◆ My Fashion Database (www.myfdb.com) An industry go-to resource which organises fashion credits of all the latest covers, campaigns, and editorials from publications and brands around the world. It holds over 50,000 professional profiles of celebrities, models, and industry pros.

◆ Gorkana (www.gorkana.com) A media database providing an accurate, in-depth and trusted source of information on thousands of journalists and media outlets in the UK, Europe and US.

It is important to know the right person to contact – for celebrities this would be the publicist or stylist, for a magazine feature, the fashion features team. Making contact is where good relationships come

in useful, so if you have them, use them. It is not easy to get through to stylists and publicists or to hold their attention so you must be confident and persistent when you do. This could be face to face, over the phone or via email. However you first make contact, talk about your clothing with enthusiasm and passion and offer to email further information. Your email should include a biography about your brand, any noteworthy information (for example, if you have made the local news, won an award or have a unique concept behind your range), a link to your website and a couple of images. A long email often does not get read because people are busy; they just want to scan the email for key information. Before you send the email, remember to use the spell check!

Don't rely solely on sending emails or calling magazine editors – make sure you are seen regularly at fashion events so that your contacts can put a face to your label. Besides, by regularly attending fashion industry events you are increasing your chance of making useful contacts in the first place.

Who are you targeting? The wish list

Aim big and create a wish list. Contact your local newspapers, and the publications you feel would suit your brand. Don't be afraid to go for the mainstream publications too. According to marketing company Stylophane,[7] the most popular fashion magazines as on Facebook as of 12th January 2012 were:

◆ *Vogue*

◆ *Cosmopolitan*

◆ *Seventeen*

◆ *Teen Vogue*

◆ *Glamour*

◆ *Vogue* Paris

◆ *ELLE*

◆ *Vogue* Italia

◆ *InStyle*

◆ *Vogue* India

Marketing and advertising

Marketing is the process of performing market research, selling products and/or services to customers and promoting them via advertising to further enhance sales.[8] It is an integrated process through which companies build strong customer relationships and create value for their customers and for themselves.[9] Marketing is a promotional activity undertaken to boost sales and connect your product – in this case clothing – with the people who will buy it.

When planning your marketing you need to be able to answer questions about who is buying your brand and who you are designing for. This information will help you to decide every detail from the best fabrics to use for your garments, to how and where your clothing will be marketed and ultimately sold, i.e. which platform will best connect with your brand.

Designers seeking to get a better understanding of marketing can consult with sales and marketing specialists to get professional feedback about creating marketable collections. For designers who do not know where to begin when it comes to connecting with their market one good idea is to try to organise a focus group. This is a form of qualitative research in which a group of people are asked about their perceptions, opinions, beliefs, and attitudes towards a product, service, concept, advertisement, idea, or packaging as a useful way to get feedback about new products.[10]

How should you get the word out about our product? Advertising

You can start by considering advertising if you have a budget, looking locally first. Local newspapers are much less expensive than high fashion magazines. Advertising is a part of the marketing process – it involves the placement of adverts, for example, in magazines, newspapers, on TV or online and is normally an expense

Definition

Lamb, Hair and McDaniel define advertising as, 'impersonal; one way communication about a product or organisation that is paid by a marketer.'[11] If you are confused about how marketing relates to advertising, it might help to use this simple analogy: think of marketing as a pie – inside the pie you have slices of advertising, market research, media planning, public relations, product pricing, distribution, customer support, sales strategy, and community involvement.[12] Advertising only equals one piece of the pie in the strategy to talk to your customer.

involved in promoting your brand. When placing an advert, a designer (or their PR in accordance with the designer's budget) will decide where to place the advert and how long the advert should run for.

Spreading the word using online marketing

Traditional forms of marketing such as e-newsletters are still seen as an effective way to connect with consumers, but with the social media movement and the likes of Facebook and Twitter, we have begun to see email signups being replaced by followers and 'likes'. Stylophane is an online marketing firm serving the fashion industry (www.stylophane.com). The company's Managing Partner, Alexander Mendoza, said in an interview with the *Los Angeles Times* about Facebook, 'you can run an ad only to people who[se birthday it is] ... I can 'hyper-target' my ads – just [to] women between ages of 18–22'.[13]

Social media marketing involves the use of social networks, online communities, blogs or any other online collaborative media for marketing, sales, public relations and customer service. The most commonly known social media marketing tools are Twitter, Facebook, LinkedIn, Flickr, Wikipedia and YouTube. Social media is a useful platform for marketing to individuals and groups of like-minded people. With these platforms, designers do not have to worry as much about the size of their marketing budget as they can take advantage of great, low-cost marketing opportunities by using social media as a tool; this means that instead of just being down to your budget, success can be determined by your creativity and persistence. By creating a professional Facebook page, using Twitter to tweet links to new products and competitions, Twitpic to share exciting images, LinkedIn to create a group for your brand or get recommendations for your company, or by blogging to provide further information and content about your products and activities, you can use social media for a multi-layered approach to connect with consumers.

CONNECT YOUR SOCIAL PLATFORMS

Connecting and linking your social media platforms where appropriate is a way to ensure that your marketing message is strengthened. This means that your platforms should be connected and linked where appropriate so that content feeds through to your multiple social network channels. For example, if you upload new content or a new video you can tweet about this and also blog about the content, whilst sharing the news with your Facebook page. Your tweets can be linked in by installing a widget

(a tool or content that you can add, arrange, and remove) onto your website and blog. Your LinkedIn page can also be connected to your blog and share your blog updates. When sharing content through each of the platforms be sure to give it a different spin so that the message is not repetitive. Each platform needs a different style of writing as bite-sized content suits Twitter but does not suit a blog as much. For example, if you write a detailed blog about your top five favourite season trends then you can tweet about two of the five and include a link to the full blog entry to find out the other three. Decide a strategy of sharing that is flexible and can change as your brand develops. See chapter 8 for more detail about connecting your social media platforms.

LET YOUR USERS DO THE TALKING

With social media you want your users to provide content in addition to your own so that your platforms are dynamic with lots of interaction, driving sales, marketing on your behalf and basically doing your promotion for you. For example, incorporating Facebook and Twitter 'share' buttons into your website is the minimum most brands do to ensure their customers can share thoughts and opinions on products. Constantly asking pertinent questions through these platforms, offering prizes for exchanges through your platforms (i.e. on Facebook, 'Like this page and tell us what you love about our new range to be in with a chance of winning a bag') and encouraging customers to share news about where they wore your brand, for example, are ways to get people talking about you.

BE PREPARED FOR HONEST OPINIONS

The very thing that makes social media exciting is also the same thing that makes it a scary prospect: its global reach. Facebook, for example, is a platform that currently has over one billion users and allows interaction between consumers and companies in the same community. Instead of coming to your website, visitors go to your Facebook space and interact with you and each other! A clothing label has no control over what its customers may say, and for this reason marketing using social media can be unsettling – you

I regularly use Twitter (@samataangel) to speak to fashion lovers, share news updates and as a networking tool.

are exposed and vulnerable to hearing the global voice that the world wide web provides. A brand may want to present a certain image of itself, but users have the right to disagree. Putting yourself out there with social media take confidence and strong products.

BE INSPIRED BY CLEVER IDEAS
In 2009, American Apparel used blog Chictopia (www.chictopia.com) to find models, using real people to model their product. This made their position in the market as being a brand for real people more believable. American Apparel is also famous for refusing to airbrush its models. Burberry's 'The Beat for Men' was, according to director Christopher Bailey, inspired by music, with various bands contributing to the perfume line including Kasabian and Razorlight, and hence has a Myspace page. Through the official Myspace page online friends could win bottles of the fragrance and exclusive prizes. Looking at innovative ideas online provides inspiration for a great idea of your own.

Branding

Branding is a combination of the images and attributes consumers associate with a product; getting it right is extremely important for the success of a clothing label. Clothing labels with strong branding are highly valued – an estimate by the British Fashion Council in 2010 placed the brand equity (the value of brand names) of the UK fashion industry at some £202 million per annum. Customers have relationships with the brands they buy and these brands evoke feelings and come with an assumed set of attributes. In a 2007 interview with the Wall Street Journal, Miuccia Prada, designer of the eponymous Italian fashion brand stated, 'For me, dressing is a versatile instrument that helps you express what's in your head and you have many different things in your head – a relationship with a man, with society. Sometimes you want to appear powerful, or serious or rich. All of us want to represent something. When you meet someone, among the instruments you have – like dialogue – you also have clothes.'[14]

The clothing people chose to wear is a personal statement, based on their personal preferences. When a consumer buys a brand, part of that buying decision is based on the feelings that brand has evoked within them. For example, in an article that appeared in *Vogue* US in March 2005 about British-born duo Georgina Chapman and Keren Craig of Marchesa, the womenswear brand is described as follows, 'If Fashion Week is like high school, Marchesa is the prom queen. She doesn't even have to compete like everyone else—she just prettily reigns, laughing and waving naturally all the way down the runway in her custom Louboutins.'[15] Reading this analogy, you understand why the Marchesa brand could be described as evoking feelings of confidence, elegance, femininity and beauty in its target customer. Of wearing the brand to the 2010 Golden Globes, actress Olivia Wilde said to *ELLE. com* in November 2011, 'It was a showstopper. I drive a '58 Chevy, and when people see it they tend to stare and smile. It's something special, evocative of another era. I get the same reaction when I'm wearing a Marchesa.'[16]

As discussed earlier, the lifestyle of a fashion entrepreneur can be all consuming and some can really become 'one' with their brand, with their persona being closely linked to that of the brand. For example, when you think of the brands Versace and Ralph Lauren, you think of the clothing but also possibly about the designer themselves. Donatella Versace and Ralph Lauren both have public images which fit their respective brand image. The Lacoste brand and logo is a great example of branding meeting passion and lifestyle. The brand's crocodile logo comes from Rene Lacoste's nickname, 'The Crocodile', which he was given for his great tennis playing skills. A keen athlete Rene Lacoste introduced the now popular Lacoste tennis shirt in 1929[17] as a comfortable casual piece to play tennis in, a style which is instantly recognisable. In 'The Brand Gap: How to Bridge the Distance Between Business Strategy and Design', author Marty Neumeier (president of San Francisco think tank Neutron) says, 'It's not what you say it is. It's what they say it is.'[18] In the fashion industry people talk about brands based on what they have experienced with a brand in addition to what they have heard second hand. According to Keller and Fay (2010), quoted on www.bazaarvoice.com, 'The average consumer mentions specific brands over 90 times per week in conversations with friends, family, and co-workers'[19] while Manage Smarter (2009) notes '74 per cent are influenced by the opinions of others in their decision to buy the product in the first place'.[20] Getting your branding right can mean that your brand name is shared regularly and positively in these conversations.

An interesting take on branding is offering by blogger and brand enthusiast Nicole Armstrong, who defines it by four key elements that work together to influence how a brand is perceived:

- A guiding purpose – why does the brand exist? In the case of the Lacoste example the brand blossomed when it sought to provide a stylish and comfortable alternative tennis shirt alongside its other products.
- The value proposition – how this purpose benefits customers. By delivering wearable, high quality and casual sport shirts Lacoste shirts became a brand of choice for comfort and style.
- Reasons to believe – how do the brands actions convince customers to believe in them? What makes the customer believe the message? This could be through a positive sales experience

Identify yourself

A start-up designer needs to define their brand – a name, term, design, symbol, or any other feature that identifies their service or product as distinct from those of other sellers,[21] making it unique, memorable and instantly recognisable.

through to what customers read about the brand in magazines features or social media platforms online.

- The brand's personality – this represents the aesthetics of the brand – the logo, the brand colours, the messaging, etc. The personality ties everything together, ensuring a consistent presentation of the brand.[22]

What does your branding say? Does it say edgy? Patriotic? Classic? Powerful? Glamorous? Athletic? It must be consistent and ring true with the clothing you design and be both memorable and unique, but it must also be consistent.

LOGO

Your logo can be anything from words to a symbol, but it must be consistent. It should not be one colour on your website, another on your business card and something different on your clothing label. These changes will leave your audience confused and unsure about the true representation of your brand. When considering your logo, think carefully about font and colour. A simple font may be more suitable for a clothing label that focuses on a minimal aesthetic rather than something elaborate and ornate. Research has shown that just like sounds and scents, colours trigger behaviour and thoughts. Red, for example, is a colour which is arousing and stimulating, where as blue has the effect of lowering blood pressure, pulse and respiration rates.[23] There are also some associations that people have with colour, for example, black can suggest a modern or sophisticated feel, green seems to say organic and pink implies a girlish feel. Think about the brands which you instantly recognise – why are they so recognizable?

Sales

Clothing is currently sold through three major channels: premises (brick and mortar), the Internet and catalogues. Examples of brick and mortar channels include independent retailers, department stores, designer stores, markets and vintage shops/boutiques, websites such as ASOS.com and mywardrobe.com and British catalogue, Littlewoods. When determining the best sales avenue for you – online, through a stockist, through your own store, through catalogue or mail order – consider which sales avenue your type and style of clothing suits best? Consider if you are selling T-shirts, these might be sold online with more ease than tailored jackets. Will you retail through a combination of platforms? For example, will you sell your old stock through a boutique and your new stock online? Determining your sales avenue involves deciding where to sell, how to present your product to the customer and who will be involved in closing the sale; will it be you, a retailer or a web page? Do your research carefully as the platform you sell your clothing through plays a huge role in the success of your brand. I always advise emerging designers to start small by 'testing' the market. Designing a few strong pieces and either selling them online or trying to get them stocked in a boutique, shop or department store is a wise first step rather than launching into producing a large collection or trying to open a store. Some designers choose to sell through markets or pop-up shops meeting customers and selling to them directly. This way provides the designer with an opportunity to meet customers, hear feedback about their designs and also to answer questions.

Tips for choosing the right store

See for yourself

Ask yourself: would your target customers enjoy buying your clothing in this store? Do they already visit this store? How is the current merchandise displayed and what condition do you find it in? Does the quality of your garments meet that of the other brands the retailer is currently stocking? Does your price range sit well amongst the other brands the retailer sells? Does your target store retail the same general type of clothing that you are offering?

Location, location, location

Footfall through your choice retailer is important as a large number of customers passing through increases the chances of you selling your clothing. If your retailer is too far from the beaten path or does not do a good job of promoting itself people may not wander far enough to discover your brand, and sales could be slow or non-existent.

Visibility

How will your goods be displayed? It is important to see how your goods will be displayed, will they be well positioned so that customers can see them or will they be tucked away in the corner where no one would see them? When you visit your target retailer do you see what they have on offer with ease?

How are sales recorded?

It is important to know the process the store uses to track sales and pay designers. For obvious reasons it is better for you if the store has an accurate and electronic system to keep receipts and records of your sales. When you sell through consignment you get paid when the clothes sell and not if they don't. You will need to know when you will receive payment for the goods sold so that you are not waiting a long time for your money, hence a monthly statement of sales is a good idea.

How will your clothing be stored?

Finding out how your garments will be stored and displayed is important, as is determining who is liable for any damage to your goods. After handing them over (in mint condition) you should find out how the condition of your garments will be maintained until sale. Check if the store has insurance and if this is against theft or damage (for example by fire); if there is no coverage at all it is worth reconsidering stocking your clothes there, especially if they are delicate and high value.

Department stores and boutiques

Selling your brand through the right kind of department store gives you exposure and access to a large customer base, which is part of the reason so many designers target them. The large number of shoppers milling around in a department store on a Saturday is an inspiring visual for many designers. In many cases, department stores have more than one location (city or country) so success through one store can lead to other stores in the chain stocking your clothing. In addition, there is the added name credibility of selling through a department store, particularly one like Berdgoff Goodman, Saks or Selfridges. These are globally known and where your clothing could share hanger time with brands like Dolce & Gabbana, Philip Lim and Stella McCartney. Understandably it is not easy to get your brand taken on by these stores as there is so much competition amongst designers to get onto these shelves. Leading department stores include Harrods, Saks, Bergdoff Goodman, Saks Fifth Avenue, Barney's, Harvey Nichols, Neiman Marcus, House of Fraser, NK (Stockholm), Steen & Ströms (Oslo), Illum (Copenhagen), Magasin du Nord (Copenhagen), Liberty, Tad (Rome), Le Bon Marché and Takashimaya in New York.

But pros aside, there are some pertinent cons. Department stores drive a hard bargain, simply because they can and may not offer you the money you believe that your clothing warrants. But in exchange for the '...stocked at...' sticker, some designers believe it a worthwhile exchange. Large

department stores can not be as flexible with the brands they stock, partly because they buy larger quantities and mistakes can be very costly. For this reason boutiques and smaller retailers are a great (and less expensive) learning ground for start-up designers to sell and structure their order process efficiently before approaching department stores (if that is the end goal).

When selling through a boutique, due to its smaller size, you are more likely to be able to build a relationship with the owner/buyer. If you become a regular face in the boutique you can start getting to know the staff and even get advice on how to increase your chances of success. In a boutique you are less likely to be competing for the customers' attention against a host of household name brands. Here you are also more likely to be dealing with small quantities which is great when it comes to manageability but may also mean you are not making a reasonable living if you only have one stockist. For example, where a department store may order anything from 30–100 pieces per style a boutique may only opt for three.

Whichever route you decide to take you can start by making a contact list of target stockists (major department stores, small retailers, boutiques or websites). Do some thorough research about the right stockist for you. In the early stages of starting up a clothing label I would not encourage a start-up designer to try to set up a shop as I think there is a great amount of risk involved in this route for an emerging brand, including the cost of running a shop. Not many designers can afford this route but to the lucky ones who can I still suggest building up your presence first by stocking within other retailers or online.

Dealing with buyers

With a department store or a smaller retailer or boutique, it may take some time for you to even get the opportunity to show your collection to a buyer so be patient and of course, prepared. You are likely to need some proven history of sales before you will be considered, demonstrating that you will be commercial and that you can sell. This is important as

if taken on you may be positioned in the same store as brands that have been established for years and years, all vying for the customers' attention. You will need to demonstrate that your brand is not a flash in the pan (even if you are hot at the moment, they want to see you will be hot in the future too). You should be able to see why it is important that you are very honest with yourself – are your target stockists the right ones? Is your clothing the right fit? Can you afford to wait, in some cases for a few months for payment? If items were to fly off the shelves you would need to be able to respond to large orders, up to 300 pieces or more, and within tight delivery deadlines and longer payment terms.

Dealing with buyers can be a nerve wracking experience so see if you can build your confidence up first. Try starting online and looking for content through a simple search by typing 'How to talk to a fashion buyer' into a search engine for useful tips and interviews with fashion buyers. Videos, articles and interviews come up alongside useful how to guides. Fashion forums are also packed with advice about how to talk to buyers and YouTube has some great video content.

The smaller retailers will be more flexible. If you manage to get into a large department store off the bat and the goods miss the deadline, you'll lose the order.[24]

Accessories Designer Bliss Lau, who now has her line in more than 40 stores worldwide.

Alternatively, if this is really not your area then you can look for an agent to represent you and do the sales on your behalf or alongside you. An agent will take a cut of the sales generated but will have a great deal more experience and strong negotiation skills. In addition they could have strong relationships with buyers that could prove beneficial to you. Their understanding of the industry could also give you insider information about the best terms to negotiate with certain stores and if your target store is actually the best one for you. Whilst working for a clothing label at university I observed the relationship the CEO had with her agent and could clearly see that the agent loved the brand, was passionate about it and wanted to see it sell. This in turn inspired the CEO and gave her confidence that she had the right person representing her brand.

Making first contact

Once you have got contact details for the buyer – this can easily be done by calling up the stockist and requesting contact details – you will need to make a good first approach. It is important to contact buyers in a professional, informed and engaging way, whether by phone, in person or by email. My suggested route is by phone and then followed up with an email. When you are emailing them, read the content of your email back to yourself before you send it, check the spelling and avoid using abbreviations such as KIT (Keep In Touch) or KR (Kind Regards) – it is lazy. Visiting the store several times to understand if your range is well suited is necessary before you make contact – if a buyer does engage in conversation with you they will want to know you have made the effort to look at the store properly. Whichever first route of communication you take introduce yourself clearly, be engaging and passionate, offer to send over material and follow up. Buyers are used to high volumes of calls asking for the same thing – a moment of their time to pitch a product that would be 'perfect for the store'. Think long and hard about how are you going to be unique and stand out before you make contact and be respectful of the fact that they are likely to be busy. If they ask you to send an email, send it and follow up after a few days with a call to make sure the information got through. Some of the best advice I ever received was from one of my former mentors, Jenny Holloway (Fashion Capital Founder). She advised me to contact buyers early, between 08:30 and 10:30 but never on a Monday as they have either had a great weekend and are busy reordering or have had a terrible one and need to cancel orders so they are quite unhappy! Think about the best time of day in a week that you would want to take sales call – more likely than not you would hate a call at lunch time or when you are getting ready to go home. Keep in touch regularly via email or phone if the buyer does not show immediate interest and let them know what you have been doing. The buyer's job is to be on top of the 'what's hot' list of designers so have confidence when you approach them with the belief that you may have what they are looking for.

Rejection

Still, there is only so much that you can do, and after you have made contact and done all of the above, the ultimate decision rests with buyer so just be keen and confident and listen to any reservations they may have. In reality your clothing may not be a

An accessories designer showcases her work to buyers and press at a trade show.

good fit for the store you have in mind, and there is nothing wrong with asking for feedback. Even if you are told that your brand is not right you should still keep in touch with buyers to let them know of any developments with your label – get permission to add them to your mailing list for updates about your news and developments.

Meeting a Buyer

If you are invited to meet with a buyer, get excited and be well prepared! This invitation is a good sign. You should know your product inside and out, from price points to delivery time. You should also be fully clued up on the latest developments within the store (information you can easily get from just visiting the company website). Be prepared to answer questions about how your clothing is made, where and by whom; consider delivery, pricing, labelling, tagging, bagging and shipping questions you may be asked. The buyer needs to know that you can manage consistent production. If not, they will be placed in the position where your collection

may sell well and then be in demand, but cannot be replenished. If you can, take a model with you to wear your pieces for the buyer. Some clothing only really comes to life when it is on a human form.

You need to be able to negotiate a fair price so that you can cover your costs and where buyers can make the purchase profitable for the store's gross profit margin. There are different deals that you can negotiate with a buyer from getting a guarantee of an order and a down payment (if possible) with full payment upon on delivery of goods across to selling your garments through consignment. This is when a retailer stocks your clothing and gets a percentage from the sale of your items when they sell (which can range between 15–50% depending on type of merchandise and the store). If they do not sell after a certain period of time your goods will be removed from the shelves and returned to you. Most designers prefer the former option as it helps with cash flow to keep their business running.

Working with stockists

Once your collection has been bought this is not the end of the hard work. Some designers put their pieces in a stockist and then tend to leave it at that and hope for the best. It is important to promote any boutique you are associated with or that stocks your collection and show an interest in seeing it do well as a business. Get your marketing machine into overdrive to direct as much traffic as you can towards wherever your clothing is being sold. Getting stock and repeat orders delivered as quickly as possible is crucial; a stockist should not end up waiting for your stock if it is in demand because this means that they are losing money and so are you.

Online retail

In April 2011, it was revealed in the *Daily Telegraph* that the market research company, Mintel had reported that £4.3 billion worth of clothes were bought over the Internet in 2010, a growth of 152 per cent in the last five years, with over a third of consumers having bough some of their clothes online in the past year.

Over the past five years, sales of online fashion have exploded. What is more, growth is set to continue, by 2015, sales are expected to increase 45% to reach a staggering £6.9 billion.[25]

Nowadays a large number of fashion houses have dedicated departments specifically dealing with their online retail, placing as high a level of importance on their online presence as they do on the actual store (if they have physical store presence). The chances are if you search online for your favourite brands you will find a sophisticated website, high-resolution pictures of clothes (with the option of close-up) and links to social media platforms. Even if the brand does not sell a full collection online, chances are some items are available to purchase online.

Leading platforms for multi-brand online retail include ASOS.com, Mywardrobe.com and Netaporter.com. The online retail boom, spearheaded by fashion websites such as ASOS. com, provides emerging and established designers with the opportunity to access millions of online shoppers around the globe at any time, instantly. Instead of being limited by the geographic location of your store designers can target and reach customers who they may otherwise not have known existed. Also, due to the nature of the Internet and online transactions, designers can get a lot more information about who their customer is through simple means such as online surveys and mandatory questionnaires when a customer is placing an order. Cost and global reach are some of the strongest selling points in the case for online retail but this depends greatly on your planned strategy. For a large number of emerging fashion designers online retail provides a slightly less difficult and complex sales strategy and is a great introduction to the market, allowing them to build up a sales history. Selling online also allows some designers to feel that they have more control over the volume and pace at which their business grows.

You can keep up-to-date accounts of your online sales and develop your brand before trying to sell your clothing to a department store or boutique. Having proof of prior sales will help your business case if and when you decide to approach a retailer; you will be able to provide statistics such as the number of website views, the number of items bought in a day and sales figures to demonstrate your success. Whilst online retail can be a more manageable way for some designers to sell to customers when starting up efficiency and speed are very important. For example, when placing an order online a customer may expect a confirmation of that order within minutes and only a small amount of time can pass before that items needs to be delivered or the customer can lose trust. If you sell online through your own website you are selling directly to your customer and hence cutting out the middleman, however, you will have to ensure that your website is easy to find online and that it receives enough visitors to make this a profitable channel for you. Having your products sold through an online shop on your behalf can help your clothing receive more visibility if you chose the right platform A website like ASOS.com has 6.3 million registered users, so selling your brand through a popular platform such as this can provide a visible route to profitability, especially if the terms of trade are fair. Terms will vary from one platform to the next but designers may need to have a minimum number of styles to sell, pay a monthly fee each month and/or a commission on each sale. Terms are best found out by contacting the company.

If you decide to sell online through an online retailer you may be responsible for delivering the goods or your online retailer may have your goods in a warehouse and be in charge of distribution on your behalf. You will still need to compete with other sellers when retailing your goods online in some of the more popular online boutiques but for an emerging designer who cannot afford the market entry presented by department stores and shops, online retail is the perfect avenue to sell, even if there are some customers you will be miss out on (those who prefer to try on the clothing from a brand they do not know before buying or who do not feel comfortable buying online).

Check out these platforms for cool insight into the world of online retail for an emerging designer:

* Style Hive (Stylehive.com): a community of style leaders, bloggers and shoppers, into fashion, beauty, design, home, technology and travel.
* Fashion Design Blog (www.fashiondesignblog. com): a collection of fashion designers and design boutiques blogging and showcasing their collections.
* The Smashing Blog (www.smashingdarling.com/ blog): a blog which spotlights young fashion designers and also has some great interviews with up and coming designers. A great place to retail collections too.

Selling through your website

Let's be honest folks, we all know a website we would or would not buy from when we see it. If you are trying to sell online you only have a short period of time for visitors to trust your platform as a place they would be willing to spend their money, be drawn in to view your products, and to stay long enough to decide to buy. Many experts believe that your website has less than 60 seconds to capture a customer's interest so if your customer is still trying to figure out how to navigate five minutes after logging on your website has not been very effective! [26]

Websites: what works – what doesn't?

Tips for online retail success:

* Information should be easy to find; e.g. there is search facility and site map;
* Make sure you have full and visible contact information – ideally visible on every page;
* Include detailed information about products with high resolution images of clothing from different angles, or even better, runway video footage of clothing on a model;
* Ensure there is clear pricing information including delivery costs and returns policy;
* Give a clear description of garments' detailing, fabric and care instructions;
* Use a clear trusted payment channel such as Paypal;
* Set up a quick and easy payment process, e.g. buy now buttons;
* Make it easy to share information: tell a friend/join mailing list.

Bad websites are:

* Confusing;
* Filled with pop-ups;
* Hard to navigate and time consuming;
* Slow to load with too much flash;
* Lack sufficient information about products;
* Have spelling mistakes and error pages/message.

NOTES

1. James E. Grunig and Todd Hunt, *Managing Public Relations* (Orlando, FL: Harcourt Brace Jovanovich, 1984)

2. Fraser P. Seitel, *The Practise of Public Relations* (Upper Saddle River, NJ: Pearson Prentice Hall, 2007)

3. Courtney Blackman, in conversation with author

4. Uche Okonkwo, 'Luxury Brand and Celebrities; An Enduring Branding Romance', Brand Channel website, http://www.brandchannel.com/papers_review.asp?sp_id=1234; accessed 23 October 2012

5. Helen Jennings, in conversation with the author

6. Nick Ede, in conversation with the author

7. Stylophane website, http://stylophane.com/fbi/; accessed 12 January 2012

8. Marketing can be defined as 'the action or business of promoting and selling products or services, including market research and advertising'. From *Oxford Dictionaries* website, http://oxforddictionaries.com/definition/english/marketing; accessed 23 October 2012

9. Gary Armstrong, Philip Kotler, John Saunders and Veronica Wong, *Principles of Marketing* (Essex: Person Prentice Hall, 2008)

10. Naomi R. Henderson, 'Managing Moderator Stress: Take a deep breath. You can do this!' in *Marketing Research*, Vol. 21 Issue 1 (2009)

11. Charles W Lamb, Joseph H Hair and Carl McDaniel, *Marketing* (Australia: South Western College Publishing, 2000)

12. 'Marketing Plans and Strategy', http://marketing.about.com/cs/advertising/a/marketvsad/htm; accessed 31 October 2012

13. Adam Tschorn, 'All the Rage: New index ranks fashion brands by Facebook fans', *LA Times* website (5 February 2010), http://latimesblogs.latimes.com/alltherage/2010/02/stylophane-launches-facebook-fashion-fan-index.html; accessed 31 October 2012

14. *Wall Street Journal* website, 'Fashion is how you present yourself to the world', http://online.wsj.com/article/SB11690706575427937.html; accessed on 5 July 2012

15. *Voguepedia* website, 'Brands: Marchesa', http://www.vogue.com/voguepedia/Marchesa; accessed 12 November 2012

16. Sarah Bernard, 'Meet Marchesa's Glamorous Designers', *ELLE.com* (18 November 2011), http://www.elle.com/fashion/spotlight/meet-marchesas-glamorous-designers-610190; accessed 12 November 2012

17. Wikipedia, 'Lacoste', http://en.wikipedia.org/wiki/Ren%C3%A9_Lacoste; accessed 31 October 2012

18. Marty Neumeier, 'The Brand Gap: How to Bridge the Distance Between Business Strategy and Design', http://www.slideshare.net/coolstuff/the-brand-gap; accessed 12 November 2012

19. Bazaarvoice website, 'Social Commerce Statistics', http://www.bazaarvoice.com/social-commerce-statistics; accessed 5 July 2012

20. Bazaarvoice website, 'Social Commerce Statistics', http://www.bazaarvoice.com/social-commerce-statistics; accessed 5 July 2012

21. Wikipedia, 'Brand', http://en.wikipedia.org/wiki/Brand; accessed 5 July 2012

22. *More than a logo* blog by Nicole Armstrong (26 May 2009) http://www.morethanalogoblog.com/2009/05/branding-is-more-than-logo.html; accessed 12 November 2012

23. Mattias Behrer and Joeri Van Den Bergh, *How Cool Brands Stay Hot: Branding to Generation Y* (London: Kogan Page, 2011)

24. *CNN Money* website, 'How fashion designers break into boutiques', http://smallbusiness.blogs.cnnmoney.cnn.com/2009/01/15/how-to-fashion-designers-break-into-boutiques; accessed 31 October 2012

25. Mintel Press Release, 'Online fashion clicks with Brits as market increases 152% over past five years', http://www.mintel.com/press-centre/press-releases/695/online-fashion-clicks-with-brits-as-market-increases-152-over-past-five-years; accessed 31 October 2012

26. International Cyber Business Services, 'Techniques to Improve your Web Site', http://icbs.com/techniques-to-improve-websites.htm; accessed 31 October 2012

27. Balderton Capital website, 'my-wardrobe.com announces Series A funding led by Balderton Capital', http://www.balderton.com/news/my-wardrobe-com-announces-series-a-funding-led-by-balderton-capital-374; accessed 31 October 2012

28. The Times 100 Business Case Studies website, http://www.thetimes100.co.uk/case-study--strategic-growth-in-the-fashion-retail-industry--134-325-4.php

Case Study

my-wardrobe.com

Launched in 2006 my-wardrobe.com is now one of the UK's leading online retailer of 'accessible luxury' designer fashion, with reportedly 100% revenue growth in recent years.[27] According to founder Sarah Curran, 'my-wardrobe.com is an innovative brand which was first-to-field with the click-to-buy video content through my-tv.' The site receives over 800,000 online visitors each month.

Retailing a comprehensive range of 'accessible luxury' womenswear and menswear ranges including brands such as Anya Hindmarch, Vivienne Westwood Anglomania, Mulberry and Phillip Lim, the company manages to retail luxury and high end clothing and accessories through a medium which usually finds it easier to sell lower-cost fashion. This could be because it was thought by many retailers that customers would not want to or would not be sufficiently confident to spend large amounts of money on products in this category online. However, my-wardrobe's

success has proved this wrong. Some clear areas where my-wardrobe.com excels are through the products they offer, the online customer experience and their online marketing strategy. mywardrobe.com only sells current season collections and may offer a selection of sale items but never at full price. The online user experience is part of the answer to the big question of why someone would choose to buy online instead of in a store. The site provides ease of contact, good customer service (available from 9am–6pm), clear terms and conditions, and an online shopping experience that is easy, clear and interactive. It has quick-to-load content and the images are clear, high resolution and give users have the option of zooming in.

Another innovation is the use of runway video footage which allows customers to see the clothing moving on a real person. Customers are able to filter through searches by key fields such as colour, style and size; they feel more in control as they

are able to use tracking tools to trace orders and track their orders online. To manage its relationship with customers my-wardrobe.com delivers editorial content through its blog, an online magazine and through regular communications with those who opt in for newsletter update.Its success to date has also ensured that my-wardobe.com has been able to secure further funding and investment to ensure the company's growth. To date the site receives over 800,000 visitors each month.[28]

Sarah Curran is the entrepreneur behind the success of my-wardrobe.com. She worked in the fashion industry as a boutique owner and a growing interest in business online encouraged her to set up my-wardrobe.com. 'Before I launched my-wardrobe.com I had a boutique in Crouch End, North London and my focus was always offering beautifully edited collections with an exceptional experience. I wanted this to be the same with my-wardrobe.com, from aspirational

styling, informative editorial and styling advice, exciting, yet authoritative magazine-style features, knowledgeable style advisors and an easy return service. We have always made sure that all of these elements are in place to reassure and build trust in mywardrobe.com and in turn loyalty to the site.'

When asked what characteristic you need to survive in the fashion industry Sarah said, 'One characteristic you need to survive in this industry? Self belief. I would say that I have always had an absolute belief in the business and the opportunity that was there in the online retail market. That belief was essential for those challenging days at the beginning raising money in the investment, but also helped to drive the passion and belief in the business among the team.'

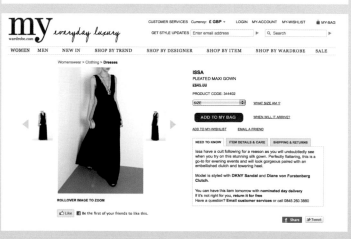

Screen shots courtesy of my-wardrobe.com

CHAPTER 8

HOW ARE YOU CONNECTING WITH THE WORLD? GETTING ONLINE

Social media and the fashion industry

Social media is 'media for social interaction, using highly accessible and scalable publishing techniques.'[1] It is extremely important and relevant in this day and age to understand social media and master it. In the fashion industry social media is used by everyone and anyone for a multitude of reasons including connecting with like-minded individuals, increasing brand visibility, increasing sales, reaching new customers and sharing a message or communicating. When you take a step back and think about the role that social media plays within in our daily lives, the figures alone are quite overwhelming. Currently Facebook has over one billion active users. LinkedIn, Twitter, Facebook, YouTube, Flickr and blogs are familiar to most people. Social media in its different forms also includes Wikipedia, Photobucket, Picassa, Xanga, Foursquare, Google Buzz, ASmallWorld and XING. Professors of Marketing at the business school ESCP Europe Andreas Kaplan and Michael Haenlein classified social media as being 'a group of Internet based applications that build on the ideological and technological foundations of Web 2.0, and that allow the creation and exchange of user generated content.'[2] These different types of social media can be grouped to include collaborative projects, blogs and micro-blogs, content communities, social networking sites, virtual game worlds, and virtual communities. Nowadays everyone from international organisations to schools, politicians, celebrities and you and I use these various platforms. Most fashion houses for example have at least a Twitter, Facebook and blog presence, with a number having a YouTube channel and Wikipedia page. These media platforms can give fashion designers and fashion entrepreneurs the opportunity to talk about their passions and to connect globally with the industry including students, models, photographers, professionals, editors, journalists and other like-minded people.

Being important on social media platforms

As with all forms of networking, being present and relevant depends on being committed and passionate to get the most out of it, whatever your motivations are. With all social media platforms, followers and fans are important, as is being able to engage people and get them talking. The 'likes' and 'fans' are important but a more powerful measure is the number who communicate and talk to you or your brand. Finding your voice online is key to being able to use the social media platforms listed below for networking. According to FreshNetworks. com 'it is typically better … to have 1 million fans, of which 5% engage with you on a regular basis, than to have 2 million fans with less than 1% engaging'.[3]

159

It is relatively easy for a person or brand to pick up numbers of 'likes', followers and fans with enough consistent communication, it is more difficult to get them to actually do something and to engage with you – i.e. pick up comments and feedback. Facebook, blogs, Twitter and customer reviews are considered the most effective tactics for mobilizing consumers to talk up products online.[4]

Key social media platforms

FACEBOOK

Millions of us use Facebook every day to keep up with friends, family and peers, upload images, share thoughts, videos and links, and learn more about the people in our personal and professional circles. In addition through most social media platforms, users are able to create and join interest groups and 'like' pages, some of which are maintained by organisations as a means of advertising. Like many working within the fashion industry, I have a professional and personal friends' page and

---

Top tips for networking with social media

- Be active;
- Give to receive – engage with others;
- Behave well;
- Have an opinion/be interesting;
- Research and look for people, search them out;
- Touch base with people, with no agenda;
- Give credit to your sources/be honest;
- Make sure all your social media is aligned with each other.

---

recommend other designers doing the same. As much as you may want to share your everyday thoughts and images with your friends, you may not want a photographer you have recently worked with to see a picture of you singing into your hairbrush. You need to decide what you want to share about yourself and with whom, which is why I definitely advocate creating clear groups. Social media platforms are discussed later with regards to advertising and marketing, but specifically when it comes to networking, these platforms provide an incomparable global reach and opportunity to build relationships with the industry you love, from your computer.

Which fashion brands rule the Facebook roost?
Observing and studying how certain fashion brands use Facebook can give you ideas about how to get the most of the platform. A great way of finding out about the leading fashion brands doing it the right way is by their ranking on social media platforms such as Facebook. This can now be done through the Stylophane Facebook Fashion Index, viewed online for free at stylophane.com/fbi. Launched by a San Francisco-based online marketing firm it shares monthly data, tracking the online popularity of fashion brands by Internet search. The index compiles data on a daily basis; measuring percentage increases or decreases in the number of fans compared to the previous month. The information can be sorted by name, number of fans and change in percentage of fans with direct links to the brands Facebook pages also being provided. As brands go up or down the index, this news is communicated.

LINKEDIN

LinkedIn is a business-networking site, which allows users to maintain a list of contacts they trust and know in business, and to invite others to connect. It is a useful site for emerging fashion designers to use as a means to connect with anyone working in the industry. In addition to useful contacts such as editors, buyers, journalists and merchandisers, fashion designers are also on this platform. Users are

Case Study

Burberry as a Facebook fashion brand

As of January 2012 Burberry was the highest ranked luxury brand on Facebook, followed closely by Gucci, Chanel, Dolce & Gabbana. Burberry has achieved this status through a strategic digital marketing strategy and heavy investment in online media, accounting for 40% of Burberry's marketing budget.[5]

If you visit the Burberry Facebook page you will see that it has regular communication through product announcements and photos, along with probing and pertinent questions asking fans regularly to give feedback and opinions therefore driving user-generated content. One example of this is the CEO to customer level relationship. In October 2010 Christopher Bailey, Chief Creative Officer of Burberry, posted a video message requesting questions and feedback on Burberry's Facebook wall, which was later responded to via video. Questions were asked about the brand's strategy in India in addition to exclusive insight being shared into Christopher's personal life and how the brand juggled modernizing itself whilst remaining traditional.[6] The original upload generated 137 comments and his response received 1,656 people likes and 75 comments.

able to build up a network of direct contacts and, through recommendations, network with connections from their existing circle (known as second-degree connections) and further. By creating an online profile through LinkedIn you are able to showcase your fashion industry experience with the collaborative input from your industry peers who can comment on your work through recommendations. LinkedIn can be used for anything from looking for a job to sourcing a manufacturer; you can also search for and join some very industry specific groups.

TWITTER

Described by some as online texting, Twitter offers a social networking and micro-blogging service. Using Twitter you are able to send tweets – messages of up to 140 characters – which display on your profile page. Tweets are fun and easy because they are online short conversations and a good way to ease into networking online. You can follow others by subscribing to their tweets and your subscribers are known as your followers.[7] Twitter can be used for networking, particularly by using searches for topics and areas of interest such as fashion design. For example, users can group posts together by topic or type by using hash tags, which are words or phrases prefixed with a # (for example #fashionlover, #fashiondesigner). Users can also message users with the @, or mention and reply to users on topics of interest. Some users provide the option of you sending them direct private messages. Once you have identified people you would like to interact with on Twitter such as fashion magazines, designers, bloggers and journalists you can use these methods to talk to them and engage with their conversation online.

Case Study

Increasing your twitter followers

by Kairi Soosaar, PR and New Media Consultant, @PRKairi

There are many ways to increase your followers on Twitter. Here are a few:

1. Every tweet you send, think of it as an opportunity to you market yourself but also to connect with people you may otherwise never have the chance to meet.

Personal tweets to people with @ mentions are great but when you do that, if possible do a retweet, then edit it so that others can also see what you are replying to. The best tool to do this with is the app TweetDeck.

Example: Tweet: @SamataAngel I love your design on this dress <link>.
Then you reply like this: Thank you, I'm glad you liked it! RT:@ PRKairi @SamataAngel I love your design on this dress <link>.

That way, others who follow you or me, will all get to click on the link to see the design that I loved so much. Easy step, but goes a long way.

2. Make a schedule for yourself showing how often you want to tweet things out. When you have a blog post out or an article, you can send that out multiple times. You shouldn't share the content on the same day repeatedly but you can send out the same message over a couple of days, once a day. It's important that people don't think you are spamming them. Three tweets a day is an optimal number. Even if you don't have any news, just tweet something that you observed, or a link from your past, or a link to one of your dresses asking, 'Where would you wear this dress?' Also, whenever someone tweets at you, reply as soon as possible. It shows you are connected and interested in what people say about you. Always try to promote discussion, if you just say 'Thanks', that ends the conversation. Better, would be

'What detail did you like the most about it?', which creates an ongoing conversation. Again, don't forget linking to content shared through other platforms!

3. To make links shorter so that I can write more text on Twitter, I use a free URL shortening and bookmarking service called bit.ly. You input the longer length tweet and it gets shortened for you.

4. When you tweet about fashion you can use hashtags, to highlight the topic of conversation. There are many to choose from and you can make your own up as well. But if you use hashtags that are pretty generic, like #fashion, #ukfashion, #eufashion, #dress, #gown etc., your tweets will end up in the stream that people follow about fashion. Fashion hashtags are an effective way to get more followers because they open you up to more

continued at bottom of p.163 (opposite)

YOUTUBE

As a means of networking, YouTube is a great platform for the visual and audio. Founded in February 2005, it allows people to discover, watch and share originally created videos.[8] Once you have created a YouTube profile you can subscribe to other users' channels, send direct messages and comment on videos. You can also share these videos with people on other social media platforms. When you create a video, label your video by category when you upload it to make it easier to find. You can also add keyword tags to individual videos such as 'fashion' or more specific words such as 'size zero debate' before you share your content. By supplying user-generated video content and personalising their channels, users can express themselves freely (as long as the content does not blatantly infringe on any copyright laws). To network on this platform you have to encourage dialogue. As great as it is to get comments you also need to comment on other people's videos and share your thoughts as this actually encourages sharing and further comments on yours. One way to do this is to use the reply to button, which allows you to reply to a video that a user has uploaded with your opinions and comments, automatically creating a linked network. Other users may see your opinion and agree/disagree and respond to you and so the cycle continues.

This is a simple way to engage and communicate using YouTube as a networking tool. YouTube was originally seen as a platform for amateur filmmakers and artists to showcase their talents but nowadays it is more sophisticated, with fashion brands and individuals using it in a range of ways, from responding to catwalk videos about collections to putting a face and voice to an opinion. The Dolce & Gabbana YouTube channel – http://www.youtube.com/user/dolcegabbanachannel – is a great example of what can be done with a fashion

continued on p.164

163

How are you connecting with the world? Getting online

people seeing your tweets (i.e. not just your followers but people who follow #fashion). Try not to overuse them on every tweet as this can break up the conversation.

Here are examples of different uses of the hashtag:

Coming to the end of a tiring week, at least next week is going to be exciting #londonfashionweek
Just met @flygirll on route to #londonfashionweek
Do you have your outfits lined up? #londonfashionweek

5. You could start a weekly or monthly Twitter chat about fashion, announcing the date and time on your Twitter stream. Also invite friends from your Facebook to join the chat and you can add a hashtag such as #fashchat on your tweets. You can make up, say, five questions for the hour of chat, and then the conversation will just flow. It is also a great way to find out what your followers like, what they'd like you to create and so on. They are your customers but you can be their fashion guide!

6. You can also add yourself to http://listorious.com, a Twitter people search on the web that enables you to find anyone by topic, region or profession. You can find people on there that you'd like to follow in the fashion world, or people who are interested in fashion, and start following them. Later, when you see that you have somehow started to follow way too many people, you can then use http://www.justunfollow.com to 'unfollow' the people who don't follow you.

7. Remember, Twitter is a very conversational tool. If you slack in posting and communicating your influence score goes down. You can check your influence score on www.klout.com

The author being interviewed for the London College of Fashion YouTube channel.

brand. The brand uploads content such as behind-the-scenes fashion week and photoshoot videos, live streaming of runway shows, designer interviews, interviews with models and party footage. The range of dynamic content uploaded encourages debate and conversation on the YouTube channel not just between the brand and users but also between users. The timely upload of runway footage during fashion week season is a good example of how releasing a video at the right time can encourage conversation. In the same way, individuals can release videos when hot or controversial topics are being discussed, for example, offering opinions on industry news.

Fashion blogs

Fashion blogs provide online content about a range of fashion topics from runway style, trends across different markets and countries, celebrity style, fashion editorial photographs and much more. You can share anything through this platform, from your

thoughts and opinions about the fashion industry, to addressing key issues and letting your voice be heard, to critiquing street style, to showcasing some of your work.

Blogs give you a voice on the world wide web and if you are good at it you can actually make money from your blog through advertising revenue; some blogs make up to £10,000 a month in advertising. Krista Peck, the Co-Founder/Chief Creative Officer of Atelier 36, a consultancy founded in 2011 that focuses on digital solutions for the luxury, fashion, beauty, and lifestyle industries, gives these guidelines for creating great blog content:

- be authentic;
- use a consistent tone;
- provide sources;
- write effectively

To establish yourself in the blogosphere you should aim to have unique content, voice your opinion and stand by it, be a little brave or outspoken occasionally, and always be yourself. You can use the comments and feedback from your users as a general suggestion to gauge what content works and what doesn't whilst still maintaining a strong direction for your blog. What should visitors expect when they visit your blog? What is the purpose of your blog existing? This should be visibly stated on your blog, for example a one-liner like 'For those of us who love to collect designer shoes', or something more original! Think about what your readers will love, which posts will be popular and why? Before starting a blog one good suggestion I was given was to sketch a diagram with the core focus of the blog in the middle and listing the categories and posts around the centre, to structure it.

To develop your network you can find blogs that you like and comment on them encouraging conversation between yourself, the blogger and other followers of the blog. When you post comments you can share your name and the URL for your blog. Guest blogging (writing for other blogs) is also a way to reach a wider audience. Take your time and think

The Sartorialist

Fashion photo blog The Sartorialist – www.thesartorialist.com – was born in 2005 out of founder Scott Schuman's desire to simply share photos of people who he saw on the streets of New York, the real people. This street style photography was seen as a pioneering and innovative way to observe and discuss fashion. Schuman had prior experience in sales and marketing, having opened his own showroom showcasing young designer collections. Starting out with the aim to shoot people, 'the way designers looked at people, and get and give inspiration to lots of people in the process,' his blog is now the leading fashion blog in the world for unique street style. To date Scott Schuman has created a street style campaign for DKNY, run a monthly page in GQ and recurring guest blogs and videos for Style.com. Scott also teamed up with Facebook to create a social networking fashion blog centred solely around the Burberry trench coat where visitors can comment and share opinions on the images, http://artofthetrench.com. In three days more than 100,000 people had joined the site.[9]

From a company brand perspective, blogs are brilliant tools for brands to build a web presence, relationships and to promote their products and services. *Vogue*, for example, currently features a blog hub with content from the likes of Savannah Miller, Henry Holland and David Gandy. *Vogue*'s 'Fashion Night In' was a great way for *Vogue*, bloggers and fashion followers to have a concentrated period of communication and shopping. *Vogue* teamed up with a number of retailers with live-blogging through the night with exclusive designer discounts and online-only offers which could be snapped up by any device with connection to the Internet.

about what you want to blog about; don't just push anything out there – quality posts are better than a quantity of posts. Having said that blogs need to be regularly updated to stay relevant so always think about what great content you can share. I am always writing any ideas I have down in my notes whenever they come to me and even if I can not think of the best way to share them then and there I give them thought and time to take shape. Setting yourself a goal of say two posts a week can be a good way to ensure you keep your blog dynamic but also keeping things manageable at your end. I believe that individual fashion blogs should mix fashion content with a personal edge so that people get a true sense of the person behind the blog and why you love blogging.

Sometimes less is more. It is not all about bells and glitter and flash html, some of the most amazing blogs look effortlessly simple and are clutterless such as the leading fashion blog The Sartorialist. The story behind The Sartorialist goes to show how a blog can be used to gain visibility within the fashion industry and become an influencer, in addition to how blogging can create opportunities in different areas.

Some of my favourite fashion blogs

THE CLOTHES WHISPERER

www.theclotheswhisperer.co.uk

This blog is run by Kristin Knox, a successful international fashion blogger and journalist with a masters degree in Classical Literature from the University of Oxford, whose work experiences include working as a stylist at Vogue Russia and Glamour. I love her because she has a lot of charisma. I quote from her bio: 'I'm a sardonic and sarcastic, half-Japanese, quarter-Danish, 100 per cent type A-New Yorker-turned-Londoner, academic-turned fashionista taking her first steps in the outside world beyond the ivory towers with a pint-size Pomeranian tucked in my Louis Vuitton and a bounce in my Margiela-obsessing hopefully Louboutin-shod step'. Kristin also wrote the stunning tribute book, Alexander McQueen, Genius of a Generation.

THE STYLE ROOKIE

www.thestylerookie.com

Tavi Gevinson started out at the tender age of eleven, featuring analysis of magazines and photographs of her daily outfits on her blog. The content looked so professional that most people were blow away when they discovered that it was maintained by such a young person. In addition to gracing the front row for countless shows during New York Fashion Week with editors and celebrities seated behind her, Gevinson has modelled for the Rodarte label, been on the cover of Pop magazine and interviewed by Love.

WHAT KATIE WORE

www.whatkatiewore.com

This blog started with the simple idea of Katie Mackay wearing a different outfit each day for a year and her boyfriend Joe Sinclair documenting these. After just one year in January 2010, the blog had maintained momentum and blossomed, reaching 7,000 hits a day.[10] I love the originality of this blog idea and the fact that a regular person's individual style can warrant so much interest. When the couple ended their blog on 1st October 2012 Joe signed off with the following text, 'Since we started this thing way back in 2009 the missus has worn over 1,000 different outfits and been seen by more than 5 million people in over 100 countries. Not bad going for something that started as a bet after Katie complained about me never writing her any love letters. I reckon I've now won that bet.'

STYLE BUBBLE

www.stylebubble.typepad.com

One of the most popular fashion blogs, this is run by Susanna Lau, a former University College London graduate who was headhunted by Dazed and Confused fashion magazine. It has around 600 clicks per month.

FASHION TOAST

www.fashiontoast.com

A personal style and fashion blog from southern California by blogger Rumi Neely, popular for her style and photography. She began her site in 2007 and combined it with an eBay vintage store called 'Treasure Chest Vintage'.

How to manage your social media platforms

On the face of it there is a social media platform for practically any need you may have but finding the time to manage them all can be the real problem. With established fashion brands online social media presence is usually maintained and updated by the marketing and customer relations team, but if you are just starting out and have very little budget then you could find yourself on your own. Social network aggregation is the process of collecting content from multiple social network services, such as Myspace or Facebook. The task is often performed by a social network aggregator, which pulls together information into a single location,[11] or helps a user consolidate multiple social networking profiles into one profile.

FriendFeed which is an easy to use social networking aggregator allowing you to share content from one place to a range of sites including Facebook, Flickr and Twitter, also integrated with blogs.

ping.fm prevents users having to post the same content individual to all of their various social media platforms. Instead you can send a message to any of your social media profiles across the web with one update.

TweetDeck works specifically with Twitter and also integrates with Facebook making it easier to manage your tweets, local trends and messages.

NOTES

1. Wikipedia, 'Social Media', http://en.wikipedia.org/wiki/Social_media; accessed 31 October 2012

2. Michael Haenlein and Andreas M. Kaplan, 'Users of the world, unite! The challenges and opportunities of Social Media' in *Business Horizons* Vol. 53 Issue 1 (2010)

3. Matt Rhodes, 'The Top Ten Brands on Facebook', Fresh Networks website (10 June 2010), http://www.freshnetworks.com/blog/2010/06/the-top-ten-brands-on-facebook/; accessed 13 November 2012

4. E-tailing Group, '1st Annual Community and Social Media Survey', the E-tailing Group website (September 2009), http://www.e-tailing.com/content/?m=200909; accessed 13 November 2012

5. Burberry page, Facebook, http://www.facebook.com/burberry#; accessed 31 October 2012

6. Jessica Salter, 'Britain's Best Fashion Bloggers', Telegraph.co.uk (21 January 2010), http://fashion.telegraph.co.uk/beauty/news-features/TMG7037668/Britains-best-fashion-bloggers.html; accessed 13 November 2012

7. Wikipedia, 'Twitter', http://en.wikipedia.org/wiki/Twitter; accessed 31 October 2012

8. Youtube, http://www.youtube.com/t/about_youtube

9. Jessica Salter, 'Britain's Best Fashion Bloggers', Telegraph.co.uk (21 January 2010), http://fashion.telegraph.co.uk/beauty/news-features/TMG7037668/Britains-best-fashion-bloggers.html; accessed 13 November 2012

10. Alice Fisher, 'The 10 best... Fashion Bloggers', *The Observer* (21 February 2010), http://www.guardian.co.uk/culture/2010/feb/21/10-best-fashion-bloggers; accessed 31 October 2012

11. Wikipedia, 'Social network aggregation', http://en.wikipedia.org/wiki/Social_network_aggregation; accessed 31 October 2012

RESPONSIBLE FASHION

Social responsibility is an ethical ideology or theory that an entity, be it an organisation or individual, has an obligation to act to benefit society at large.[1]

Can a designer create with compassion for people and the planet? This is a question being asked with increasing frequency in the face of a glaringly obvious fact – that our resources on this planet are finite. Currently the fashion industry is producing, consuming and throwing away at a quite terrifying rate. One single, shocking statistic is that in 2009 in the UK ,over two million tonnes of fashion were thrown away, items which were worn on average just six times.[2] Can we, as designers, place as much importance on the resources we use and what happens to them when we are finished, as we do on designing creative and exciting fashion? I believe so.

Left: Author with entrepreneur and former model Suzy Amis Cameron, wearing sustainable fashion by Lindee Daniel.

It is food for thought when you consider the following:

- Clothing is now cheaper than any time in history, largely driven by demand for fast, as opposed to slow, fashion;
- We are producing more clothing than ever before – now some brands often have up to 6 collections each year (in addition to S/S and A/W);
- There is demand for a faster turnaround from clothing manufacturers, with lead times down from 3–4 months to as little as 28 days;
- Quicker productions often mean a lower quality product, which is easier to discard;
- The large scale offender is cheap and fast fashion where the real costs (financial, people and planet) tend to be carried at the start of the supply chain – with the manufacturers.

In the face of pressing issues such as climate change and material and water scarcity, it is time for designers to think about the future of the fashion industry. An organisation that has helped me to understand the key aspects of what I call 'responsible fashion' is the Cradle to Cradle Products Innovation Institute (http://c2ccertified.org/product_certification), which uses a rating system to assess how safe and healthy a product is for humans and the environment, based upon the five categories listed overleaf.

1. safe and appropriately sourced materials;
2. material reutilization;
3. renewable energy;
4. release of clean water; and
5. social fairness.

When applied to clothing production this means:

- The fabrics used need to be safe i.e. not manufactured with toxic chemicals;
- The fabrics should be able to be reused and there must be consideration of how to dispose waste material;
- How manufacturing is powered must be considered (reduction of carbon footprint for example, through use of hand sewing where possible, or a solar powered manufacturing unit);
- The quality of water used and released must be considered;
- There must be a socially responsible approach to manufacturing, i.e. how well the manufacturers are treated and paid.

AN EXAMPLE: WHY DOES MATERIAL HEALTH MATTER?

The manufacture of conventional cotton over organic cotton uses more water, releases more CO$_2$ and often puts the cotton farmers at risk. The pesticides used to grow conventional cotton are often dangerous and when these are released into the environment often result in a range of illnesses from numbness of legs, feet to a worse case scenario, infertility, for the farmers and local community.[3]

Sustainable and eco-fashion terminology

Terms we often hear in the same breath as sustainable fashion are 'social responsibility' and 'fairtrade'. Why? Well if you read the definitions you can see why both are a hugely important part of sustainability within fashion. Social responsibility is an important element of the business model for many designers, impacting their creative and business decisions, such as which materials (organic, natural,

sustainable) are sourced and where these are sourced (locally, internationally). For some designers creating fashion responsibly means designing clothes which are not part of the fast, throwaway fashion group, i.e. cheap clothing which lasts for only a few wears, but clothing that can be endlessly recycled and worn. For others social responsibility can mean ensuring there is complete visibility along the supply chain so that consumers can find out all about the process, from where fabrics are bought, to the conditions existing in the manufacturing premises and how the clothing is transported.

Fairtrade is a term often used in close association with social responsibility, as by definition 'fairtrade is about better prices, decent working conditions, local sustainability, and fair terms of trade...'.[4] In the UK, the Fairtrade mark, which can be seen on some garments is an independent consumer label, acting as a guarantee for meeting internationally agreed Fairtrade standards. The mark indicates that the product has been certified to give a better deal to the producers. As a designer you would think that it should go without saying that you would try to ensure that producers are paid fairly but so much of the time designers are trying to cut already high costs and this important consideration falls in the wayside. It is an issue we can all do much more to address.

THE FACTS: WHY IS FAIRTRADE NEEDED?

A large amount of the clothing for sale in the Western world is made in Bangladesh where clothing exports account for 70% of the GPD. The industry is responsible for 3 million jobs yet as of 2010 the minimum wage was just 1,662 taka/month = 80 cents/day.

Sustainable fashion is part of a growing design philosophy and trend of sustainability, which supports environmental and social responsibility. Sustainable design is where a product is created and produced with consideration for the environment and the social impact the garment has throughout its product life cycle. The term 'eco-fashion' is often used interchangeably with 'sustainable fashion', however sustainable fashion places emphasis on renewable and sustainable design. Sustainable fashion can refer to recycling and non-waste fashion such as vintage or using fabric made from renewable sources (such as bamboo or soy). Eco-fashion, on the other hand, is often applied when the fabric or materials used are harvested with little or minimal negative impact on the environment/eco-system, for example, minimal use of harmful chemicals and pesticides or little waste of water. Eco-fashion can also be used to describe clothing made from organic fabrics (all-natural, non-synthetic materials) such as organic cotton, organic silk and hemp. If manufactured in the right way, these fabrics can do minimal damage to the environment, for example, by not exposing humans and animals to chemicals, or by not damaging the earth when thrown away. The Organic Trade Association in the USA and Canada is the membership-based business association for the organic industry in North America which plays an important role in shaping

the regulatory and market environment for organic products. The official website is a useful resource for organic facts and definitions: www.ota.com.

Although the definitions and understanding of eco-fashion and sustainable fashion may differ greatly in discussion, it is clear that both terms refer to fashion that avoids being wasteful of natural resources and damaging to the environment or 'fast throwaway'.

CASE STUDY: ECO-FASHION BRAND PEOPLE TREE

An example of a sustainable and eco-fashion clothing brand is PeopleTree, who creates organic clothing and accessories by forming partnerships with organic producers in developing countries. People Tree works to ensure that the people involved in the production process – growing cotton, weaving, dyeing, embroidery, stitching etc. are fairly paid and treated. The brand champions the use of eco-

friendly production methods and only uses natural and recycled material, which is dyed using natural dyes. In addition to careful fabric selection the brand also designs garments which can be produced by hand rather than machinery as much as possible, so that their products have minimal carbon-footprints. The label also runs a number of organic cotton programs to help ensure that farmers and the local communities are not exposed to the pesticides used in conventional cotton manufacturing. According to People Tree's website, 'if there's a green way to do something, that's the way we try to do it', and this includes shipping more than 98 per cent of their clothing by sea when possible.
www.peopletree.co.uk

How can a start-up designer incorporate sustainable or eco-fashion values?

Start-up designers can make changes to their activities even on a small and affordable scale, so that they can contribute to positive change within the industry and adopt a more sustainable approach to design. This might include:

- Using a sampling process that uses a 'no-waste' pattern where little fabric is thrown away or wasted;

- Using hand sewing as much as possible and hence reducing the carbon footprint;

- Using fabrics that have been manufactured with minimal impact to environment;

- Avoiding or reducing the use of synthetic fibres;

- Using natural, chemical free or low-impact (azo-free) dyes;

- Reducing the length of the supply chain and hence reducing the carbon footprint – this can be done by sourcing fabrics locally or reducing the number of locations a garment has to travel to and from;

- Reusing and recycling surplus materials such as fabrics and trim instead of throwing away.

For a start-up designer, manufacturing may involve input from companies in different locations and time zones – fabric could come from India, tags, labels and packaging from China, clothing may be manufactured in the UK and packaging supplied by a company in Italy. It is easy to see how challenging it can be to ensure that all production is done in an environmentally friendly way and that at every stage of clothing development there are fairtrade processes if manufacturing is so spread out. One solution for this is to reduce the length of your supply chain, meaning that designers should get what they can manufactured as close to home as possible. It may cost a little more, but for many designers minimising the impact on the environment is a huge part of the decision to do this and a worthy trade off.

If you would like to find out more about ways you can take a more eco-friendly or sustainable approach towards design, here are some useful key organisations:

- Source for Style – an online directory of sustainable fabric suppliers
  www.source4style.com
- Centre for Sustainable Fashion – a supportive resource which connects research, education and business to encourage innovative approaches to fashion
  http://www.sustainable-fashion.com
- Fairtrade Foundation - the website of the Fairtrade Foundation, home of the FAIRTRADE Mark
  www.fairtrade.org.uk
- Clean Clothes – campaign to improve working conditions and empower workers
  www.cleanclothes.org
- Global Organic Textile Standard (GOTS) – organisation sharing expertise on organic farming and sustainable textile processing
  www.global-standard.org
- MADE-BY – works with fashion and textile brands to improve sustainability across the supply chain
  www.made-by.org
- Ethical Fashion Forum – a network of organisations, designers and businesses offering information and

guidance on social and environmental sustainability in the fashion industry
www.ethicalfashionforum.com

◆ [re]design – connects designers with people, products, services and information on sustainable fashion
http://www.redesigndesign.org

■■

Designers not only have a responsibility to show consideration towards the environment when designing, but they also have the ability. As an inherently creative group designers can lead the way to a fashionable future which is slow and considered, not fast and throwaway, inspiring and thought provoking, not repetitive and which brings value and self-esteem to the lives of all of those who work in the industry, particularly the manufacturers.[7]

Suzy Amis Cameron, Co Founder of Muse School, California and founder of Red Carpet Green Dress

■■

Giving something back: *pro bono* work

Pro bono publico (usually shortened to *pro bono*) comes from the Latin and means 'for the public good'.[6] Some of the pro bono or charity/volunteer work I have done has included a charity fund raising fashion show in Sierra Leone. The show was a music festival combined with a fashion catwalk show and I was in charge of coordinating the fashion show, sourcing models and musicians, and assisting with scheduling the show. I also worked on the

Eva Longoria Noble Gift Gala in London, a charity gala working on raising funds for Eva's Heroes and Make-A-Wish UK. At this event I helped source models and makeup artists who all had an amazing time and got some fantastic credentials and work for their portfolios. Doing *pro bono* work does not take that much of your time because you slot it in when you can and take on what you know you can deliver, hence it can help you to improve your time management skills. *Pro bono* work also encourages creativity as it makes you think of innovative ways to solve problems or a lot of the time, figure out how to get things done for free and encourages you to think outside of the box. At the same time you develop interpersonal skills and learn about more effective ways to communicate with others to get the desired result. The feel good factor is undeniable. Knowing that you are assisting on a project which may otherwise have greatly struggled is a really great feeling. This is part of the reason why when you volunteer to assist on a project you should make sure it is a project you actually care about. Completing a project and being able to walk away with a thank you reminds you of the skills you do have (as often as you may get caught up in the ones you don't).

NOTES

1. Wikipedia, 'Social Responsibility', http://en.wikipedia.org/wiki/Social_responsibility; accessed 6 November 2012

2. Sass Brown, *Eco Fashion* (London: Laurence King, 2010)

3. Safia Minney, *Naked Fashion: The New Sustainable Fashion Revolution* (Oxford: The New Internationalist, 2011)

4. http://www.fairtrade.org.uk

5. Safia Minney, *Naked Fashion: The New Sustainable Fashion Revolution* (Oxford: The New Internationalist, 2011)

6. Wikipedia, 'Pro bono', http://en.wikipedia.org/wiki/Pro_bono; accessed 19 October 2012

7. Suzi Amis Cameron, in conversation with the author.

Case Study

My Red Carpet Green Dress experience

I have learned a lot about sustainable fashion from my involvement in the Red Carpet Green Dress challenge (redcarpetgreendress.com). On the 14 January 2011 I saw an advert for a competition online called Red Carpet Green Dress, which challenged new designers to create a dress suitable for a red carpet event using only sustainable fabric, such as natural, organic or recycled material. The use of notions such as buttons, crystals and beads was allowed in the design.

My initial passion has always been for fashion design, and particularly red carpet fashion, so I thought I would enter it and see what happened. I was blown away when I received a call from Suzy Amis Cameron, the founder of the contest (and the wife of Hollywood Director James Cameron) to let me know I had won. I didn't have time to celebrate because I had only ten days to get the dress made before I was due to be flown to LA with it. There was lots to be done, from sourcing the fabric, dying it, sewing and cutting, to fitting my model, and everything in between – and it took nearly two days to find the fabrics! In the end I found a company in the UK specialising in organic silk bridal fabrics, who sent me a sample of organic chiffon in the post. I used the Internet to source the fine hemp silk (again after having been sent a sample in the post) and I decided to buy it to make the dress. I ended up dying the fabric myself in my bathroom! The challenge of designing a sustainable dress also showed me that although sourcing the fabric was difficult the next steps weren't. I tried my best to make the dress as 'green' as possible. I did as much hand sewing as I could, made the belt from scratch and beaded it using cranberry-dyed pearls and beads from other jewellery I had, took my own carrier bags to the fabric supplier, used a no-waste pattern so that no excess fabric was wasted and even recycled an old belt buckle. With the help of a pattern maker and seamstress brought in at the last minute we pulled it together and I boarded a plane to LA.

The hemp silk and organic chiffon two-layered dress

The dress with a beaded belt was inspired by a classic silhouette which enhances the beautiful feminine form. A beautiful hemp silk fabric formed the under-dress and provided the necessary structure to showcase the hourglass silhouette. I then added an ethereal soft edge by over-layering this under-dress with an organic chiffon fabric. This over-layering fabric grazed the model's body. I selected the fabrics I used for their sustainable nature – the hemp silk was harvested in an animal cruelty-free way and the organic chiffon was naturally dyed – but also due to their luxurious feel and lightweight movement, which I think is crucial for a red carpet dress. I wanted the model to be able to move freely and with elegance, to be able to breathe through the fabric and to look elegant and unique. The beaded belt enhanced the hourglass silhouette and added that special red carpet glamour through sparkle and beautiful craftsmanship. The belt was handmade to ensure as minimal a carbon-footprint as possible. Another beautiful feature was the delicate gathering of the organic chiffon on the model's left shoulder, which created an elegant drop down to the bust, and enhanced the model's collarbones and neckline (this is also why I styled the model with her hair tied back). The hemp-silk under-dress had darts at the bust and waist to ensure a beautiful fit and a concealed popper fastening and side zip. Both dresses, under-dress and over-dress, had a flare at the hem for an elegant 'kick-out' with the organic chiffon over-dress having a wider flare. The dress was cream with a pink overlay but the exact hue of pink was decided based on the model's skin tone to really make the dress stand out. I only submitted one design because I felt this design was strong enough to stand-alone and make an impact on such a glamorous occasion.

I loved being involved in the competition because as well as being such an exciting project the Red Carpet Green Dress Contest is an international fund raising competition where money raised goes towards the MUSE School Ca (a school co-founded by Suzy Amis Cameron and her sister) and MUSE Global Program. The MUSE Global Program fully funds a school in Mae Sot, Thailand for children who have escaped the genocide in Burma (Myanmar). The fact that the competition was fund raising for such as positive cause made me even happier to be involved, and this ties in nicely to one of the key messages in this book. As an industry often referred to as being superficial, it is not that surprising that you have to work hard to retain a sense of who you are and not allow yourself to

My winning entry on my model, Aine.

get swept up in the glamour of it all. Good karma is important. This applies to everything, from treating everyone you meet with equal respect (as you would like to be treated); and not allowing yourself to believe your own hype; to seeking out ways to assist and support others in the industry who are also trying to

make it. This could be anything from volunteering to work at the weekends (I did volunteer work at a fashion boutique whilst at university), to assisting at a fund raising charity fashion show, to organising networking groups at university.

CHAPTER 10

EMOTIONAL WELLBEING

The life of a fashion designer or fashion entrepreneur is often romanticized. It is definitely not all about glamorous parties, dressing celebrities and getting into magazines. It starts with long hours, little income, hard work and slow progress. Fashion designers and entrepreneurs eat, sleep and breathe fashion, and that lifestyle can be all consuming. They will often work long hours and weekends to meet deadlines – fashion weeks in particular are killer times. Working as a designer is not a 9–5 job. There are no official hours as you often work when inspiration hits you, in response to a changing demand or trend – which can happen overnight – and to the fashion industry's global timetable. I have found that a lot of creative people, not just fashion designers, never really have proper 'down time' or switch off. It is hard to switch off from something that surrounds you everywhere you go. And yet, if you're going to succeed you need to stay motivated and inspired. This chapter explains how to get and stay inspired, how to deal with creative block and how to cope with stress through relaxation.

Motivation

I touched on motivation in chapter 2, when defining what motivates you to want to work in the fashion industry. This is your intrinsic motivation, that is, the incentive to undertake an activity based on the expected enjoyment of the activity itself, rather than external benefits that might result. In *The Midnight Disease: The Drive to Write, Writer's Block, and the Creative Brain* the neurologist and writer, Alice Flaherty describes hypergraphia, the compulsion to write (from which she suffers). Flaherty attempts to explain the biology behind inspiration and the physical relationship found by neurologists between emotion and creativity, or between fatigue and creativity. She explains that:

> In psychological terms, it seems that drive is more important than talent. But the type of motivation is important. Teresa Amabile at Harvard has done a number of studies to show that intrinsic motivation, such as enjoyment, is more likely to produce creative work. And, paradoxically … extrinsic motivation [such] as money hurts creativity. This may be because money is distracting or because the person stops working the instant money comes in.[1]

From this we can learn that, simply put, the more we enjoy ourselves, the more we are likely to be intrinsically motivated and hence create! But if we allow factors such as money or peer acknowledgement to be our motivators we could actually be doing our creativity a disservice. Flaherty also talks about the importance of rest, explaining that power naps of less than 15 minutes are 'more effective than coffee' but that any longer than this and you can wake up feeling worse than if you had stayed awake! According to Flaherty, 'sleep deprivation itself seems to decrease creativity, rather than increasing it.'

Get inspired!

Any creative person will tell you that there is not really any set place or way to 'get inspired'. Inspiration is all around you but your ability to access it depends on your emotions, what is going on in your life, the time you have to create and so many other factors. But although inspiration cannot be prescribed it can be helped along, I believe that adding new elements into your daily routine is a brilliant way to help you find inspiration. This could simply involve taking a new route to work, trying a book from a genre you have never read before, rearranging your sleeping space, rotating or introducing new art on your walls, or dipping into another related area of the arts such as a visit to an art gallery or a museum. For me, visiting museums such as the Tate Modern or the V&A gives me the added inspiration I need to be creative. Another great idea is to have a board in your creative space somewhere where you can pin images, quotes or articles you have come across which inspire you. Some artists have a 'vision' board full of images of things they would like to see in their future.

I also find dance inspires me, and when I was happy to have been invited by a friend to Sadler's Wells theatre in London to watch the Alvin Ailey Dance Theatre. I came out absolutely full of inspiration. The costumes were a fitting kaleidoscope for the dance moves, dancer's shapes and music and I was enthralled to see how dances, movement and costume married so well together, so effortlessly. For a visitor to London there is always a popular show on at Sadler's Wells (www.sadlerswells.com) and in my opinion it is well worth a visit for some art, dance and inspiration. For more ideas of inspiring places to go, see pp.180–1.

A playlist for inspiration

Playlists for different states of mind are a great idea. You can put together different ones for making, getting inspired and when you have your business hat on. I have an eclectic taste in music and have found that some songs help me whilst sketching and visualising my fashion show, for casting models and so on. I have listed some of the sounds I enjoy listening to and hope that some of them strike a chord with you or encourage you to create your own play lists for different creative mind sets.

My top suggestions to help you get inspired

- Exercise;
- Rest;
- Visit an art gallery;
- Listen to classical music (I am a huge fan);
- Connect with nature: the sky, clouds, stars, sunrise and sunsets (the start of a new day and the end of one) – spend some time at the beginning of your day or the end, appreciating the nature around you, go to a zoo!

- Read old diaries if you have any – Yes, you may cringe slightly but in many ways you can be re-inspired by your goals and dreams of yesteryear and the ambitions which once seemed quite huge to you. This also can remind you of how far you have already come;
- Travel;
- Write anything, draw anything – just for fun and with no intention to use it.

ARTIST	TRACK
Frou Frou	Let Go
Fray	Say When
Simon & Garfunkel	Bookends
Feist	Honey Honey; Mushaboom
Regina Spektor	Hero
Idlewild Blue	Outkast
Local Natives	Eyes Wide
My Girls	Animal Collective
Kelis	4th July
Scissor Sisters	Any Which Way
Madonna	Lucky Star
Tina Turner	Proud Mary
Ellie Goulding	Starry Eyed
Snow Patrol	The Golden Floor
Janet Jackson	Rock With You

One of my personal favourites is the Royal Philharmonic Orchestra (RPO; www.rpo.co.uk), a British orchestra based in London which tours widely.

Textures and colours

I love interior design and playing with textures so looking through interior design websites can be fun and inspirational, you see amazing use of texture – from the wallpapers to the cushions and inspirations ranging from Persian to Victorian, from natural textures such as linen to luxurious velvets. Clever use of colours and textures can create atmospheres in rooms from calm and tranquil to vivid and exciting. Try visiting a home décor store; most big cities have them. Whilst in New York recently I disappeared for two hours in ABC Carpet & Home, it is the retail Mecca for all artists especially those in fashion, interior, and industrial design! There are ten floors offering an inspired collection of rugs, furniture, antiques, home textiles, accessories and sustainable furnishings. Hotels can offer the same kind of inspiration so I often meet friends for drinks in some

continued on p.182

Beautiful destinations: places to go for inspiration

FRANCE

CENTRE GEORGES POMPIDOU, PARIS

The cultural and artistic centre named after Georges Pompidou, has sparked many a lively debate about its daring and strange architecture (designed by architects Rogers, Piano and Franchini). It houses one of the leading collection of modern and contemporary art in Europe, as well as a vast public reference library, a cinema, performance halls, educational activity areas, bookshops, a restaurant and a café.

www.centrepompidou.fr

MUSÉE D'ORSAY, PARIS

The Musée d'Orsay holds mainly French art – painting sculptures, furniture and photography dating from 1848 to 1915. It is known for impressionist and post-impressionist pieces and work by of Monet, Renoir, Sisley and Van Gogh.

www.musee-orsay.fr

MUSÉE DU LOUVRE, PARIS

Once a royal palace, the Louvre has a long history of artistic and historic conservation. The museum, located in the centre of Paris, holds some of the world's most famous works of art including Leonardo da Vinci's *Mona Lisa*.

www.louvre.fr

ITALY

UFFIZI GALLERY, FLORENCE

Built in 1581 the Uffizi Gallery, is one of the oldest and most ancient museums in the modern world. The gallery holds a comprehensive and fine collection of Florentine art from the Late Gothic through the Renaissance and Mannerist periods. It holds a collection of painting including work by Leonardo da Vinci, Michelangelo and Rembrandt Van Rijn.

www.uffizi.com

VATICAN MUSEUMS, ROME

This is where the Sistine Chapel and Michelangelo's famous ceiling frescos are to be found. As seen today, the Vatican Museums are a complex of different pontifical museums and galleries that began under the patronage of the popes Clement XIV (1769–74) and Pius VI (1775–99) displaying works from the extensive collection of the Roman Catholic Church and spanning from antiquity to modern religious art. The museums, which include Museo Pio-Clementino and Museo Gregoriano Etrusco house by Caravaggio, Leonardo da Vinci's and Raphael bring over four million visitors annually.

http://mv.vatican.va/3_EN/pages/MV_Home.html

RUSSIA

THE STATE HERMITAGE, ST PETERSBURG

The State Hermitage is made up of six buildings, situated in the centre of St Petersburg consisting of the Winter Palace, the former state residence of the Russian emperors, the buildings of the Small, Old (Great) and New Hermitages, the Hermitage Theatre and the Auxiliary House. With over three million works of art it holds the Guinness World Record for world's largest painting collection. It includes works of Western and Russian art. In amongst the collections are paintings, graphic works, sculptures and works of applied art and archaeological finds.

www.hermitagemuseum.org

SPAIN

MUSEO DEL PRADO, MADRID

The Prado Museum houses collections of European art from Goya to El Greco. Although it houses paintings and sculptures it also contains important collections of other types of works including prints. Velazquez's painting *Las Meninas* is certainly the best known piece of work in the collection and has been recognised as one of the most important paintings in Western art history. Other artists on display include El Greco, Goya, Peter Paul Rubens and Hieronymus Bosch.

www.museodelprado.es/en

UK

THE DESIGN MUSEUM, LONDON

To date the Design Museum has staged over 100 exhibitions. It aims to celebrate design across platforms from furniture to graphics, fashion and architecture. The word 'design' is used to include all genres and forms and focuses on it as a tool for creative thinking and inspired problem solving.

www.designmuseum.org

SAATCHI GALLERY, LONDON

This gallery for contemporary art was opened by Charles

Saatchi in 1985 to exhibit his own collection to the public. It is considered by many to be one of the most influential art galleries in London and has displayed work by the likes of Damien Hirst and Tracey Emin. I love its beautifully airy galleries, diverse collection of stimulating (and often controversial) work and the space it gives you to think about what you have seen. What I like most about the Saatchi is that you will see emerging talent. In the words of the gallery's head of development, Rebecca Wilson, 'The gallery's guiding principle is to show what is being made now, the most interesting artists of today. It's about drawing people's attentions to someone who might be tomorrow's Damien Hirst.'[2]

www.saatchi-gallery.co.uk

TATE MODERN

The Tate Modern is Britain's national gallery of international modern art. The collection is of contemporary and modern art including work by the likes of Picasso and Matisse. It also has significant collections of Pop art, including major works by Warhol, and Conceptual Art.

www.tate.org.uk/modern

THE VICTORIA & ALBERT MUSEUM, LONDON

The Victoria & Albert Museum is currently the world's largest museum of decorative arts and design, housing a permanent collection of over 4.5 million objects. When in London I love going to the beautiful V&A at the weekend for a stroll, to look at the collections and explore the many cultures celebrated, from Europe, North America, Asia and North Africa. The fashion and jewellery, and the theatre collections are also definitely worth a view! In 2002, the Museum acquired 178 Vivienne Westwood costumes as well as pieces by Coco Chanel, Yves Saint Laurent Mary Quant and Christian Lacroix, Jean Muir and Pierre Cardin.

www.vam.ac.uk

USA

J PAUL GETTY CENTRE, LOS ANGELES

The J. Paul Getty Museum has two locations, one in Los Angeles, California and another in Malibu. In Los Angeles, the Museum houses European paintings (including *Irises* by Vincent Van Gogh), drawings, sculpture, illuminated manuscripts, decorative arts and European and American photographs. The J. Paul Getty Museum at the Getty Villa in Malibu, is home to approximately 44,000 works of art and is dedicated to the study of the arts and cultures of ancient Greece, Rome, and Etruria.

www.getty.edu

MUSEUM OF MODERN ART, MANHATTAN

Located in the middle of Manhattan, MOMA is often called the most important and influential museum dedicated to modern art in the world today. The collection has works in almost all the major areas of fine and contemporary art, from painting and sculpture to film and new media. You can see Van Gogh's *Starry Night,* Warhol's *Campbell Soup Cans* and Picasso's famous *Les Demoiselles d'Avignon.*

www.moma.org

NATIONAL GALLERY OF ART, WASHINGTON

The National Gallery is located on the National Mall and is made up of two buildings. The West Building has a huge collection of sculpture and paintings from Europe from medieval times up to the 19th century, but also includes some American artists. The usual names like Monet, Rembrandt, da Vinci and Van Gogh grace the walls with amazing masterpieces. The East Building is more concerned with contemporary and modern art such as Pollock, Picasso, Warhol and Lichtenstein. Be sure to check out the sculpture garden with works by Alexendar Calder and Joan Miro.

www.nga.gov

THE METROPOLITAN MUSEUM OF ART, NEW YORK

The Metropolitan Museum of Art is one of the world's finest and largest art museums. Its collections include more than two million works of art spanning 5,000 years of world culture, from prehistory to the present day. Past exhibitions have included Alexander McQueen's 'Savage Beauty' exhibition, which celebrated the late designer's contribution to fashion. Fashion lovers will also know it as host to the Costume Institute Gala Benefit, an annual fund raiser that celebrates the opening of the spring exhibition each May. Under the leadership of Trustee Anna Wintour (Editor in Chief, *Vogue*) the gala is a highly anticipated event in the industries of fashion, film, society, business, and music.

www.metmuseum.org

of the cutting edge hotels around London. Another fantastic place to look for textures and colours is of course the great outdoors. Botanical gardens are great places to find a wide range of beautiful plants and flowers.

Dealing with creative block

All designers face the reality of a creative block at some stage or another. Being consistently creative is difficult, especially considering you probably have a life outside of work which often directly or indirectly affects your creativity, sometimes causing it to just dry up. If you are going through personal problems you may not have enough inspiration in you to create. It is frustrating when the ideas stop flowing and everything you produce feels as if it's no good. Creative block can drive some creatives to become depressed, which may not seem understandable to many, but when your main form of self-expression stops working it can dent your confidence. Self-doubt haunts creative minds. Creative block is like writers block and can be defined as, 'A periodic lack of inspiration that can descend on the most experienced of writers and that results in an almost pathological inability to put pen to paper.'[3] If this happens to you I can reassure you that you are definitely not alone. Everyone goes through periods when they feel less creative than usual so it is really important to know when to put the needle, pencil or scissors down and take a time out. In the poet Shelley's words, 'A man cannot say, "I will compose poetry"',[4] essentially it composes itself. It is unrealistic to believe you will always be in the right frame of mind to create because what is the right frame of mind to create? For some, their best work comes in times of turbulence, for others in times of complete bliss, for some brilliant work arises from the mundane. Sometimes forcing creativity can ruin something that could be brilliant whilst others will suggest pushing through as the resulting work could grow on you and you could start to like it.

You can try to make the optimum conditions for creativity by observing the things that cause and ease your block but a sure way to deal with a creative block is to take time out and come back to your work at a later date, approaching things with fresh eyes. You want to reach a state of flow, described by Csíkszentmihályi (author of *Flow: The Psychology of Optimal Experience*), as 'a state of concentration or complete absorption with the activity at hand and the situation'. For creatives being in flow is being totally absorbed and engaged so that time feels like it is flying and the creative juices are flowing. In flow you are being productive and you are happy in this state. According to Csíkszentmihályi,

> 'To achieve a flow state, a balance must be struck between the challenge of the task and the skill of the performer. If the task is too easy or too difficult, flow cannot occur…skill level and challenge level must be matched …'[4]

Flow is losing yourself in your work and enjoying it, and to me it is important to appreciate the moments you can get into this state because it is a desirable place to be and not always an easy place to reach.

Coping during stressful times

My experiences of the fashion industry have taught me how overwhelming and daunting it can be and feel. Without outlets to vent frustrations and problems we can really internalise a great deal and feel quite lonely. Hopefully some of the suggested ways to chill out will help you combat those feelings if and when they arise.

The long hours and seemingly slow progress as you establish yourself can leave you feeling tired and stressed; that feeling of still having so much to do can sometimes seem like it is never going to go away. Even when your work is good you can feel it is not good enough and you can be blind to your own potential. Your confidence levels can dip, ebb and flow. Sometimes you may feel like throwing away your sketches and work all together. During some of the busiest times of your year, for example during fashion weeks, you can come the closest to having a panic attack and feeling like you do not have enough time or money. Money, or the lack of it, is one of the greatest causes of stress as it can take away from the freedom you feel to deliver work you are proud of. If you are a start-up designer you may not be able to afford to employ much-needed help and can therefore end up doing everything yourself. As many say, being an impoverished designer is a rite of passage!

I think that at times like this it is important to remember that you can only do so much. When you are very stressed it can cause you to question why you are doing this in the first place and feel that surely there is an easier career path that you could pursue! I have had these conversations with myself endlessly and still do at times. In truth, the main things which will get you through will be perseverance, patience and passion. The busiest times on the fashion calendar (such as fashion weeks) can be extremely draining both physically, emotionally and mentally for an emerging designer. This, coupled with the anxiety you might feel ahead of showcasing your collection and opening yourself up to industry criticism and feedback, can leave you feeling down and anxious. During these times it is likely that you will not eat well, not get enough sleep and have a mind that is in overdrive, so massages, exercise and a good diet all play an important part in keeping you relaxed, happy and at your optimum.

My relaxation corner...

WELCOME DISTRACTIONS
I love trawling the Internet for inspirational blogs and websites when I am having an unproductive day. Two of my favourite websites for this are Monomoda. com and the blog Unconventionally Beautiful (samanthashorey.blogspot.com).

MONOmoda.com is a place to find thoughtful articles, useful resources and a unique selection of design

Inspired Magazine's Top 10 Tips to Avoid a Creative Block[5]

- Doodle in your sketchbook;
- Visit inspirational galleries on the web;
- Take a walk;
- Search for new fonts;
- Stop doubting yourself;
- Get away for a day or two;
- Take your work to the nearest coffee shop;
- Go out with some friends;
- Listen to some music;
- Follow some tutorials.

Reproduced courtesy of inspiredm.com

inspiration daily. If you log on to Creativeblock. monomoda.com you get inspirational quotes to help you fend off creative block, such as 'Let it solve itself'; 'It will become what it wants to become'; 'Does it make you say "WOW?"'; 'Everything you can imagine is real'; and 'Make it inspiring'.

The Unconventionally Beautiful blog, is by Samantha Shorey and contains her personal writing and art portfolio. It's a great example of a simple, clutter-free blog.

SENSE SOOTHERS

No one should ever underestimate the power of a long relaxing bath! It is priceless after a long and stressful day. Classical music on low volume, a vanilla and coconut scented candle burning and bubbles up past your nostrils – easily created and perfect! When you need to switch off you need to try to forget about everything and one way to relax is with sense stimulators which feel, taste, sound or smell good such as warm water, delicious food, soothing

music and essential oils or incense. My favourite food is chocolate, and I like bergamot, sandalwood and mandarin essential oils. Scent is very powerful. I love bergamot for its warm citrus scent – it has the effect of making me feel refreshed, happy and relaxed and therapeutically it is used to treat depression, tension and stress. Sandalwood from India is my favourite; it works to relieve nervous tension and helps you to wind down. It has an intense woody and exotic smell and is said to have a calming and harmonising effect on anxiety and nervous energy. There are two types of mandarin – green and red varieties – and both are used as remedies to aide sleep. It is also known to increase circulation and help relieve stress. You can try mixing different scents to come up with something of your own.

ASK YOUR FRIENDS AND FAMILY WHAT THEY DO TO RELAX?

People often call their friends or family to talk about their problems when they are stressed. Try asking them for their practical tips on how to unwind. I asked a group of my friends and here are some of the suggestions that they came back with.

- 'I would avoid the crowded tube and people with negative or overly intense energy. I also do yoga'
- 'I try going to the gym and completely switching off from anything negative going on.'
- 'Run until you forget you're running.'
- 'Music, baby!'
- 'Looking at window displays, I look at all types of window displays. That's the key!'
- 'Scented candles and a cool playlist – being near water also!'
- 'Poetry or audiobooks!'

Take care of yourself, and enjoy creating!

For me, managing your lifestyle is one of the most important skills of a fashion designer or entrepreneur because it gives you the foundation and energy to be able to carry out the suggestions in this book with a level of peace and calm. I hope that this book will act as a useful resource and guide, helping you to succeed in your ambitions within the fashion industry, whatever they may be. I truly believe that this is one of the most exciting and fun industries to work in, so enjoy yourself, be brave and go for it!

NOTES

1. Alice Flaherty, *The Midnight Disease: The Drive to Write, Writer's Block, and the Creative Brain* (New York: Houghton Mifflin Harcourt, 2004)

2. Robert Barr, 'London's new Saatchi Gallery looks to China's emerging artists', *The Associated Press* (7 October 2008), http://humantimes.com/articleaction/printnow/44519; accessed 13 November 2012

3. John Ayto and Ian Crofton, *Brewer's Dictionary of Modern Phrase and Fable* (Chambers, 2009)

4. Mihaly Csíkszentmihályi, *Flow: The Psychology of Optimal Experience* (London, Harper Perennial Modern Classics, 2008)

5. *Insipred Magazine*, '10 Tips to Avoid a Creative Block', Jacques van Heerden (@an1ken), http://inspiredm.com/creative-block/; accessed 17 October 2012.

ACKNOWLEDGEMENTS

First and foremost I would like to thank Bloomsbury and Davida Forbes for having faith in this project and working with me every step of the way to deliver this beautiful book. My thanks also to Susan James for agreeing to take me on over lunch in Bloomsbury Square after I had babbled on excitedly about this project. Thank you for seeing its potential. I have been lucky enough to meet some hugely inspirational people in an industry that is largely misunderstood and at times trivialised by those who do not understand its innovative qualities, far-reaching contribution to society, or what makes it tick. I would also like to thank photographer Alex Maguire for supplying so many fantastic images; our random meeting at the V&A for the London College of Fashion BA Shows was of great significance for this book. In addition I would like to thank the wonderful staff at the London College of Fashion for their support over the years, particularly since I moved to London. Specifically: Dean Frances Corner; Adam Watling and Clare Douglas, who are constantly striving to find ways to give their students the best start possible; and Events Coordinator Gillian Evans, who makes pulling together a fashion show of over 20 designers look easy. For their contributions to this book, Anti Copying In Design, Nigel Barker, Courtney Blackman, Sarah Curran, Sombo Dakowah, Rajeeb Dey, Nick Ede, Aneeqa Flynn, Helen Jennings, Alex Leonhardt, Anne Look, Bekka Payack, Kairi Thornton, Harold Tillman CBE and Simon Whitehouse. For proving what I already knew – that it is definitely possible to work in this fast-paced industry and remain an authentic person – Jessica B at *Vogue*, Cat S at Christian Louboutin and Eilidh MacAskill at *InStyle*.

In particular I am blown away by the women I meet who juggle a career with their personal lives: Robbie Myers, Editor-in-Chief of *ELLE* US is one such woman; another is Suzy Amis Cameron, co-founder of Muse School California and founder of Red Carpet Green Dress, who has taken me on a life-changing journey of discovery about sustainability by way of Hollywood and the Oscars. I deeply appreciate your friendship. I would like to thank my close friends who have always supported me and offered me words of encouragement from the bottom of my heart including my brother Ronnie. To the Pattinsons, thank you for your acceptance and enthusiasm for my project. To my Mum, Dad and two sisters, Habiba and Mariama, I am lucky to come from such an impressive, talented and yet humble family, who have always stressed the importance of treating people kindly, a good education, hard work and prayer. To my future husband, thank you for reminding me why I was writing this book and encouraging me with each single chapter, I know it was not easy. Thank you.

INDEX

PICTURE CREDITS

Page 2 © Alex Maguire; Page 6 © Alex Maguire; Page 10 © andrea michele piacquadio/Shutterstock.com; Page 12 © Alex Maguire; Page 13 (above) © rockey/Shutterstock.com, (below) © markrhiggins/Shutterstock.com; Page 14 © Lucian Coman/Shutterstock.com; Page 16 © Alex Maguire; Page 19 © Alex Maguire; Page 20 © Samata Angel; Page 21 © r.nagy/Shutterstock.com; Page 22 © nito/Shutterstock.com; Page 23 © /Shutterstock.com; Page 24 © F.C.G. /Shutterstock.com; Page 25 © conrado/Shutterstock.com; Page 26 © aaleksander/Shutterstock.com; Page 27 © ssguy/Shutterstock.com; Page 28 © Alex Maguire; Page 34 © Gromovataya/Shutterstock.com; Page 37 © Darqowski/Shutterstock.com; Pages 38 and 39 © Losevsky Photo and Video/Shutterstock.com; Page 40 © Alex Maguire; Page 41 (right) FIASCO magazine cover issue 8, 2011 © FIASCO Publishing; Page 43 © Gary Yim/Shutterstock.com; Page 44 © wrangler/Shutterstock.com; Page 46 © Alex Maguire; Page 51 © Samata Angel; Pages 52–3 © Alex Maguire; Page 54 portfolio images courtesy of Matthew Fox; Page 56 © Alex Maguire; Page 64 © Yuri Arcurs/Shutterstock.com; Page 67 (above) © CandyBox Images/Shutterstock.com, (below) © illustrart/Shutterstock.com; Page 68 © CandyBox Images/Shutterstock.com; Page 70 © Niall McInerney/Bloomsbury Fashion Photography Archive; Page 71 (above) pcruciatti/Shutterstock.com, (below) © 101imges/Shutterstock.com; Page 73 © Alex Maguire; Page 76 © Samata Angel; Page 77 © Samata Angel; Page 78 © Samata Angel; Page 82 © Maksim Shmeljov/Shutterstock.com; Page 83 © Samata Angel; Page 85 © SVLuma/Shutterstock.com; Page 86 © Samata Angel; Page 88 © Boris Bushmin/Shutterstock.com; Page 89 © Samata Angel; Page 92 © Yuri Arcurs/Shutterstock.com; Page 97 © Gromovataya/Shutterstock.com; Page 98 © Samata Angel; Page 103 © Patrick Wang/Shutterstock.com; Page 104 © Samata Angel; Page 106 © Kiselev Andrey Valerevich/Shutterstock.com; Page 112 © Zhukov Oleg/Shutterstock.com; Page 113 © jennyt/Shutterstock.com; Page 114 © GoodMood Photo/Shutterstock.com; Page 115 © Levent Konuk/Shutterstock.com; Page 116 © Samata Angel; Page 117 © Ragne Kabanova/Shutterstock.com; Page 118 © Moreno Soppelsa/Shutterstock.com; Page 119 © StockLite/Shutterstock.com; Page 122 © Levent Konuk /Shutterstock.com; Page 124 © Alex Maguire; Page 126 © Samata Angel; Page 127 (above and below) © Kean Diao; Page 128 © Alex Maguire; Page 129 © Jordan Tan/Shutterstock.com; Pages 131–3 © Alex Maguire; Page 134 © Luba V Nel/Shutterstock.com; Page 135 © Diego Cervo/Shutterstock.com; Page 137 © Alex Leonhardt; Page 138 © Alex Maguire; Page 142 © Bennett Raglin; Page 145 © ra2studio/Shutterstock.com; Page 149 © MJTH/Shutterstock.com; Page 150 © Samata Angel; Page 152 © Samata Angel; Page 157 images courtesy of my-wardrobe.com; Page 158 © Aliaksei Lasevich/Shutterstock.com; Page 162 © Kairi Soosar; Page 164 © Samata Angel; Page 168 © Brandon Hickman; Page 171 © 58763899/Shutterstock.com; Page 175 © Brandon Hickman; Page 176 © AISPIX by Image Source/Shutterstock.com; Page 179 © Alex Maguire; Page 182 © Ant Clausen/Shutterstock.com; Page 184 © Mayer George/Shutterstock.com; Page 188 © Alex Maguire.